Woman's Athletic Club
COOKBOOK

Copies of
"The Woman's Athletic Club Cookbook"
can be obtained by writing to:
Woman's Athletic Club of Chicago
626 N. Michigan Ave.
Chicago, Illinois 60611

$5.50 per copy
$6.25 per copy postpaid
Illinois residents must add tax

Illustrated by
A. Philbin Schulz

Printed in the United States of America
by
Heitman Printing Co.

TO

IONE RHYNSBURGER
(Mrs. Henry Russer)

Since March 2, 1936 Miss Rhysburger has faithfully and efficiently served as kitchen manager of the Woman's Athletic Club. It is with great appreciation to her that the members proudly dedicate this book.

The Woman's Athletic Club of Chicago has the distinction of being the first athletic club for women in this country. Emphasis on athletics has always been important but since its inception the club has been noted for its excellent cuisine. It seems fitting therefore to commemorate the club's 75th anniversary year by recording menus and recipes from the club's kitchen as well as selected favorites from the membership. The illustrations represent likenesses of interior rooms and treasures found in the club.

TABLE OF CONTENTS

Section I
Recipes from the W.A.C. Kitchen

Section II
Favorite Recipes from the Membership

SECTION I

Favorite Club Menus

CLUB TEA

CLOSED TEA SANDWICHES
Ripe Olive & Cream Cheese
Minced Chicken
Minced Lobster

~

OPEN TEA SANDWICHES
* Cucumber and Green Pepper
* Rolled Watercress
Cream Cheese with Whole
Strawberry & Mint
Cream Cheese with Ripe Olive
filled with Anchovy Paste

* Lilly Cookies
* Lace Cookies
* Rolled Cookies
Crescents
Small Macaroons

* Salted Nuts
Yellow & White Mints

* Date Nut Bread
* Anna Rolls
Petit Fours (yellow-white)
Tiny Coconut Balls
Punch Bowl with Fruit Ice Mold

* Denotes recipes found in this book

CHRISTMAS TEA DANCE

* Burgundy Beef Patties in
Tiny Buns
* Hot Cheese Puffs
* Hot Mushroom Puffs
Minced Ham on Tiny Rounds of Rye
* Hot Crabmeat
Chicken Salad Finger Sandwiches
Quiche Lorraine
* Date Nut Bread
Cocoanut Balls
Christmas Cookies
* Salted Nuts   Red & Green Mints
Tea—Coffee

CHRISTMAS HOLIDAY LUNCHEON

* Tomato Aspic Ring filled with
Diced Avocado
* W.A.C. Special Dressing
* Cheese Straws
* Artichoke Bottoms filled Crabmeat—
Mornay Sauce
Buttered Peas with Mushroom Slices
* Orange Rolls—Plain Rolls
* Frozen Almond Ball—
* Butterscotch Sauce

PAST PRESIDENT'S LUNCHEON

* Tomato Bouillon—Horseradish Cream
Cheese Straws
* Almond Chicken or Lobster
Buttered and Parsleyed Rice
Broccoli Polonaise

* W.A.C. Tossed Salad with
Marinated Mushrooms
* Orange Rolls
* W.A.C. Coconut Cake

LUNCHEON for VISITING COLUMNIST

Tomato filled with Fresh Shrimps—
Mustard Mayonnaise
Cucumber Finger Sandwiches
*Breast of Chicken Jubilee
Green Beans Almondine
* Orange Rolls
*Baked Pear Sabayon

BRIDGER'S LUNCHEON

* Cream of Mushroom Soup—
* Melba Toast
* Individual Cheddar Cheese Souffle—
Lemon Butter
Fresh Asparagus
* Vinaigrette Salad
* Anna Rolls—Plain Rolls
* Lemon Souffle Pudding

INVESTMENT DAY–SPECIAL EVENT

Chicken Consomme with Rice—
Chopped Parsley
* Curried Toast
Combination Lamb Chop Grill—
Lamb Chop, Bacon & Mushroom
Broiled Tomato Slice Topped with Corn
Sliced Avocado on Assorted Greens—
* Lemon Oil Dressing
* Chocolate Marshmallow Cake

～

BOARD MEETING LUNCHEON

Fresh Fruit Cup with Port Wine
* Filet of Chicken in Almond Batter
Buttered Peas & Waterchestnuts
Tossed Green Salad with Tomato Wedges
* Special W.A.C. Dressing
* Orange, Pecan and Plain Rolls
* Fresh Lime Tart

～

FALL NEEDLEWORK SHOW

* Molded Beet Salad—Sour Cream Dressing
Breast of Chicken
* Mornay sauce
Peas with Mushroom Slices
* Blueberry Muffins
* Pineapple Ice Box Cake

BEFORE the MATINEE

*Molded Spring Salad—
* Sour Cream Dressing
* Rolled Melba Toast
* Crabmeat or Lobster Alaska
* Braised Cucumbers
* Pecan Rolls
* Heavenly Strawberries—Tiny Coconut Ball

~

THE COOKING CLASS LUNCHEON

Jellied Tomato Madrilene a la Hales +
Melba Toast
* Breast of Chicken Citron
* Baked Zuccini with Onion & Bacon
Meringue with Vanilla Ice Cream—
* W.A.C. Special Fudge Sauce

+½ egg with curried sour cream, Red Caviar
over Bibb Lettuce

~

LUNCHEON BEFORE
PRESBYTERIAN-ST. LUKE'S FASHION SHOW

*Sour Cream Dressing
Melba Toast
* Italian Baked Breast of Chicken
Parsley Rice
Assorted Rolls
* Angel Pie

BRIDAL SHOWER LUNCHEON

*Consomme with Orange Slice
Crepes filled with
* W.A.C. Creamed Chicken
Buttered Peas with Celery
* Beet Mold with Sour Cream Dressing
Cocoanut Rolls
* Frozen Lemon Angel

&

KATE GREENAWAY DAY

* Molded Bing Cherry Salad—
Whipped Cream Dressing or
* W.A.C. Mayonnaise
Toasted Wafers
* Calf's Sweetbreads Saute
* Spinach Timbales
* Bavarian Cream with Melba Sauce

&

SPRING FASHION SHOW LUNCHEON

* Molded Spring Salad—
* Sour Cream Dressing
Breast of Chicken with Curry Sauce
Rice topped with Chutney and Almonds
* Orange Rolls
* Lemon Angel Tart

ZODIAC LUNCHEON

* Artichoke Bottom topped with
Crabmeat Salad Tyrolienne &
Chopped Ripe Olives on Tossed Greens
* Breast of Chicken Veronique—
Pimiento Rice
* Anna Rolls
Christmas Snow Ball +
Christmas Wreath Cookie and Star Cookie
(on each side of ice cream ball)

+Ice Cream Ball of New York and Lemon Ice on
bed of Coconut

Poolside Luncheon
SWIM'N TRIM

* Hot Consomme with Orange Slice
* Hollywood Salad Bowl—
* Diet Dressing

CORPORATION BUFFET LUNCHEON

*Baked Chicken Breast—Veronique
Lobster Newburg
Mushroom Rice
* Molded Bing Cherry Salad
Ripe & Green Olives
Tossed Green Salad
Cottage Cheese
Tomato Slices
* Strawberries Romanoff
Tiny Coconut Ball

SKI STYLE SHOW

Oyster Bisque—Toasted Wafers
Breast of Chicken in
Mushroom Wine Sauce
* Spinach Timbales
W.A.C. Tossed Salad—Croutons
Assorted Rolls
* Chocolate Rum Tart—
Whipped Cream

~

BEFORE THE CONCERT

* Cream of Watercress Soup—
* Cheese Straws
London Grill—Beef Tenderloin—
Mushroom Cap—Bacon
* Baked Eggplant with Tomato, Onion, and
Green Pepper
Mimosa Salad
* Burnt Sugar Cake with Caramel Icing

~

HOT SUMMER DAY LUNCHEON

* Tomato Aspic Ring filled with
Chopped Egg Salad—
Topped with Crisp Bacon
Artichoke Hearts with
* Marinated Mushroom Slices
* Blueberry Muffins
* Lime Chiffon Tart

LUNCHEON FROM SANTA'S KITCHEN

Smile Cheeseburger+
Tomato and Lettuce Garnish
French Fried Potatoes
Ice Cream Snowball—Christmas Cookie
Chocolate Milk

Smile Cheeseburger+

Broiled chopped steak
American Cheese Sliced size of Round steak
Sliced black olives for eyes
Ripe olive ring for mouth
Place on half buttered toasted bun. On other half
bun place lettuce, tomato and mayonnaise.

DUCK DINNER

* *Poached Filet of Sole—Chantilly*
* *Rolled Melba Toast*
Roast Duck a la Orange
* *Hunters Baked Rice*
Bibb Lettuce
* *Wine Dressing*
* *W.A.C. Rolls*
Peach Melba

SPRING DINNER DANCE

*King Crabmeat * Tyrolienne en Coquille*
Assorted Wafers
* W.A.C. Au Gratin Potatoes
*Baked Zuccini with Onion & Bacon
* Pecan Rolls
* Fresh Fruit Compote with
Orange Curacao
* Million Dollar Cookies
and
* Thin Ginger Cookies

~

CLUB DINNER
Preceding a Travelogue Program

* Cold Curried Crabmeat Bisque
Marinated Roast Beef Tenderloin
* Rice with Peas and Mushrooms
* Zucchini Slices with Onion and Bacon
Tossed Green Salad—
* Thousand Island Dressing
Sesame Seed Rolls
* Baked Orange Alaska—Sugar Cookies

~

BASEBALL DINNER–AFTER BALL GAME

Marinated Cucumbers on
*Tossed Greens * Sour Cream Dressing*
Assorted Wafers
* Swiss Chicken Divan
Glazed Belguim Carrots
*¹ Chocolate Angel Tart
Assorted Rolls

CANDLELIGHT DINNER

*Consomme Royale— * Cheese Straws*
Individual Crabmeat Souffle—
Lemon Butter
(Pouilly Fumme de la Douchette 1969)
** Escallops of Veal Bonne Femme*
(Chateau Las Combes 1967)
** Duchess Potatoes*
Broccoli Hollandaise
*Bibb Lettuce with * Red Wine Dressing*
Sweet and Plain Rolls
(Wehlener Sonnenbhr Auslese 1970)
** Fluffy Pumpkin Chiffon Tart*
Demi Tasse

ANNIVERSARY of CHICAGO FIRE
DINNER DANCE

** W.A.C. Green Salad with Tomato Slices*
Special Dressing
Brisket of Corned Beef with
Buttered New Cabbage
Irish Potatoes—
** Shredded Carrots with Sherry*
(Calcannon)
Croissants
** Apple Pie Ala Mode*

VISITING DIGNITARY DINNER

* Tomato Bouillon—Horseradish Cream
* Cheese Straws
* Poached Filet of Sole Chantilly
Roast Tenderloin of Beef—
Mushroom Slices
* Pommes de Terre Espagnole
* Artichoke Bottom Veronique
Tiny Parkerhouse Rolls
Tossed Green Salad—
* Cooked Salad Dressing—Croutons
* Bavarian Cream with
Fresh Sliced Strawberries
Cappuccino

NEW ENGLAND DINNER

*Shrimp Bisque - Toasted Wafers
Yankee Pot Roast - Carrots
Potatoes - Onions
Boston Baked Beans
* W.A.C. Tossed Salad Bowl
*Special Dressing
*W.A.C. Whole Wheat Bread
Boston Brown Bread
*Blueberry Crisp—
Topped with Vanilla Ice Cream

CANADIAN CONSULAR DINNER

*Puree of Mongole Soup—
Maple Leaf Cheese Wafers
Boneless Prime Rib Roast
Yorkshire Pudding
Buttered Brussel Sprouts
Green Salad with Hearts of Palm—
* W.A.C. Special Dressing
Croissants
* Fruit Crisp*

FOUNDERS DAY DINNER

*Sherried Oysters in Heavy Cream
* Filet of Chicken with almonds
Artichoke Bottoms topped with
Spinach and Riced Egg
Tropical Salad +
Plain Rolls
* Cold Chocolate Souffle*

+Molded salad with Pineapple, Mandarin Orange
and Seedless Grapes

A NIGHT IN VIENNA

Tomato filled with Chopped Aspic,
Filet of Sole and Caviar
Melba Toast
Veal Princess
(Veal scallops, Asparagus and
Hollandaise Sauce)
* Duchess Potatoes
Bibb Lettuce with Artichoke Hearts—
* Vinaigrette Dressing
* Anna Rolls

Cheese Platter
French Roquefort—Brie—Port Salut

* Mocha Angel Food Torte

Hors d'Oeuvres and Appetizers

BLEU CHEESE DIP

3 3-oz. packages cream cheese
¼ lb. Bleu cheese
1 T. onion juice
1 T. Worcestershire sauce

Mash cream cheese and add bleu cheese crumbled. Blend in onion juice and Worcestershire sauce. Mix thoroughly. Pile lightly in dish and serve with toasted wafers or potato chips. If you like a softer mixture add a little cream.

MUSHROOM PUFFS   (10 or 12 appetizers)

1 cup chopped mushrooms
½ tsp. grated onion
Salt to taste
Enough finely ground bread crumbs to absorb moisture.

Toast one side of a buttered bread round or square. Spoon on mixture. Top with chopped bacon or Parmesan cheese. Broil until brown. Serve hot.

FRUIT ICE MOLD FOR PUNCH BOWL

Small bunch of grapes
Whole solid stemmed strawberries
Another fruit
Water

Freeze a 1 quart round pan filled ¾ full of water.
Wash a small bunch of grapes and put in center of
ice. Place strawberries in and around grapes. Use
any other fruit in season, Kumquats are very nice
to add color. Spoon water over fruit, return to
freezer until set. Then add about ½ cup of water to
hold fruit and freeze until needed.

BACON CRISPS

Slice bread, remove crust and cut into 4 pieces.
Cut bacon slice into 4 pieces (overlap bread).
Wrap a slice of bacon around bread and secure
with toothpick. Bake in 375 degree oven until
brown. Remove toothpicks. These can be done
ahead and warmed before serving.

CHEESE STRAWS

Use regular pie crust recipe.
Sharp cheddar cheese (grated)

Roll out pie crust to a rectangle, sprinkle grated
cheese over half of pastry. Fold end to end and
press edges together. Roll out pastry again to
rectangle and repeat with grated cheese. Roll out
again so you have layers of pastry and cheese. Cut
in strips 4 inches by ¼ inches. Bake on cookie
sheet at 425 degrees 5 to 8 minutes. Watch closely
that they do not burn. Remove from pan while hot.

HOT CRABMEAT APPETIZERS

8 oz. of crabmeat (chopped fine)
½ tsp. of lemon juice
1 dash of tabasco sauce
¼ tsp. Worcestershire sauce
Salt to taste
Bind with a small amount of cream sauce
2 T. Parmesan cheese

Toast one side of a buttered bread round or square. Pile crabmeat on the untoasted side. Top crabmeat with Parmesan cheese. Place under broiler until brown.

CHEESE PUFFS   (12 to 16)

1 cup sharp Cheddar cheese (grated)
½ tsp. dry mustard
1 dash of tabasco sauce
¼ tsp. Worcestershire sauce
1 whole egg

Combine ingredients and beat in electric mixer until light and fluffy. Toast buttered rounds on one side. With teaspoon cover toast rounds with cheese mixture. Place under broiler until brown. These may be made ahead of time and kept in the refrigerator or you may freeze them.

SALTED PECANS OR ALMONDS

½ lb. whole shelled pecans
4 T. butter
Salt

½ lb. blanched whole almonds
4 T. butter

Place pecans in shallow pan and dot with butter. Toast in 350 degree oven about 15 min. Stir constantly so the nuts will brown. When crisp remove from oven and drain on paper towels to remove butter. Sprinkle with salt. If doing both pecan and almonds do in separate pans because it takes longer to toast the almonds.

ROLLED WATERCRESS SANDWICH
Makes 8 whole or 16 ½ rolls

6 oz. cream cheese (room temperature)
1 T. butter (soft)
1 large bunch of watercress
¼ tsp. Beau Monde seasoning
1 loaf of fine textured bread (solid and a day old)

Clean watercress saving the nice tops for the sandwich. Chop the remaining watercress for the filling. Squeeze to remove all liquid. Mix cream cheese, butter and seasoning. Slice bread very thin and remove crust. Spread with mixture and roll like a jelly roll. Wrap in wax paper. If you have trouble rolling bread thin, place between a slightly damp towel and roll with a rolling pin. When ready to serve, cut sandwich in half. Use toothpick to make a hole in the end to insert watercress top.

CUCUMBER, CREAM CHEESE AND GREEN PEPPER TEA SANDWICHES   (18 to 20)

4 oz. cream cheese (room temperature)
1 medium cucumber (peeled, seeded and chopped)
½ large green pepper (chopped fine)
1 T. soft butter
Salt, onion juice, Beau Monde seasoning to taste.

18 to 20 bread rounds, cut and buttered.

Mix cream cheese, seasonings, butter and well drained cucumber (squeeze in cloth to remove water). With teaspoon, pile cucumbers on rounds. Edge round with chopped green pepper.

BURGUNDY BEEF PATTIES FOR APPETIZERS   (20 to 30)

1½ lb. ground chuck—ground twice
2 T. chili sauce
¼ tsp. Worcestershire sauce
½ tsp. minced onion
½ tsp. prepared mustard
¼ tsp. horseradish
¼ cup red burgundy wine
Salt and pepper to taste

Combine ingredients and chill. Form into patties the size of 50 cent pieces. Dampen your hands so meat will not stick. Flatten. Place on a cookie sheet and broil 2 minutes on each side. Serve in tiny buns.

Soups

TOMATO BOUILLON

Chicken broth—1 qt.
Tomato paste—2 T.

Simmer.

Serve with thin lemon slice or Horseradish cream (whipped cream with horseradish).

Variation:

Add ½ cup finely chopped sauteed mushrooms.

COMMODORE SOUP   (Serves 8)

3 cups chicken broth
1 cup clam broth (strained)
Salt to taste
¼ tsp. celery salt
1 tsp. lemon juice
¼ cup sherry
Sliced lemon
Chopped parsley

Combine all ingredients. Serve with thin slice of lemon topped with chopped parsley.

CHILLED FRESH TOMATO SOUP
(6 Cup servings)

7 large ripe tomatoes

Grind or use blender. Season with ½ tsp. onion juice, 1 T. salt, ¼ tsp. ground black pepper. *Chill thoroughly.*

Top with:
5 T. mayonnaise combined with
½ tsp. curry powder and
2 T. parsley

CREAM OF WATERCRESS SOUP   (Serves 6)

3 T. butter
1 T. flour
3 cups chicken broth (HOT)
1 cup cream
Salt and pepper to taste
1 large bunch of watercress chopped fine
¼ cup whipped cream

Melt butter until bubbly, add flour and stir. Add to hot broth and continue to cook 6 to 8 minutes. Add cream and seasoning. Drain chopped watercress. Before chopping watercress save 6 nice little tops to garnish. Use leaves and stems for flavor. Add watercress to soup mixture. Garnish with whipped cream and sprig of watercress. May be served hot or cold.

CREAM OF MUSHROOM SOUP   (Serves 10)

½ lb. fresh mushrooms chopped fine
4 T. butter
3 T. flour
4 T. butter
1 qt. milk
2 cups chicken stock or beef stock
2 cups cream
1 egg yolk

Saute chopped mushrooms in 4 T. butter. Make roux of 4 T. butter and 3 T. flour. Heat milk and stock, add roux, and cook to a slow boil. Add sauteed mushrooms, add beaten egg yolk, and cream.

BASIC CREAM SOUP   (Serves 4)

2 T. butter
1 T. flour
1 cup cream
1 cup soup stock

Melt butter, add flour and stir. Gradually add cream and soup stock, stirring constantly. Season to taste. If a thinner soup is desired, add a little more cream.

Variations:

Cream of almond—add ¼ tsp. almond extract, garnish with whipped cream & toasted slivered almonds.

Cream of Spinach—add ½ pkg. frozen spinach, cooked & chopped very fine. Garnish with whipped cream.

Cream of Asparagus—add ½ pkg. frozen asparagus, cooked & cut small.

Cream of Tomato—add 2 T. of tomato paste, cook gently.

CHICKEN STOCK (CONSOMME)

1-5 lb. to 6 lb. Hen
2 stalks of celery with leaves
1 carrot
1 parsnip
1 small onion
1 T. of mixed whole spice
1 tomato washed and cut
A little parsley

Use chicken for salad or creamed chicken.

Wash and clean chicken thoroughly. Be sure that all the blood has been removed. Put in a deep kettle, add remaining ingredients and cover with boiling water. Cover and simmer for 2 or 3 hours, until tender, turn occasionally. Remove chicken from stock. Strain stock in collander. Refrigerate overnight, fat will become hard. Carefully remove fat next day. Strain stock through two thicknesses of cheesecloth. Return stock to fire, bring to a boil and add a washed egg shell to clear, skim off any sediments that come to the top. Remove shell and simmer stock to about ¾ to ½ the amount. When you have the strength you want add salt to taste. Note variations.

   1. With Avocado slice (soak avocado in lemon juice)
   2. With sherry (1 T. per 4 oz. cup)
   3. With rice
   4. With Chopped Mushrooms
   5. With Chopped Watercress
   6. With Orange Slices
   7. With Lemon Slices
   8. Sauteed julienne of celery and carrots
   9. Tiny noodles
   10. Peeled, seeded and cubed tomatoes
   11. Royale (See recipe)

MONGOLE SOUP (Serves 6-8)

1 10-oz. pkg. peas
¼ cup butter
¼ cup flour
1 cup milk
1 cup cream
1 cup stock
½ cup tomato paste
Salt
Pepper
¼ cup sherry

Cook peas, drain and put through a blender to a smooth paste. Melt butter, add flour and stir and cook a few minutes. Heat milk, cream and stock, add flour mixture and simmer, gently making sure it does not stick. Add tomato paste, stir until blended. Add salt and pepper to taste. Before serving add the puree of peas and sherry. Be very careful that the tomato mixture does not curdle.

CHILLED W.A.C. AVOCADO SOUP (Serves 6)

2 small avocado, ripe
1 cup chicken stock
1 cup heavy cream
¼ tsp. onion salt
Salt to taste
¼ cup whipped cream

Cut skin of avocado in 4 pieces and pull off from meat (do not cut away), this will give you the nice green part of avocado. Put in blender to mash, add chicken stock, heavy cream and seasonings. Blend well. Garnish with salted whipped cream.

COLD CURRIED CRABMEAT BISQUE
(Serves 8)

3 T. butter
1 T. flour
1½ cup fish stock or consomme
1½ cup cream
1 tsp. curry or more to your taste
1 tsp. lemon juice
2 T. chopped celery sauteed
1 T. grated onion sauteed
1 cup crabmeat chopped fine
1 tsp. chopped parsley
Salt
¼ tsp. Worcestershire sauce
½ cup whipped cream

Bring butter to bubble, add flour, cook for a few seconds. Heat stock and cream, add to flour mixture. Beat until smooth. Cook for 6 or 8 minutes. Make a paste of curry and lemon juice. Add to the stock, add sauteed celery and onion, blend well. Add crabmeat, chopped parsley, salt and Worcestershire sauce. If the bisque is too thick to your liking add a little more cream. Chill in bouillon cups, top with whipped cream.

ROYALE FOR CONSOMME

½ cup milk (scalded)
⅛ tsp. salt
⅛ tsp. onion salt
1 slightly beaten egg

Combine milk and seasoning and add to slightly beaten egg. Strain. Pour into small pyrex dish, place in water bath and bake at 325 until firm. Do not over bake. Test with silver knife. Chill and cut into small cubes. Serve in hot consomme with a little chopped parsley.

SHRIMP BISQUE

3 T. butter
1 T. flour
1½ cup consomme
1½ cups Half and Half cream
2 T. chopped celery sauteed
1 T. grated onion sauteed
1 tsp. lemon juice
1 cup Madeira wine
¼ tsp. Worcestershire sauce
1 T. chopped parsley
1 cup cooked shrimp chopped fine
¼ cup whipped cream

Bring butter to a bubble, add flour and cook for a few seconds. Heat stock and cream and add to flour mixture. Beat until smooth and cook for about 6 or 8 min. Add celery and onion, lemon juice, wine and seasonings. Add chopped cooked shrimps. Bring to a boil and serve with a dab of whipped cream. If bisque is too thick, add a little more cream or wine. May be served hot or cold.

Bread and Rolls

W.A.C. BASIC ROLLS

1 oz. yeast
¼ cup lukewarm water
¾ cup milk
¼ cup sugar
¼ cup melted butter
¾ tsp. salt
¼ cup sugar
3 slightly beaten egg yolks
3½ to 4 cups flour

Dissolve yeast in lukewarm water (112 degrees). Scald milk, dissolve sugar and salt and add ¼ cup melted butter. Cool, then add dissolved yeast and beaten egg yolks. Add flour and stir until well blended, and enough for a stiff dough and beat well. Turn out on floured board and knead until smooth and elastic. Place in buttered bowl and let raise double in bulk. Proceed to make rolls. For plain rolls, just shape as you wish. For sweet rolls follow auxiliary recipes for orange rolls, etc. Bake at 350 degrees for sweet rolls and at 400 degrees for plain rolls for 15 to 20 minutes.

ROLLED MELBA TOAST

Day old bread (unsliced)
Butter
Beau Monde seasoning or parmesan cheese

Slice bread into thin slices and remove crust. Roll
out thin with rolling pin. Butter bread and
sprinkle with Beau Monde seasoning or parmesan
cheese. Roll bread from corner to corner and
secure with toothpick. Let dry and remove toothpick and brown in oven.

Serve with soups or salads.

W.A.C. CINNAMON TOAST

1 cup sugar
1 T. cinnamon
Mixed together, you can always keep it on hand.

Slice bread and remove crust and toast. Butter
toast quite heavily and sprinkle cinnamon and
sugar over the toast and be very generous. Put
under the broiler until sugar boils. Cut in 3 fingers
and serve hot.

CURRIED TOAST

Mix softened butter, curry powder, salt and onion
salt to taste.
Slice fine textured soft bread very thin and
remove curst.

For easy rolling, roll bread out on a slightly
damped towel. Spread with curry butter, roll each
slice and fasten with a toothpick. Toast on all
sides, remove toothpick and allow to dry.

Serve with soup or salads.

PECAN ROLLS

W. A. C. basic roll recipe
Butter
Cinnamon
Sugar
6 T. butter
6 T. brown sugar
1 T. Karo syrup
¼ lb. broken pecans

Roll dough into rectangle about ¼ inch thick. Spread with butter, mix cinnamon and sugar together and spread over the dough. Roll jelly roll style and cut into ¾ inch pieces. Mix butter, brown sugar and Karo together. Butter muffin tins and place a small amount of mixture in bottom of pans and a few pecans. Place dough on top of mixture. Let rise double in bulk then bake at 350 degrees for 15 to 20 minutes.

BLUEBERRY MUFFINS

¾ cup sugar
½ cup butter
2 eggs
½ cup milk
¼ tsp salt
2 cups cake flour
2½ tsp baking powder
¾ cup blueberries

Cream sugar and butter, add eggs. Sift flour, salt and baking powder and add alternating with milk. Put batter into muffin tins, a little more than half full. Sprinkle with blueberries so they sink into the butter. Bake at 400 degrees for 20 minutes.

ANNA ROLLS

1 cup cold milk
1 egg
2½ cups flour
¼ tsp. salt
1 oz. fresh yeast (dissolve with 3 T. sugar)

Mix all ingredients. Chill for ½ hour. Then knead.
Roll dough, about ½ in. thick. Spread with 1/3
cup butter and fold over in thirds. Refrigerate for
½ hr. Repeat this last step two more times. Then
roll out and cut into strips about 3 inches long by 1
inch wide and tie into bow knots. Place on pans
and let rise. When they have doubled in size,
brush with mixture of ¼ cup cream and 1 egg
white. Bake in hot oven—475 degrees for 10 min.
Brush with melted butter and sprinkle with sugar
icing.

W.A.C. WHOLE WHEAT BREAD   (3 loaves)

2 cups scalded and cooled milk
3½ T. dry yeast
1 cup warm water (108 to 112 degrees)
1 T. molasses
¼ cup brown sugar
½ T. salt
½ cup shortening
3 cups whole wheat flour
6½ to 7 cups pastry flour

Soak yeast in water. Mix all ingredients and
knead. Let rise till it doubles in size then knead
again. Let rise again and then divide into 3 loaves.
Put into greased pans and bake about 50 minutes
at 350 degrees.

DATE NUT BREAD   (2 loaves)

1½ cups pitted dates (cut up)
4 T. shortening
1½ cup sugar
1 tsp. salt
1½ cup boiling water
2¾ cups sifted flour
1 tsp. soda
1 tsp. cream of tartar
1 egg slightly beaten
1 cup chopped nuts
½ tsp. vanilla

Put dates, shortening, sugar and salt in a mixing bowl and pour the 1½ cups of boiling water over them. Stir to dissolve and set aside to cool. Sift flour, baking soda and cream of tartar together and blend. When date mixture is room temperature, add the egg and flour mixture and beat until blended. Fold in nuts and vanilla and pour batter into greased loaf pan 9x5x3. Bake at 350 degrees until loaf pulls away from edge of pan and toothpick comes out clean (about 1¼ to 1¾ hours).

ORANGE ROLLS

W. A. C. basic roll recipe
¼ lb. melted butter
1 cup granulated sugar
1 orange (grated rind)

Pinch dough off into pieces about 1¼ inches in diameter. Roll in melted butter. Mix sugar and orange rind together and roll buttered dough in mixture. Place in buttered muffin tin and let rise double in bulk. Bake at 350 degrees for 15 or 20 minutes.

Sandwiches

SANDWICH LOAF

(Serves 8)

1 loaf unsliced day old bread
1 cup minced chicken salad
1 cup minced ham salad
1 cup ripe olive and cream cheese spread
1 cup minced egg salad
10 oz. cream cheese at room temperature
Watercress, firm peeled tomato, and
   creamed butter

Trim crusts from bread. If you prefer three fillings, cut loaf of bread into 4 slices lengthwise. If you want 4 fillings, cut bread into 5 slices lengthwise. Butter one side of bread for top and one side for bottom. The other three slices must be buttered on both sides and use plenty of butter. On bottom layer spread minced chicken salad, then a slice of buttered bread on top, butter, and repeat for the remaining salads. End with the top slice buttered on the bottom side. Refrigerate until set. Put a light weight on top of loaf to press. Remove from refrigerator, trim off salads that have pressed out of loaf. Mix cream cheese well with wooden spoon and add a small amount of cream for easier spreading. Place sandwich loaf on serving tray and put wax paper strips around bottom of loaf. Spread cream cheese on sides of loaf and avoid mixing salads in with cheese. Then spread the top of loaf with cream cheese. After loaf has been covered with cheese, pull wax paper away from loaf. Garnish top of loaf with tomato cut in 6 pieces. Garnish platter with watercress.

626 NORTH MICHIGAN SANDWICH

1 slice rye bread
Lettuce nest
1½ oz. sliced swiss cheese
2 oz. sliced chicken breast
1/3 cup 1,000 Island dressing
1 slice tomato
1 slice hard cooked egg
1 strip crisp bacon

Butter bread and remove crust. Place lettuce over bread then cheese over the lettuce. Put chicken over the cheese and put dressing over center of chicken only. Top with egg, tomato, and bacon. Garnish with parsley and ripe olives.

50TH ANNIVERSARY SANDWICH

3 slices of buttered toast

On first slice:
4 slices of tomato sliced thinly. Spread mayonnaise over the tomato and salt. Put chopped celery over mayonnaise. Sprinkle chopped bacon over celery and bacon.
On second slice:
Cover with thin slices of chicken breast. Repeat mayonnaise, chopped celery and bacon.
Third slice:
Cover sandwich, trim crusts and cut into four triangles.

GRILLED ROQUEFORT AND CHICKEN SANDWICH

1 slice of trimmed toast
mayonnaise
2½ oz. sliced white chicken meat
4 oz. Roquefort cheese topping

Butter bottom of toast and place in a ramekin dish with buttered side down. Spread top with mayonnaise. Place chicken over toast and spread with mayonnaise. Completely cover chicken with cheese topping. Bake in 350 degree oven for 15 to 18 minutes until bubbly and golden brown. Garnish with ripe olive and parsley.

ROQUEFORT TOPPING FOR GRILLED OR CHICKEN ROQUEFORT SANDWICH SANDWICH

1 lb. grated Roquefort cheese
  at room temperature
8 oz. cream cheese at room
  temperature
2 whole eggs
1½ tsp. worcestershire sauce
¾ tabasco sauce

Beat in mixer until light and fluffy.

EGG SALAD AND BACON SANDWICH
(Serves 3)

6 hard boiled eggs
W.A.C. Mayonnaise
Salt to taste
Lettuce
Butter
Bread
3 slices of cooked crisp
  bacon, chopped and drained

Chop eggs, add salt to taste, and enough W.A.C. mayonnaise to moisten. Slice bread thinly and butter from crust to crust. Place crisp lettuce on one side of bread, top with egg salad and sprinkle with hot chopped bacon. Top with other slice of buttered bread, remove crust and cut sandwich in half. If toasted, reheat sandwich in oven before serving.

BAKED FLUFFY CHICKEN SALAD SANDWICH

1 slice buttered toast
4 oz. chicken salad
1 egg white beaten stiff
1 beaten egg yolk
1 tsp. mayonnaise

In a ramekin dish place toast, buttered side down to avoid sticking. Spread chicken salad over the toast. Fold egg white into egg yolk and add mayonnaise. Cover the chicken salad with the egg mixture and bake at 350 degrees for about 15 minutes.

W.A.C. GRILLED CHEESE SANDWICH

1 slice bread (remove crust)
3 or 4 thin slices of peeled tomato
4 oz Wispride cheese (room temperature)
2 strips crisp bacon

Butter one side of bread and place buttered side down in a shirred egg dish or small casserole. Place tomato slices over top of buttered side of bread and season with salt. On top of tomatoes place Wispride cheese. Put in 350 degree oven for 15 minutes. Be sure that the bottom of bread is brown and the cheese is bubbling. Serve with crisp bacon.

You may substitute Ye Old Tavern or Kaukauna cheese.

Salads and Salad Dressings

ARTICHOKE HEARTS IN ASPIC

½ cup cold stock
1 T. gelatin
1½ cups hot stock
2 T. lemon juice
4 T. dry sherry
¼ tsp. Worcestershire sauce
¼ tsp. celery salt
¼ tsp. onion salt
6 artichoke hearts
6 or 8 pitted ripe olives
1 T. cubed pimento
1 T. chopped celery

Dissolve gelatin in ½ cup cold stock and add to the hot stock. If it doesn't dissolve heat for a few minutes but do not boil. Remove from flame and add lemon juice, sherry and seasonings. Cool until slightly thickened. If using individual mold put 1 T. of gelatin in bottom until almost gelled. Cut artichokes in half and drain well. Place in mold cut side down and add a few sliced ripe olives, pimento and celery. Pour remaining gelatin over and chill. Serve on Bibb lettuce and garnish with watercress.

TOMATO ASPIC   (1 pint mold)

1 envelope of Knox gelatin
  dissolved with
½ cup tomato juice
2 T. tomato paste plus tomato
  juice to fill 1 cup
¼ cup catsup
¼ tsp. salt
2 T. lemon
½ tsp. Worcestershire sauce
⅛ tsp. tabasco
½ tsp. celery salt

Heat catsup, tomato paste and tomato juice to
dissolve gelatin. Add spices and lemon juice,
cool and mold in 1 pt. mold or individual molds. To
make a crisp salad mold, add 1 cup of finely
chopped celery.

MARINATED MUSHROOM SLICES

1 lb fresh mushrooms
1 cup oil
2 T. vinegar
2 T. lemon juice
½ tsp. celery salt
¼ tsp. onion salt
¼ tsp. Worcestershire sauce
¼ tsp. Beau Monde seasoning
Salt to taste
1 T. chopped parsley

Wash and dry mushrooms. You may cut stems off
to use for sauce or soup or slice the whole
mushroom very thinly. Put in bowl. Mix oil,
vinegar, lemon juice and seasonings. You may do
this by putting into a jar and shaking until mixed
well. Pour over mushrooms and mix lightly. You
may do this the day before but do not add parsley
until serving as it turns dark.

SHRIMP AND VEGETABLE BOWL
(Serves 8)

2 lbs shrimp cooked and diced
½ cup cooked carrots julienne
½ cup cooked peas
½ cup cooked french green beans
½ cup chopped celery
1 cup mayonnaise (thinned with whipped cream)
¼ tsp. Worcestershire sauce
¼ tsp. Tabasco sauce
Salt and Pepper

Mix and refrigerate for one hour and serve in a
large lettuce cup.

RICE AND VEGETABLE SALAD   (Serves 4-6)

1½ cups cooked rice
¼ cup cooked green peas
¼ cup cut celery
1 tomato, peeled, seeded
   and cut in squares
6 ripe olives sliced thin
season to taste
½ small cucumber, peeled,
   seeded, cut in squares
¼ tsp. Beau Monde seasoning
½ tsp. salt and pepper to taste
¼ tsp. celery salt
¼ tsp. onion salt
1 tsp. chopped parsley

Combine all ingredients turning lightly. Marinate
with lemon and oil dressing. Garnish with tomato
wedges, whole ripe olives and bunches of
watercress.

CURRIED CHICKEN SALAD BOWL WITH
TOASTED ALMONDS   (Serves 4)

1 pint cubed chicken
¼ cup celery chopped
Salt and pepper
¼ tsp. curry
½ cup mayonnaise
2 T. whipped cream
Sliced toasted almonds

Combine chicken, celery and seasonings. Let
chicken absorb the seasonsing. Dissolve the curry
in a small amount of mayonnaise then add to the
remaining mayonnaise. Fold in whipped cream
and fold into chicken. Always fold, do not stir
because this will keep the chicken from breaking.
Suggestion: Be very careful of curry, some is
very strong. Serve on crisp lettuce and sprinkle
almonds on top and garnish with watercress and
ripe olives.

MOLDED BEET SALAD   (6 individual molds)

1 pkg lemon gelatin 3¼ oz.
1 No 2 can beets, drain and save juice
chop beets not too fine and drain again
    to remove all liquid
1 T. lemon juice
2 T. horseradish

Measure beet juice, lemon juice and horseradish.
Add enough water to make 2 cups liquid. Heat
liquid to dissolve gelatin, salt to taste. When
gelatin begins to set stir in well drained chopped
beets and mold. For a firmer mold add ½ tsp.
Knox gelatin to hot liquid and dissolve.

HOLLYWOOD SALAD BOWL

Line a large glass bowl with ½ cup of assorted greens. Sprinkle in this order:
1 T. chopped celery
¼ cup cooked french green beans
¼ cup cooked carrots, julienne
1 oz. julienne cooked chicken
1 oz. julienne ham
1 oz. julienne swiss cheese
¼ cup cooked peas

Garnish with tomato wedge, radish, ripe olive, sprig of watercress, and endive.

ASSORTED SALAD PLATE WITH CHICKEN SALAD   (Serves 1)

1 watermelon ball
1 cantaloupe ball
1 honey dew melon ball
1 grapefruit segment
1 orange segment
1 tomato slice
1 scoop of cottage cheese
1 scoop of chicken salad

Line a large glass shallow bowl with head and bibb lettuce. On 1/3 of bowl place first 6 items. On 1/3 of bowl place the tomato and cottage cheese. On 1/3 of bowl place the chicken salad. Garnish with 1 olive, 1 radish, ¼ hard boiled egg, parsley and watercress.

MOLDED SPRING SALAD

1 pkg of lemon gelatin
1 ¾ cup hot water
¼ cup lemon juice &
  vinegar mixed
½ tsp. salt or more
½ tsp. Worcestershire sauce
½ tsp. celery salt
½ cup finely chopped cabbage
2 T. finely chopped celery
2 T. finely grated carrots
1 T. chopped green pepper
1 T. chopped ripe olive
1 tsp. chopped chives
1 tsp. chopped parsley

Dissolve gelatin in hot water, add lemon juice and vinegar. Mix well and add seasoning. Cool, when slightly gelled add your very well drained vegetable mix. Pour in damp molds to gell. Serve on crisp lettuce nest. Garnish with endive and watercress. Serve with sour cream dressing.

BING CHERRY MOLD

1 box strawberry gelatin
1-1 lb. can pitted bing cherries
Port wine

Drain cherries and save juice, cut cherries in half. Follow recipe on box. (Small box of gelatin calls for 2 cups liquid.) Pour cherry juice in cup and fill remainder of cup with port wine. Use 1 cup hot water to dissolve gelatin, stir well. Add your cherry juice and wine. Cool, and when it begins to thicken add well drained cherries. Mold in a damp mold.

SOUR CREAM DRESSING   (1 cup)

1 cup commercial sour cream
1 T. W.A.C. mayonnaise
1 tsp. lemon juice
½ tsp. celery salt
¼ tsp. Worcestershire sauce
¼ tsp. Spice Island Beau Monde Salt
1 tsp. chopped parsley
You may add:
½ cup seeded chopped cucumber
1 tsp. onion juice

Combine all ingredients and blend well by folding gently until thoroughly mixed. Do not beat.

COOKED SALAD DRESSING   (2 cups)

2 T. flour
2 T. sugar
1 tsp. salt
1 tsp. dry mustard
1 whole egg slightly beaten
¼ cup vinegar
¾ cup water
1 T. butter
½ cup whipped cream

Combine flour, sugar and seasoning. Add vinegar and water and cook in double boiler until thick. Add beaten egg and continue to cook for a few moments and add butter. Remove from fire and pour into a bowl and cover with wax paper to avoid crust. Before using fold in whipped cream. For fruit salad substitute fruit juice and lemon juice for vinegar and water, and omit the mustard.

DIET DRESSING (1¼ cup)

1 cup oil
¼ cup lemon juice
½ tsp. Worcestershire sauce
½ tsp. salt
½ tsp. celery salt
½ tsp. onion salt
½ tsp. sugar substitute

Combine all ingredients in glass jar and shake well.

RED WINE DRESSING

2 cups oil
1 cup red wine
½ cup wine vinegar
1 tsp salt or more

Combine all ingredients and beat well.

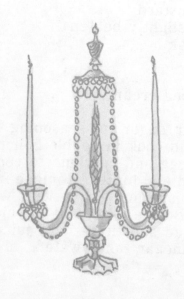

WARM SAUCE TO BE USED IN 1/2 AVOCADO
(Yields ¾ cup)

4 T. butter
2 T. water
4 T. catsup
3 tsp. sugar
2 tsp. Worcestershire sauce
½ tsp. salt
Dash of tabasco

Combine ingredients and bring to a boil. Serve hot.

VINAIGRETTE DRESSING
(Yields 1¼ cups)

1 cup lemon oil dressing
½ cup chopped sweet pickles
2 T. chopped pimiento
1 tsp. chopped chives or grated onion
1 tsp. chopped parsley
salt to taste

For variety add 1 chopped egg, 2 T. green pepper chopped.

LEMON OIL DRESSING

1 cup oil
6 T. lemon juice
4 tsp. Worcestershire sauce
½ tsp. salt
½ tsp. celery salt
½ tsp. onion salt
¼ tsp. Beau Monde seasoning

Combine all ingredients in glass jar and shake well.

W.A.C. MAYONNAISE

(5 cups)

4 egg yolks or 2 whole eggs
4 cups oil
¼ cup lemon juice
⅛ cup vinegar
1 tsp. salt
¾ tsp. paprika
¾ tsp. dry mustard

Beat eggs slightly with electric mixer at medium speed. *Slowly* add ½ of the oil. Mix paprika, dry mustard, and salt into vinegar and lemon juice. As oil and egg mixture begin to thicken add a *small* amount of the lemon juice-vinegar mixture. *Slowly, alternately,* in small amounts at a time add remaining oil and lemon-vinegar mixture.

W. A. C. SPECIAL DRESSING

1 whole egg
1 qt. oil
¾ cup spiced vinegar (below)
¼ cup celery seed
2 T. granulated sugar
1 tsp. tabasco sauce
1 tsp. Worcestershire sauce
1¼ tsp. salt or more to taste

Slightly beat one whole egg in electric mixer at medium speed. Beat in oil slowly a little at a time. Combine spiced vinegar, celery seed, sugar, salt, tabasco and Worcestershire sauce. As dressing thickens add a small amount of vinegar to thin. Repeat process until finished.

THOUSAND ISLAND DRESSING   (1½ cups)

1 cup mayonnaise
¼ cup chili sauce
3 T. chopped sweet pickles
2 hard cooked eggs chopped
1 tsp. chopped parsley
½ tsp. Worcestershire sauce
Salt to taste

Fold all ingredients into the mayonnaise very carefully. Do not beat.

SPICED VINEGAR USED FOR SPECIAL DRESSING

1 qt. cider vinegar
¼ cup Tarragon vinegar
¼ cup celery seed
¼ cup whole black pepper
¼ cup white mustard seed

Combine vinegar and spices and let age for 3 or 4 weeks. Shake bottle once a week to mix.

Entrees

CHEESE SOUFFLE   (Serves 4)

¼ C. butter
¼ C. flour
1 C. whole milk
½ tsp. salt
¾ C. grated sharp cheddar cheese
4 egg yolks beaten
4 egg whites
2 T. Parmesan cheese

Melt butter and blend in flour, cook a few moments. Heat 1 Cup whole milk, combine with flour and butter. Cook until thick, add cheese and stir until cheese is melted. Remove from heat. Add beaten egg yolks. Cool mixture. This can be made ahead of time and beaten egg whites folded in when ready to bake. Spoon into 4 buttered individual casseroles, sprinkle with Parmesan cheese. Bake in pan of water 25-30 minutes at 375 degrees.

ARTICHOKE BOTTOMS FILLED WITH
CRABMEAT TYROLIENNE SAUCE (Serves 4-6)

6 artichoke bottoms
1 lb King crabmeat cut in pieces
2 T. chopped celery
Tyrolienne Sauce
Lettuce
Watercress
Lemon wedge
Ripe olive
Endive

Make nest of lettuce in center of plate. Do not go over ridge of plate. Place artichoke bottom on top of lettuce. Top with crabmeat—sprinkle chopped celery over the top. Garnish with watercress, lemon wedge and ripe olive. Before serving, top the crabmeat with Tyrolienne sauce.

MUSHROOM FILLED ARTICHOKE
BOTTOMS   (Serves 6)

12 artichoke bottoms
1½ lbs. chopped mushrooms (cooked)
2 T. finely chopped celery
1 tsp. finely chopped onion
2 T. butter
¼ tsp. Worcestershire sauce
Salt to taste
Bread crumbs (fine)
2 T. Parmesan cheese
Mornay Sauce (Approx 3 C.)
12 strips crisp bacon

Saute celery and onions in butter. Drain the cooked mushrooms and combine all ingredients with seasoning. Add a few bread crumbs to bind. Fill artichoke bottoms with mushroom mixture. Top with Parmesan cheese. Serve on toast and top with mornay sauce and crisp bacon.

ARTICHOKE BOTTOMS FILLED WITH CRABMEAT MORNAY
(Serves 3-4)

6 artichoke bottoms
1 lb. crabmeat cut in pieces
1 T. lemon juice
1 T. sherry
2 C. Mornay sauce
¼ C. Parmesan cheese

Mix crabmeat with lemon juice, sherry and ½ C. of Mornay sauce (enough to bind crabmeat). Sprinkle Parmesan cheese over and brown in oven at 375 degrees for 25-30 minutes.

To serve, place on platter and cover artichoke bottoms with 1½ C. Mornay sauce.

EGG CUTLETS WITH MUSHROOM SAUCE
(12 cutlets)

10 hard cooked eggs
1 C. white sauce
Salt to taste
½ tsp. dry mustard
½ tsp. onion salt
Flour
1 egg beaten
2 T. cream
Bread crumbs for coating

Cut eggs criss-cross with egg slice or chop. Add seasoning. Add white sauce to bind eggs. Chill overnight. Shape into cutlets about one Tablespoon each. Flour cutlets, then dip into beaten egg and cream, then into bread crumbs, Chill until ready to use. Fry in deep fat at 400 degrees—until golden brown. Drain on paper towel. Serve with a mushroom sauce.

CALVES SWEETBREADS SAUTE   (Serves 4)

2 pairs of calves sweetbreads
1 tsp. salt
2 T. vinegar
Flour
Paprika
Butter
1 T. flour
½ C. sherry
Mushroom slices cooked

Cover sweetbreads with boiling water, add salt and vinegar. Simmer for about 20 min. Remove from fire, drain and run cold water over them to cool. Drain. Pull off the thin membrane, the thick membrane and the darker tubes. You may press or leave round. Dip in a little flour with salt and a few grains of paprika. Saute both sides in hot butter, add sherry & cover. Continue to cook about 5 min. Remove sweetbreads, strain drippings, return to fire, add flour and sherry to thicken. Cook well. Pour over sweetbreads and garnish with sliced mushrooms.

CORNED BEEF HASH   (Serves 4)

3 C. cooked lean chopped corned beef
1 C. cooked and diced potatoes
Cream
½ T. grated onion
Salt
Pepper

Combine all ingredients enough cream to moisten. Add seasoning to taste. Bake in a buttered casserole in pan of water. Brown to your liking about ½ hour at 350 degrees. Serve with crisp bacon.

ESCALLOPS OF VEAL BONNE FEMME
(Serves 4)

12 veal scallops cut very thin
  coated with a mixture of flour
paprika
salt
pepper
½ C. dry wine
¼ C. stock
1-16 oz. jar tiny white onions
½ lb. firm, fresh mushrooms
sweet butter
1 T. cornstarch
Chopped parsley

Remove fat and skin from veal. Dip veal slightly in flour mixture. Brown quickly in sweet butter. Put in baking pan, season and add dry white wine and a little stock. Cover with foil. Bake at 375 degrees about 30 min. Strain drippings and carefully mix in 1 T. of cornstarch for the sauce. This will give a clear sauce. Cut mushrooms in quarters, saute in butter. Place veal on platter, pour sauce over veal, add mushrooms and onions.

FRESH MUSHROOMS MORNAY CRISP BACON
(Serves 4)

1 lb. mushrooms, whole
1 tsp. lemon juice
¼ C. butter
1 C. Mornay sauce
8 slices-crisp bacon

Wash and remove stems. Cook in ¼ C. butter with 1 t. lemon juice (chop stems and cook, may be used for soup or sauce). Serve mushrooms in rice ring or on toast. Cover each serving with Mornay sauce and slices of crisp bacon.

W.A.C. BREAST OF CHICKEN JUBILEE
(Serves 6-8)

6 breasts of chicken
1 1 lb. can pitted bing cherries
1 cup sherry
2 T. chopped sauteed onion
2 T. brown sugar
2 T. chili sauce
½ tsp. Worcestershire sauce
¼ cup brandy
1 T. cornstarch

Drain cherries, pour brandy over them and set aside. Mix cherry juice, sherry, sauteed onion, brown sugar, chili sauce and Worcestershire sauce. Bring to a boil and add 1 T. cornstarch, stir and continue to let boil. Sprinkle a little flour and paprika over breasts and put into another pan, pour the sauce over breasts, cover with foil and bake for 45 minutes or until tender. Heat cherries. Place breasts on platter, pour over sauce and spoon on the brandied cherries. Garnish with watercress or parsley.

W.A.C. BAKED CHICKEN   (Serves 1)

½ broiler chicken
Bread crumbs to cover
Butter
Salt and Pepper

Coat chicken with melted butter. Season with salt and pepper and dip into bread crumbs. Bake in a 375 oven for 50 minutes. Serve plain or with sauce prepared from juices.
Variation: Add wine or mushrooms to sauce.

SWISS CHICKEN DIVAN (Serves 6-8)

2 pkg. frozen broccoli spears (cooked)
¼ cup butter
¼ cup flour
1 tsp salt
⅛ tsp pepper
1 cup chicken stock
1 cup cream
1 5-6 lb. stewing hen cooked
1 cup grated swiss cheese
1 tsp minced sauteed onion
3 T. sherry & dash of brandy
1 egg yolk
½ cup cream whipped
Parmesan cheese

Heat butter until it bubbles. Add flour and cook for a few minutes. Heat liquids and add to butter mixture, add seasoning and bring to boil. Add grated cheese and onion and continue to cook until cheese is melted. Add sherry and fold in whipped cream. Drain broccoli on towel to remove water. Place broccoli on serving platter. Top with chicken and cover with sauce and sprinkle with cheese. Brown under broiler.

BREAST OF CHICKEN VERONIQUE

(Serves 6)

6 boneless chicken breasts
1 cup supreme sauce
1 cup drained seedless grapes
Paprika
Salt
2 T. butter
Butter
Chopped parsley

Dip chicken breasts in flour, salt and small amount of paprika for browning. Butter baking pan and place chicken in pan, skin side up. Baste as chicken cooks and add ¼ cup of chicken stock. Turn chickens over—cover with foil. Bake at 350 degrees for 60 minutes.Remove to serving platter, ribbon with supreme sauce. Heat grapes in butter, drain and sprinkle grapes over chicken. Sprinkle a little chopped parsley over the top.

ITALIAN BAKED BREAST OF CHICKEN
(Serves 6)

6 boneless ½ breasts of chicken
3 T. butter
2 tsp. Beau Monde Seasoning
4 small white onions
1-4½ oz. can artichoke hearts
1 lg. firm ripe tomato
1 tsp. Spice Island Italian Herb seasoning
1 T. chopped parsley
2 T. water
¼ cup Marsala
¼ cup grated Parmesan cheese

Season chicken with salt and pepper, Beau Monde, paprika and sprinkle lightly with flour. Brown chicken in butter until golden brown. Transfer chicken to a 2 qt. casserole. Peel onions and quarter. Drain artichokes and cut in half. Cut tomato in 6 or 8 wedges. Saute onions and artichokes in same pan where chicken was browned. Add Italian Herb seasoning, parsley and water. Cook stirring constantly until all drippings clinging to pan have been dissolved. Add tomatoes and Marsala. Pour mixture over chicken and cover and bake at 350 degrees for 50 minutes or until chicken is tender. Remove cover, sprinkle with cheese and bake for 5 minutes longer until cheese is melted.

BREAST OF CHICKEN CITRON

(Serves 4)

4 large single, boned chicken breasts
½ cup butter
Salt and pepper
Flour
1 T. sherry
1 T. white wine
1 orange—juice and rind
1 large lemon
2 tsp. lemon juice
Salt and pepper
1 cup thin cream
12 very thin slices of lemon
Grated Parmesan cheese

Season chicken breasts with salt and pepper, dust with flour, dot with butter and brown at 400 degrees for about 25 minutes. Lower the temperature to 325, cover and continue to bake until nearly done, about 20 to 25 minutes. Combine sherry, white wine, and orange juice and pour over chicken. Continue to bake until tender. When done, turn up fire and add cream. Put lemon slices on a flat broiler proof pan, sprinkle with Parmesan cheese and put under broiler till cheese browns slightly. Put chicken on serving platter and garnish with lemon slices.

W.A.C. CHICKEN AUGUSTA
(Serves 6)

6—5 oz. boneless, skinless, raw chicken breasts
½ lb. ground round steak
¼ cup fine bread crumbs
1 T. grated sauteed onion
1 well beaten egg
1 cup cream
Salt to taste
¼ lb. butter and
1 T. chopped parsley mixed together to make small butter balls

Grind chicken breasts with fine blade, then grind the chicken and steak together 3 times. Mix the crumbs, onions and cream together and let stand a few minutes. Then combine all ingredients, beat well with a wooden spoon and add beaten egg. Continue to beat until fluffy. Mixture should be quite soft, if needed add more cream; make the day before so it will be easier to handle. Shape into patties about 3 by ½ inches. The mixture will be easier to handle with damp hands. Chill again. Heat skillet and add butter. Sear patties quickly on both sides and let simmer for 15 min. After removing patties to platter add about ½ cup stock to skillet and bring to a boil. Pour this over patties. Place a butter ball on each patty when they are served.

MANDARIN CHICKEN   (Serves 8-10)

10 single chicken breasts
¼ cup butter
Salt and pepper
1 11 oz. can mandarin oranges, drained
½ tsp. grated orange rind
Juice 2 medium oranges
¼ cup soy sauce
2 T. honey
1 tsp. dry mustard
1 tsp. chopped onion
1½ cups half & half
1 cup frozen orange juice
3 cups chicken stock
Flour to thicken

Season the chicken breasts with salt and pepper.
Dot with butter and brown in oven at 400 degrees
for ½ hour. Combine orange juice, soy sauce,
honey, mustard, onion, orange rind, and chicken
stock. Pour this sauce over the chicken breasts.
Lower the oven to 325 degrees and continue to
bake for 35 to 40 minutes. When tender remove the
chicken breasts to a heated serving dish. Thicken
the pan juices with flour. Remove the sauce from
the heat and add the half & half. Pour this sauce
over the chicken which has been sprinkled with
the mandarin orange sections.

ALMOND CHICKEN OR LOBSTER (Serves 2-4)

½ lb. cooked lobster or
1 boneless chicken breast
½ cup Chinese pea pods
   cut diagonally
½ cup Chinese waterchestnuts
   sliced thin
½ cup green peppers cut in
   thin strips
½ cup fresh mushrooms quartered
   and sauteed in butter for 3 min.
½ cup pascal celery,
   cooked slightly
¼ cup peanut oil (heat)
Salt & pepper
onion salt to taste
¾ cup chicken stock
   cooked and combined with
   1 T. cornstarch

Blanch green pepper in hot water. In pan with
hot oil, put lobster or chicken and vegetables.
Cook for 5 or 6 minutes, carefully turning not to
break ingredients. Place in serving dish and keep
warm. Add chicken stock and cornstarch mixture
and cook until thick.

FILET OF CHICKEN IN ALMOND BATTER
(Serves 6)

12 1 oz. slices cooked white meat
6 1 oz. slices cooked dark meat
Batter:
  ¾ cup flour
  2 eggs
  ½ cup milk
  ¾ tsp. salt
  1 tsp. baking powder
  1 tsp. almond flavoring
  Beat all ingredients well

Dip chicken in batter and fry in deep fat. Serve 2
slices white and 1 dark meat covered with ½ cup
of supreme sauce flavored with almond extract.
Garnish with sliced almonds and parsley.

CHICKEN MARAGITA   (Serves 10)

¼ cup onions, chopped fine
1 T. butter
1 cup milk
2 T. flour
2 T. butter
½ cup dry sherry
1¼ lbs. diced chicken (4 cups)
1 / 3 cup chopped stuffed manzanilla olives
2½ cups raw fine noodles
  (7½ cups cooked)

Saute onions in butter. Heat milk, flour, and
butter to make cream sauce. Add onions, sherry,
diced chicken and chopped olives. Cook noodles
and drain well. Butter individual casseroles or 2-2
qt. casseroles. Layer the noodles and the chicken
in the casseroles, ending with layer of noodles.
Sprinkle with parmesan cheese, dot with butter
and bake for 20 min. at 350 degrees.

FAR EAST CHICKEN   (Serves 8-10)

1 stick butter
½ cup flour
½ tsp salt
1 cup cream (½ & ½)
2 cups chicken stock

Melt butter in top of double boiler, add flour and salt. Cook until bubbly. Add chicken stock stirring constantly until smooth. Then add cream. Cook over hot water for 30 minutes. Then add:

2 cups chicken diced large
½ cup sauteed sliced mushrooms
1 cup sliced waterchestnuts
¼ cup pimiento—cut in strips
¼ cup dry sherry

Serve over parslied rice and sprinkle with blanched sliced almonds.

W.A.C. CREAMED CHICKEN   (Serves 8)

4 T. butter
3 T. flour
2 cups milk
½ cup sherry
1 tsp Worcestershire sauce
Dash of onion salt
Few drops of Tabasco sauce
2/3 cup cream
Salt and pepper to taste
2 cups cooked cubed chicken

Blend butter and flour to make a roux. Add milk, stirring constantly till it boils. Then add wine and seasonings and cook gently for a few minutes. Then add cream and diced chicken. Serve in pastry shells, over toast points or rice.

CHICKEN TURNOVERS   (Serves 8)

Pie crust (See recipe)
Creamed chicken (recipe)
Mushroom sauce (recipe)

Roll out pastry dough and cut out eight 5 inch rounds. Fill with creamed chicken which has been chilled overnight and fold over, crimping edges tightly so filling does not escape. Bake for 45 minutes to 1 hour at 400 degrees. Serve with mushroom sauce.

SOUR CREAM CHICKEN CASSEROLE
                                       (Serves 10)

1 pkg 8 oz. cream cheese
2 cups dairy sour cream
2 cups chicken cut in cubes
½ cup sliced sauteed mushrooms
2 T. grated sauteed onions
2 T. chopped parsley
1 tsp. salt
¼ tsp. Worcestershire sauce
¼ tsp. Spice Island Beau Monde
1 8 oz. pkg. fine noodles
¾ cup buttered bread crumbs

Have cream cheese at room temperature, blend in sour cream. Add the remaining ingredients except noodles and crumbs. Cook noodles in salt water until tender, wash with cold water and drain. Butter baking dish, pour noodles in dish, and dot with butter. Top with well blended chicken mixture. Sprinkle buttered bread crumbs on top. Bake in water bath in 350 degree oven for 30 to 40 minutes.

FILET OF SOLE–ALMONDINE (Serves 6)

1½ lb.. filet of sole
1 cup milk
1 / 3 cup sauterne
3 T. butter
2 T. flour
½ tsp. dry mustard
½ tsp. salt
½ tsp. Worcestershire sauce
¾ cup shredded swiss cheese
1 beaten egg yolk
1 T. whipped cream
¼ cup sliced almonds

Roll filets, place in shallow baking dish. Pour milk over fish and cover with foil. Bake at 350 degrees for 15 min. or until tender but do not overcook. Melt butter and blend with flour, mustard and salt. Pour milk off fish and strain and blend into flour and butter. Cook until thickened and add swiss cheese and wine. Stir until cheese is dissolved, stir in beaten egg yolk and fold in whipped cream. Pour sauce over fish and sprinkle with sliced almonds.

SEAFOOD MORNAY (Serves 6)

1½ cup Mornay sauce
½ lb. crabmeat (cut)
½ lb. deveined cooked shrimps (cut in half)
½ lb. lobster meat
3 T. butter
2 T. sherry
2 T. Parmesan cheese

Heat seafood in butter and sherry, combine with mornay sauce. Pour in buttered baking dish and sprinkle with Parmesan cheese. Bake in pan of hot water at 350 degrees, 40 to 50 minutes.

POACHED FILET OF SOLE–CHANTILLY
(Serves 4)

1 filet of sole
Juice of ½ lemon
¼ cup sauterne
½ cup hollandaise sauce
2 T. whipped cream
8 cooked shrimp
4 broiled mushroom caps
Parsley (chopped)

Steam filet of sole with lemon juice and sauterne about 10 min. Do not over cook. Save ½ cup fish stock and fold in hollandaise sauce. Just before serving fold in whipped cream. Spoon sauce over sole and top each serving with 2 cooked shrimps, 1 broiled mushroom cap and sprinkle with chopped parsley.

FILET OF SOLE, IN WHITE WINE (Serves 2-4)

1 lb. filet of sole
Salt
1/3 cup white wine
Juice of 1 lemon
¼ cup water
1 egg yolk (beaten)
2 T. butter
1 T. flour
1 T. Parmesan cheese
1 lemon, sliced thin

Cut filets lengthwise in half. Roll each piece and place in a buttered pan. Season with salt and add 1/3 cup white wine, lemon juice, and water. Cover pan tightly with aluminum foil and steam in oven at 350 degrees for 15 or 20 minutes. Remove from oven, pour off liquid and strain. Melt butter, add flour and hot stock to make sauce. Add egg yolk. Arrange filets on platter and pour sauce over it.

CREAMY SHRIMP SCALLOPS   (Serves 4)

1 lb. bay scallops
½ lb. cooked and deveined shrimps
  cut in quarters
3 T. butter
1½ T. flour
1 cup cream
1 egg yolk
¼ tsp. onion salt
1 tsp. lemon juice
¼ cup whipped cream
¼ cup dry sherry
¼ tsp. paprika
Season to taste
4 slices of toast
Chopped parsley

Season scallops and sprinkle with paprika, sautee
quickly in sweet butter. Bay scallops should only
be cooked seconds or they will be tough. Make
white sauce: Melt butter, and flour, stirring until
bubbly. Add cream, onion salt, salt and pepper.
Cook until thickened and smooth. Heat shrimp in
sherry and lemon juice. Add to white sauce and
fold in whipped cream. Place scallops on toast
and pour creamy shrimp sauce over and sprinkle
with chopped parsley.

DEVILED CRABMEAT EN COQUILLE
(Serves 6)

3 T. butter
1 T. finely chopped onions
½ cup chopped celery
1 lb. crabmeat
2 hardcooked eggs cut fine
3 T. chopped parsley
3 T. diced pimento
2 T. dry sherry
¼ tsp. Worcestershire sauce

Sauce:
3 T. flour
2/3 cup milk
2/3 cup half and half
¾ tsp. salt
½ tsp. prepared mustard
Pepper to taste

Saute onions and celery in butter and set aside.
Sauce: melt 3 T. butter, add flour and stir well.
Add milk and half & half, stirring constantly.
Cook until thick and smooth. Add crabmeat, eggs,
sauteed onions and celery, parsley and pimentos.
Combine mixture lightly. Serve in coquille shells
and sprinkle with sliced toasted almonds.

LOBSTER ALASKA   (Serves 4)

1 cup lobster meat
3 T. butter
2 T. flour
1 cup coffee cream
1 T. lemon juice
1 T. Madeira
1 T. Brandy
Salt to taste
⅛ tsp. paprika
2 egg yolks
4 egg whites beaten
1 T. thick mayonnaise
½ tsp. salt
1 tsp. chopped parsley

Make cream sauce with flour, butter and cream.
Cook until smooth. Heat lobster in lemon juice,
brandy, wine, salt and paprika. After combining
sauce and lobster, add 2 slightly beaten egg yolks;
stir over low heat for a few seconds. Pour into
buttered casserole. Beat egg whites stiff, fold in
mayonnaise and chopped parsley. Cover lobster
casserole with egg white mixture. Do not make
smooth—peak the egg whites. Place casserole in
pan of hot water. Bake 10 or 15 minutes at 350-375
degrees until lobster is hot and egg whites are a
golden brown.

Just before serving spoon hollandaise sauce over
top and sprinkle with chopped parsley.

SEAFOOD CUTLETS   (Serves 4-6)

1 cup chopped cooked shrimps
1 cup chopped crabmeat
1 tsp. lemon juice
Salt to taste
4 T. butter
2 T. flour
½ cup milk (heated)
½ cup cream (heated)
2 T. water
1 egg beaten to blend
Fine bread crumbs

Melt butter, add flour and stir until well blended.
Add warm milk and cream and bring to a boil.
Cook about 2 minutes then add seasoning and
lemon juice. Combine seafood and chill—this
may be done the day before. Shape into cutlets.
Blend beaten egg and water. Cover cutlet with
flour then dip in egg and water mixture, then
bread crumbs. Chill formed cutlets. Fry in deep
fat 390 to 400 degrees. When nicely browned, drain
on paper towel to absorb fat. Serve with Newburg
sauce.

BASIC SUPREME SAUCE   (2 cups)

¼ cup butter
¼ cup flour
1 tsp salt
⅛ tsp pepper
1 cup chicken stock
1 cup cream
3 T. Madeira
1 egg yolk
3 T. whipped cream

Heat butter until it bubbles and add flour and cook for a few minutes stirring to avoid sticking. Heat liquids and add to butter mixture. Add seasoning and bring to a boil. Cook about 5 min. and taste to see that there is no flour taste. Add Madeira and beaten egg yolk. Cook 5 min. longer and then fold in whipped cream before serving.

MUSHROOM SAUCE   (1 cup)

1 cup supreme sauce
½ cup chopped or sliced sauteed mushrooms.

Mix.

HOLLANDAISE SAUCE   (1¼ cups)

3 egg yolks
2 T. lemon
½ cup butter, melted
¼ tsp. salt
¼ cup whipped cream

Make in a double boiler. Beat egg yolks with a wooden spoon until smooth but not fluffy. Add lemon juice. Add melted butter a small amount at a time. Cook until sauce begins to thicken. Add salt. Remove from heat, and add whipped cream.

MORNAY SAUCE   (3½ cups)

¼ cup butter
¼ cup flour
1 tsp salt
⅛ tsp pepper
1 cup chicken stock, heated
1 cup cream (half & half)
1 cup grated swiss cheese
  (pack slightly)
1 tsp. minced onion
1 egg yolk beaten
3 T. sherry
½ cup whipped cream

Bring butter to bubble and add flour and cook for
a few seconds. Add chicken stock and cream,
continue to cook until thick. Add grated cheese
and stir until melted. Add minced onion, beaten
egg yolk and sherry. Remove from heat and fold
in whipped cream before serving.

TYROLIENNE SAUCE FOR COLD CRABMEAT
OR SHRIMPS
                            (Yields 1½ pints)

2 cups mayonnaise
1 cup chili sauce (strained)
1 T. finely cut chives
½ tsp. worcestershire sauce
¼ tsp. tabasco sauce
2 T. whipped cream

Fold chili sauce and other ingredients into
mayonnaise.

NEWBURG SAUCE

4 T. butter
2 T. flour
1 egg yolk
½ cup hot milk
½ cup hot cream
White pepper
Paprika
Salt
2 T. sherry
2 tsp. brandy
¼ tsp. Worcestershire sauce

Melt butter and add flour, blend well. Add hot milk and cream, salt, pepper and enough paprika to turn sauce a delicate pink color. Add sherry and brandy and Worcestershire sauce and cook until flavors are well blended. Add beaten egg yolk last.

Vegetables

EGGPLANT, TOMATO, ONIONS & GREEN PEPPER CASSEROLE   (Serves 6)

6 slices eggplant, ½" thick
6 slices peeled tomato ½" thick
6 slices thin bermuda onion
6 thin slices green pepper
¼ cup parmesan cheese
¼ cup olive oil or butter
1 tsp. Beau Monde seasoning
salt & pepper to taste

Wash and peel eggplant, slice and soak for 10 mins. in salted water. Drain on a paper towel. Saute eggplant in oil or butter. When slightly brown, place in oiled baking dish or pan, season with Beau Monde, salt and pepper. Place sliced tomato over eggplant and repeat seasoning. Place sliced onion and green pepper over tomato and season. Next pour a small amount of oil over all to glaze. Sprinkle with parmesan cheese. Bake at 350 degrees for 45-60 minutes (until vegetables are tender). For a luncheon entree, top with mushroom cap and crisp bacon strips.

BRAISED CUCUMBER STRIPS   (Serves 4)

2 large firm cucumbers

Peel cucumbers with vegetable peeler. Cut cucumber in half lengthwise, then cut each half in thirds to make strips. Cut out seeds. Put in a sauce pan. Add just enough water to keep covered. Cook slowly until tender, turning gently to avoid breaking (5 to 10) minutes. Drain on a paper towel. Serve with lemon parsley butter or hollandaise.

SPINACH TIMBALES   (16 Timbales)

5 whole eggs
2 cups whole milk
¾ cup cooked chopped spinach
onion salt
salt
⅛ tsp. Worcestershire sauce

Beat eggs slightly. Strain to remove the egg white threads. Add milk and seasonings. Mix spinach into egg mixture. Butter timbale molds. Spoon in the mixture. Bake in pan of water at 300 degrees for 45 minutes. Test with silver knife as you would a custard.

SHREDDED CARROTS IN   (Serves 4-6)
SHERRY

1 lb. carrots
3 T. sherry
¼ cup butter

Wash and scrape carrots. Grate carrots with the long grater edge.

Cook in pan with ¼ C. butter and 3 T. sherry. Stir constantly. Do not overcook.

BAKED ZUCCHINI WITH   (Serves 4-6)
ONION AND BACON

2 lbs. zucchini squash
4 young green onions chopped
½ cup chopped bacon
½ cup chicken stock
Salt & pepper
½ tsp. Beau Monde seasoning
1 T. diced pimento

Wash and cut zucchini on slant—¼" thick. Place
slightly overlapping. Season. Pour chicken stock
over zucchini. Place in 350 degree oven for 10 to 15
minutes (or until transparent.). Saute onions in
butter. Remove zucchini to platter and sprinkle
with seasonings, onion, bacon and pimento.

FILLED ZUCCHINI–MORNAY SAUCE (Serves 6)

6 small firm zucchini
1 T. chopped onion
4 strips crisp bacon, chopped
1 T. celery chopped
¼ cup mushrooms, chopped
2 T. butter
¼ cup bread crumbs
½ tsp. Beau Monde seasoning
2 T. Parmesan cheese
salt and pepper to taste

Scrub zucchini with brush, dry and cut ¼ off top
lengthwise. Scoop out the pulp and chop. Cook
the large portion of zucchini 8 to 10 mins. in salt
water. Remove from water and drain on paper
towel, cut side down. Saute onions, celery,
chopped squash and mushrooms in butter. Add
crisp bacon and toss. Add seasonings and fill
zucchini. Mix cheese and crumbs together.
Sprinkle over top. Bake in buttered baking dish at
350 degrees for 25 to 30 minutes.

ARTICHOKE BOTTOMS VERONIQUE

(Serves 3-4)

6-8 Artichoke bottoms
1 2 lb. can seedless grapes
2 tsp. Brandy
1 T. Karo
1 tsp. butter—melted
Chopped parsley

Place artichokes in buttered flat baking pan. Drain grapes. Heat.

Mix brandy, karo and butter together. Mix with the grapes to glaze. Spoon into artichoke bottoms—sprinkle with chopped parsley before serving.

POMMES DE TERRE ESPAGNOLE

Peel and wash potatoes. Cut with a large melon ball cutter. Cook about 5 minutes in salted water. Drain and pour into a well buttered baking dish. Coat potatoes with finely ground bread crumbs mixed with parmesan cheese. Drizzle with butter and brown in the oven at 400 degrees until golden brown. Sprinkle with finely chopped pimento, chives and parsley before serving.

W.A.C. AU GRATIN POTATOES

4 medium sized red potatoes
2 T. butter
1 T. flour
½ cup cream
¾ cup milk
¼ cup cheddar cheese, grated
2 T. parmesan cheese
salt & pepper to taste

Peel potatoes and cut into ¼ inch cubes. Rinse in cold water to remove starch. Cook potatoes in salted water. Do not overcook. Melt butter, add flour, cook a few seconds. Heat milk and cream then add gradually to the butter and flour mixture stirring constantly until it bubbles. Add cheddar cheese, salt and onion powder to taste. Butter a 1 qt. baking dish, put cooked potatoes in and cover with sauce. Sprinkle parmesan cheese over top. Bake at 350 degrees for 30 to 40 minutes.

DUCHESS POTATOES   (Serves 8-10)

4 cups hot mashed or riced potatoes
1 T. butter
2 egg yolks or 1 whole egg beaten
Seasoning to taste (onion salt and pepper)

Combine all ingredients and blend well. Put mixture thru a pastry bag with a star tube to make a large rosette. Place on a well buttered cookie sheet. Drizzle with melted butter and sprinkle with a little paprika. Bake at 450 degrees for 15 to 20 minutes.

HUNTER'S BAKED RICE   (Serves 6)

1 cup rice
3 cups water
1 tsp. salt
1 green onion chopped
1 T. chopped green pepper
1 T. chopped pimento
4 T. butter
1 T. parsley, chopped

Cook rice in water and salt until rice is tender.
Remove from fire. Pour rice in strainer and run
cold water over rice to remove starch. Return to
fire and add onion and green pepper which have
been sauteed in butter. Stir in pimento. Blend
well. Before serving add parsley.

SAVORY RICE   (4 servings)

1 cup raw rice
2¼ cups broth
½ cup cooked & chopped mushrooms
½ cup sauteed onion
½ tsp. Beau Monde seasoning
1 tsp. chopped parsley
Salt and pepper to taste

Combine all ingredients and bake covered at 350
degrees for about 40-45 minutes.

RICE WITH PEAS AND MUSHROOMS

1 cup rice
½ tsp. salt
2 cups water
½ cup cooked, chopped mushrooms
¾ cup peas, cooked
¼ cup butter
2 tsp. chopped parsley
½ tsp. onion salt

Cook rice until tender, wash in cold water to remove starch. Return to fire add butter, mushrooms and cooked peas. Toss lightly. Add chopped parsley before serving.

Cookies

MILLION DOLLAR COOKIES

½ cup white sugar
½ cup brown sugar
1 cup butter
1 egg unbeaten
1 tsp. soda
½ tsp. salt
1 tsp. vanilla
½ cup finely ground nuts
2 cups sifted all purpose flour

Cream butter and sugar, and add the egg and beat until fluffy. Sift flour and dry ingredients together, add nuts. Add to the butter and sugar. Add vanilla. Mix thorougly. Roll into small balls, the size of quarters, dip in sugar, Press with bottom of a glass. Do not butter cookie sheet. Bake at 350 degrees 10-12 minutes. After cookies are cooled, swirl with caramel icing. Let icing dry before storing cookies.

LILLY COOKIES FOR TEA

4½ oz. cream cheese
1 cup butter
2 cups all purpose flour

Combine ingredients. Chill dough. Roll on pastry cloth or slightly floured board, cut with 1½" round cutter. Bring lower end together and press with fingers. Spread top part to look like a lily. Put a small amount of orange marmalade in the center. Bake on buttered cookie sheet at 375 degrees for 10-15 mins. Cool and sprinkle with powdered sugar.

ROLLED PECAN COOKIES

¼ C. butter
½ C. brown sugar
1 egg beaten
2 T. flour
¼ C. chopped nuts
Salt

Cream butter, sugar, add beaten egg. Blend in flour, chopped nuts, and salt. Drop by teaspoonfuls on buttered cookie sheet and spread thin. Bake in slow oven 300 degrees for 10-12 minutes. Watch closely so they do not burn. Remove cookies one at a time and roll over a wooden spoon handle. They must be warm to roll.

PECAN TEA BALLS

1 C. butter
4 T. powdered sugar
1 tsp. vanilla
¾ tsp. salt
2 C. all purpose flour
1 C. coarsley chopped nuts

Cream butter and sugar, add vanilla. Mix nuts with flour and salt and add to butter mixture. Chill dough for ½ hour. Roll into balls or crescent shape. Bake on buttered cookie sheet at 300 degrees for 10 minutes, then turn to 375 degrees to brown slightly. Remove from oven and while still hot roll in powdered sugar. If to be stored for future use roll in powdered sugar later.

W.A.C. OATMEAL LACE COOKIES

½ C. butter
¾ C. sugar
1 whole egg
¼ tsp. baking powder
⅛ C. flour
1 C. coarse oatmeal

Cream butter, sugar and whole egg until fluffy. Add dry ingredients and blend well. Drop by teaspoonfuls onto a buttered cookie sheet, 2 inches apart. Bake in hot oven—400 degrees 6-8 minutes. Watch carefully so cookies do not burn. Cookies should spread and be very thin.

FROSTED LEMON BARS

¾ C. sifted all purpose flour
1/3 C. butter
2 whole eggs
1 C. brown sugar
¾ C. shredded coconut
½ C. chopped nuts
⅛ tsp. vanilla

Mix together flour and butter to consistency of
fine crumbs. Sprinkle evenly on 11"x7" pan. Bake
in moderate oven (350 degrees) for 10 minutes.
Beat eggs with brown sugar, coconut, chopped nuts and vanilla. Spread over first mixture.
Return to oven and bake 20 minutes longer.
FROSTING: 1 tsp. grated lemon rind, 1½ tsp.
lemon juice, 2/3 C. powdered sugar. Combine all
ingredients and ribbon over cookies while still
warm. Cut into small squares.

ALMOND MACAROONS

½ lb. almond paste
1 cup granulated sugar
2 egg whites

Beat almond paste and sugar until smooth. Add
one egg white at a time, beating well after each
addition. Use a star pastry tube to form macaroon
or shape with a teaspoon. Form each macaroon
on a cookie sheet covered with brown paper.
Sprinkle each with a little granulated sugar.
Place the macaroons in the refrigerator a few
hours to dry. Bake in a 300 degree oven for 25-30
minutes. When macaroons are baked pull the
paper from the cookie sheet onto a wet towel and
let them steam to remove from paper.

THIN WHITE SUGAR COOKIES

1 C. butter
1 C. sugar
1 egg
1 tsp. vanilla
2 C. and 2 T. unsifted all purpose bread flour
½ tsp. soda
½ tsp. cream of tartar
Pinch of salt

Cream butter and sugar. Add egg and beat until fluffy. Add vanilla. Sift dry ingredients and combine with butter and sugar mixture. Chill for 1 hour. Roll into tiny balls, dip in sugar. Press down with glass. Do not grease cookie sheet. Bake at 350 degrees for about 10 or 12 minutes.

SUGAR COOKIES FOR CUT OUTS   (5 or 6 doz.)

½ lb. butter
1 cup sugar
2 whole eggs
3 cups flour
½ tsp. soda
½ tsp. cream of tartar
½ tsp. vanilla

Cream butter and sugar, add eggs beat until fluffy. Mix in dry ingredients. Chill dough for easier handling. Roll out on pastry canvas or slightly floured board. Cut with floured cookie cutter. Bake on buttered cookie sheet, 8 to 10 minutes at 375 degrees.

MRS. GEVERT'S WAFERS

½ lb. butter
1 cup sugar
1 egg yolk
2 cups flour
¾ cup chopped nuts
1 beaten egg white

Cream butter and sugar, add egg yolk and continue to beat until fluffy. Add the flour and mix well. Butter a cookie sheet, pat dough very, very thin on sheet. Beat egg white slightly and brush on top of the dough. Sprinkle chopped nuts over the top and cut unto squares. Bake at 250 degrees for 15 or 20 minutes.

THIN GINGER COOKIES

¾ cup butter
½ cup granulated sugar
½ cup brown sugar (packed)
1 egg
4 T. molasses
2 cups flour and ¼ cup extra
2 tsp. soda
1 tsp. cinnamon
1 tsp. ginger
½ tsp. nutmeg

Cream butter and sugar, add egg and beat until fluffy, then add molasses and beat. Sift flour, soda, and spices together and add to butter and sugar mixture, chill. Roll into small balls, dip in sugar and press thin with bottom of a glass. Do not butter cookie sheet. Bake at 350 degrees ten minutes or until lightly browned.

W.A.C. BROWNIES

½ cup butter
1 cup sugar
2 sq. melted chocolate
2/3 cup sifted flour
2/3 cup chopped nuts
2 slightly beaten eggs
1 tsp. vanilla

Cream butter and sugar, add melted chocolate. Mix thoroughly and add beaten eggs and vanilla. Mix chopped nuts with flour and blend into the butter and sugar mixture. Pour mixture into an 8" square pan lined with waxed paper. Bake 25 min. at 325 degrees. Do not overbake.

PAPER THIN CHOCOLATE BARS

2 sq. bitter chocolate
½ C. melted butter
1 C. sugar
½ tsp. salt
½ C. flour
2 eggs beaten
1 tsp. vanilla
½ C. chopped nuts

Melt chocolate in top of double boiler, add butter & sugar. Mix well. Remove from fire, add dry ingredients and beat until well blended. Add beaten eggs and vanilla, thoroughly mixing all ingredients. Roll in chopped nuts. Spread very thin on a well buttered baking sheet. Sprinkle nuts on top. Bake 10 min. at 400 degrees. Do not over bake. Cut in squares while still warm.

Pies and Cakes

W.A.C. BASIC PIE AND PASTRY CRUST

Flour	2½ cups	5 cups	6¼ cups
Lard	½ lb.	1 lb.	1¼ lb.
Ice water	½ cup	1 cup	1½ cups
Salt	½ tsp.	1 tsp.	1¼ tsp.
Yield:			
Pies (9")	1 double crust 1 single crust	3 double crusts 1 single crust	4 double crusts
Tarts (3"x1")	24	48	60
Turnovers	8	16	20

Blend the flour and salt with the lard until crumbly. Add the ice water and mix until a ball can be formed. WAC crust is rolled out very thin for pies and tarts.

W.A.C. APPLE PIE

Prepare plain pastry dough
6 or 8 firm Jonathan apples
  (peeled, cored and sliced)
¾ cup sugar
¼ tsp. salt
½ tsp. cinnamon
2 T. butter
1 T. minute tapioca

Line a 9 in. pie tin with pastry and fill with apples. Mix sugar, salt and cinnamon together and sprinkle evenly over apples. Dot with butter. Sprinkle tapioca over top. With brush, moisten ridge of pie before putting on top crust. With fork or fingers press top crust to bottom. Brush cream over pie to remove excess flour. Sprinkle with sugar. Put a few fork holes in top crust to allow steam to escape. Bake at 425 degrees until apples are tender, about 50 minutes.

INDIVIDUAL DEEP DISH APPLE PIE (Serves 8)

8 Jonathan apples
8 Baked pie rounds
1 cup sugar
1 cup water
¾ tsp cinnamon
2 T. butter
⅛ tsp salt

Wash and peel apples and save the skin. Cut each apple into 8 sections or more if they are large. Remove core. Cook apple peelings and cores in 1 cup of water, 1 cup of sugar and ¾ tsp cinnamon until a nice pink color. Put apples into long pan with a small amount of water, cover and bake at 350 degrees for 20 to 30 minutes. Do not overcook. Fill individual deep dishes and place the baked pie round on top. Strain juice from peelings and pour over apples when served.

LIME CHIFFON TART

1 T. plain gelatin
¼ cup cold water
¾ cup sugar
½ cup lime juice
½ tsp salt
1 tsp grated rind
4 eggs separated
Green food coloring
6 tart shells (see basic pie & pastry recipe)

Soften gelatin in cold water. Combine ½ cup sugar, salt, lime juice and rind. Beat egg yolks and blend into lime mixture. Cook over hot water until spoon is coated. Remove from heat and add gelatine and stir until dissolved. Cool until slightly thickened. Beat egg whites stiff but not dry and gradually add ¼ cup sugar beating constantly. Add a little green coloring and fold lime mixture into egg whites. Fill pastry shells. Top with whipped cream and thin slices of lime.

FLUFFY PUMPKIN CHIFFON TART

3 egg yolks beaten
¾ cup brown sugar
1½ cups pumpkin
½ cup cream
½ tsp. salt
1 tsp cinnamon
¼ tsp ginger
1 T. gelatin
¼ cup cold water
3 egg whites beaten stiff adding
¼ cup granulated sugar

Cook egg yolks, sugar, pumpkin, cream and spices in double boiler and add the gelatin, soaked in water. Stir until dissolved. Cool and when mixture begins to thicken fold in beaten egg whites. Spoon lightly into tart shells. Chill for a couple of hours. Top with a dab of whipped cream.

CHOCOLATE RUM CREAM TART   (10 tarts)

½ cup sugar
1 / 3 cup flour
¼ tsp salt
3 oz. melted chocolate
2 cups warm milk
2 whole eggs slightly beaten
1 T. butter
1 T. rum
¼ tsp vanilla
¼ cup pecans
½ pt whipping cream

Combine sugar, flour, salt and milk. Cook in double boiler. Add melted chocolate, stirring until well blended. Add slightly beaten eggs and blend well. Cook until mixture coats spoon. Remove from fire, add butter, rum, vanilla and stir until blended. Put wax paper over top of filling to avoid crust. Chill and fill tart shells. Top with whipped cream and toasted pecans.

MERINGUE FOR ANGEL TARTS

2 cups sugar
¾ cup water
5 egg whites
½ tsp vanilla

Boil sugar and water to 244 degrees. Beat egg whites until stiff and rather dry. Pour sugar syrup with fine stream over beaten egg whites. Do this slowly until all syrup is added. Continue to beat until mixture holds peak. Place meringue mixture in pastry bag with star tube. Have brown paper lined cookie sheet ready to shape meringues. Make a circle on paper 1½ to 1¾ in. and with pastry tube go around the outside of circle building up to about 1½ in. Place in preheated 200 degree oven. Let bake until dry to touch but not brown—about 25 minutes. Turn off heat if they start to color and open the oven door. Do not over bake because they will dry a little after removing from oven. They should be dry on the outside and creamy on the inside.

ANGEL TART FILLING   (Serves 6-8)

4 egg yolks
½ cup granulated sugar
2 tsp grated lemon rind
3 T. lemon juice
1 cup whipped cream
8 meringues

Cook in double boiler 4 slightly beaten egg yolks, ½ cup sugar, 2 tsp grated lemon rind, and 3 T lemon juice, until thickened. Cool, then fold in 1 cup of whipped cream. Spoon into meringue shells.

LEMON CURD TART

Yield:	6	36	48
Lemons, juice and rind	2 T.	12 T.	16 T.
Butter	6 T.	1¼ lbs.	1¾ lbs.
Sugar	1 cup	6 cups	8 cups
Whole beaten eggs	3	18	24
Egg whites	4 T.	24 T.	32 T.
Sugar	6 T.	2¼ cups	3 cups

Put lemon juice, rind, butter, sugar and whole beaten eggs in a double boiler. Stir over a slow fire until mixture thickens and coats back of spoon. Cool and fill tarts. (See basic pie and pastry recipe). Stiffly beat egg whites. When dry, carefully fold in sugar. Take pastry bag which has been fitted with a rose tube and fill with egg white mixture. Cover top of each tart making certain meringue extends over tart shell. Sprinkle with granulated sugar and put in a slow oven about 350 degrees to set and until golden brown. Remove, cool and serve.

LEMON ROLL

5 eggs (separated)
1 cup sugar
1 cup cake flour
2 tsp. baking powder

Beat egg whites until stiff and add sugar slowly,
continue to beat. Add one egg yolk at a time
beating well after each addition and continue to
beat until fluffy. Sift flour and baking powder
together and add slowly. Butter a cookie sheet
and cover with wax paper, pour out batter. Bake
at 350 degrees for 12 to 15 minutes. Do not over
bake. Turn out cake on towel covered with confectioners sugar. Pull off wax paper and with
sharp knife cut off crisp edges, then roll the cake
in a towel until cooled. Unroll and fill with lemon
filling & wrap in waxed paper.

LEMON FILLING FOR LEMON ROLL

¾ cup sugar
2 T. cornstarch
¾ cup water
2 egg yolks beaten
3 T. lemon juice
1 T. lemon rind
1 T. butter
Salt

Combine sugar, cornstarch, water and lemon
juice. Cook in double boiler until thick and
transparent. Add beaten egg yolks and rind. Cook
about 5 min. Remove from heat and add butter
and cover with wax paper. Serve with shipped
cream.

W.A.C. COCONUT CAKE

1½ cups granulated sugar
½ cup butter (flavored with a little grated orange peel)
1 cup milk
2¼ cups cake flour
2 tsp. baking powder
5 egg whites—large (6 if small)

Cream butter and sugar and add orange peel, milk, 2 cups sifted flour and beat well. Add remaining ¼ cup of flour into which the baking powder has been sifted. Last—fold in whites of eggs, beaten dry. Bake in 3x9 inch layer pans 25-30 minutes. Before frosting cut all the brown crusts off to make the cake completely white.

COCONUT FROSTING

2 cups granulated sugar
½ cup water
2 egg whites (beaten dry)
1 tsp. vanilla
Juice of ½ lemon
1 whole fresh coconut grated. Let stand 2 hrs. or so after it has been grated and shake roughly several times to dry it out. (Substitute canned sweetened coconut if fresh not available.)

Boil together the sugar and water until it spins a thread. *Slowly* beat this into the egg whites, lemon juice, and vanilla.
To Frost Cake:
Spread frosting on bottom layer and sprinkle with grated coconut. Place center layer. Put frosting on both sides of top layer and sprinkle top heavily with coconut.

BURNT SUGAR CAKE

Melt: 1 cup granulated sugar. After it is melted, add 1 cup of boiling water.

1½ cup sugar
½ cup butter
4 eggs—beaten separately
1 cup milk
2½ cups flour
2 tsp. baking powder
4 T. burnt sugar syrup

Cream butter and sugar and add yolks. Add sifted flour and baking powder alternating with milk. Add burnt sugar syrup and fold in beaten egg whites. Bake in 2-9 inch pans at 350 degrees for 30 minutes. Frost with caramel frosting.

CHOCOLATE DATE CAKE   (2-9 in. layers)

1 cup butter
2 cups sugar
4 eggs
4 squares chocolate
2 cups buttermilk
3 cups cake flour
2 tsp. soda
1 tsp. salt
1 tsp. vanilla

Cream butter and sugar, add eggs one at a time.
Sift flour, salt, soda, and add alternating with
buttermilk. Add melted chocolate and vanilla.
Bake in 2-9 in. layers at 350 degrees. Make filling.
Filling:
1¼ cup pitted chopped dates
1 cup cold water
½ cup chopped nuts

Cook in double boiler until thick. Place filling
between layers and frost with caramel icing.

CARAMEL ICING

3 cups brown sugar
1½ cups Half & Half
1 cup butter
Another ½ cup Half & Half and approximately 2
cups powdered sugar.

Bring first three ingredients to a boil and cook for
10 minutes. Cool. Stir while cooking.

After it cools, put brown sugar mixture into
mixer. Add gradually Half & Half and powdered
sugar until mixture reaches spreading consistency.

DARK ORANGE CAKE

1 cup butter
1½ cups sugar
3 eggs
1½ cups sour milk
1½ tsp. soda
3 cups flour
1 cup raisins—ground
Peel of 2 oranges

Cream butter and sugar and add 3 eggs, one at a time. Sift soda and flour and add gradually alternating with sour milk. Last add ground raisins and ground orange peel. Bake at 350 degrees in 2-9 inch layer pans 25-30 minutes. (Pour boiling water over raisins and pat dry before grinding.) Frost with orange butter frosting.

ORANGE BUTTER FROSTING

½ cup soft butter
2 T. frozen orange juice or juice of 1 orange
Grated orange rind of 1 orange
2 cups of powdered sugar
Pinch of salt

Beat butter until fluffy, add powdered sugar a little at a time, thin with orange juice. Add orange rind and blend well.

W.A.C. SPICE CAKE   (2 layers)

1 cup sugar
¾ cup butter
3 eggs
½ cup buttermilk
2 cups flour
1 tsp. soda (mix in buttermilk)
1 tsp. baking powder
1 tsp. cinnamon
½ tsp. allspice, ground
1 cup stewed, strained prunes

Cream butter and sugar, add eggs one at a time. Sift flour, salt, baking powder and spices and add to butter mixture, alternating with buttermilk. Last, fold in strained prunes. Bake in 2-9 inch layer pans at 350 degrees 25 to 30 minutes. Frost with fluffy butter icing 25 to 30 minutes.

CHOCOLATE MARSHMALLOW CAKE (3 layers)

¾ lb. chocolate—grated (Maillards)
¼ cup hot water
4 eggs
½ cup butter
2 cups pastry flour
1 cup milk
1½ cup granulated sugar
1 tsp. vanilla
2 tsp. baking powder

Mix chocolate and water and cook over asbestos mat, (it brings out a gloss). Use half of mixture for cake and half for frosting. Cream butter and sugar together and add 4 egg yolks, 1¼ cups sifted flour, 1 cup milk and half the melted chocolate. Beat well. Last, add remaining ¼ cup flour into which baking powder has been sifted. Add 4 egg whites beaten dry. Bake in 9 inch round pans 30 minutes at 350 degrees. Use 2 layers for this cake and use the 3rd layer for a "half" cake frosted.

CHOCOLATE FROSTING FOR CHOCOLATE MARSHMALLOW CAKE

3 cups confectioners sugar
¼ cup hot water
½ tsp. vanilla
9 oz. large marshmallows cut in quarters
chopped pecans

Combine first 4 ingredients. Spread layer of frosting on one layer then put a thick layer of marshmallows on top of frosting, arrange as closely as possible. Then spread more frosting on top of marshmallows. Top with second layer of cake and cover all with frosting. Again, press a layer of quartered marshmallows over top of second layer and cover with remaining chocolate. Sprinkle with chopped pecans.

FLUFFY BUTTER FROSTING

1 / 3 cup butter
4 cups sifted confectioners sugar
1 egg white
1¼ tsp. vanilla
Coffee cream
A few grains of salt (optional)

Beat butter until light and fluffy. Add about 1 cup of sugar and continue to beat. Put in the egg white and beat until butter and sugar mixture is fluffy. Continue to add powdered sugar at a slower speed. Add enough cream for easy spreading.

FILLING AND TOPPING FOR MOCHA ANGEL FOOD TORTE

1 Angel food cake
1¼ T. gelatin
¼ cup cold water
1 cup powdered sugar
2 T. powdered coffee
2 T. hot water to dissolve coffee
8 egg yolks
1 pint whipping cream—whipped
1 tsp. vanilla
¼ tsp. salt
¼ lb. toasted sliced almonds

Soak gelatin in cold water, put over boiling water to dissolve; then add sugar and coffee mixture and cool. Beat egg yolks until light and fluffy and add salt and vanilla and gelatin mixture. Let gell until consistency of egg white, fold in whipped cream. Chill until stiff enough to spread. With a fork, divide cake in half. Put filling between layers and frost the whole cake. Refrigerate until ready to use. Cover cake with toasted sliced almonds before serving.

Desserts

FROZEN ALMOND BALLS–BUTTERSCOTCH SAUCE

Vanilla ice cream
Sliced toasted almonds
Butterscotch sauce

Make a ball of vanilla ice cream. Roll in sliced toasted almonds pressing ice cream against almonds. If you cannot buy almonds already sliced, blanch whole almonds in hot water to remove skin. Cool and while still soft slice thin with sharp knife. Dry and toast in oven at 350 degrees until brown. Stir so they will brown evenly. After almond balls are made, roll in foil and freeze until needed.

Serve with Butterscotch Sauce.

BUTTERSCOTCH SAUCE   (Yields 2 qts.)

2 lbs. brown sugar
4 cups white Karo syrup
¼ lb. butter
1 cup whipping cream

Mix brown sugar and Karo syrup, bring to a boil and let boil for 5 minutes. Remove from heat and add butter. Stir to keep crust from forming. When cool add the whipping cream.

STRAWBERRIES ROMANOFF

2 qts. whole strawberries
1 pint vanilla ice cream
½ pint whipping cream
Juice of 1 lemon
2 oz. Cointreau
2 oz. Bacardi rum
Powdered sugar

Wash and stem strawberries and dry on paper towels. Whip ice cream slightly to soften and fold in whipped cream. Mix lemon juice, cointreau and rum. Carefully fold into ice cream mixture, taste and if it is not sweet enough add a bit more powdered sugar. Pour mixture over strawberries and combine carefully as not to mash the strawberries. Mix only once before serving. Serve in stemmed sherbet glasses and top with whole strawberry dipped in powdered sugar.

HEAVENLY STRAWBERRIES   (Serves 6)

1 qt. strawberries
¼ lb. powdered sugar
1 orange juice and rind
¼ cup orange curacao
1 cup whipped cream
6 strawberries, whole
6 springs of mint

Wash and stem strawberries and dry on paper towel stem end down. Mix sugar, orange juice, rind and curacao. Pour mixture over strawberries, let stand 1 hour. Serve in a lovely stemmed glass and top with whipped cream, a whole strawberry and spring of mint.

LEMON SOUFFLE PUDDING (Serves 6)

1 cup sugar
¼ tsp. salt
3 T. lemon juice
2 tsp. grated lemon rind
3 eggs separated
1 / 3 cup sifted all purpose flour
2 T. melted butter
1½ cup milk

Mix together sugar, salt, lemon juice and rind. Add egg yolks and beat. Add flour mixing well, blend in melted butter and milk. Beat egg whites until stiff and fold into egg yolk mixture. Pour into 6 buttered custard cups and set in pan of hot water and bake in moderate oven 350 degrees for 30 to 40 min Chill before serving. When turned out into serving dishes, custard will be on top. Top with whipped cream.

PINEAPPLE ICE BOX CAKE (Serves 6-8)

½ lb. Macaroon crumbs
½ cup grated coconut
½ cup butter
1½ cups powdered sugar
2 eggs, unbeaten
1-9 oz. can crushed pineapple drained
½ pt. whipping cream

Roll the macaroons into crumbs, add coconut. Put ½ of crumb mixture in the bottom of 8x8 inch pan. Cream butter and sugar. Add eggs one at a time and beat until smooth and creamy. Pour this mixture over the crumbs. Whip cream and fold in pineapple, pour this over the butter and sugar mixture. Cover with remaining crumbs and put in the refrigerator overnight.

FRESH ORANGE COMPOTE   (Serves 6-8)

8 large oranges (sections and rind)
1 cup sugar
½ cup water
Juice of 1 orange
2 T. orange curacao

Peel oranges and save the rind. Cook rind in water until tender then remove from heat and cool. With spoon remove white membrane. Cut orange rind into fine strips either with knife or scissors. Bring to a boil sugar, water, and orange juice. Add orange strips and cook for 10 min. until rind is glazed. Remove from stove and cool and add 2 T. of orange curacao. Pour over orange sections and let stand for a few hours in the refrigerator.

BLUEBERRY CRISP

1 lb. frozen blueberries
2 T. butter
¼ cup brown sugar
1 lemon (juice)
¼ tsp. cinnamon

Topping:
¼ cup butter
½ cup brown sugar
½ cup flour

Pour blueberries in buttered shallow baking pan. Sprinkle with brown sugar and lemon juice. Combine butter, brown sugar and flour into a crumb mixture. Sprinkle over top of blueberries. Bake at 350 degrees for 30 to 45 minutes. Serve with a dab of whipped cream. You may use any other fruit of your choice. When using apples, cook a little before making the crisp.

BAVARIAN CREAM WITH MELBA SAUCE
(Serves 6-8)

1 T. gelatin
¼ cup cold water
2 eggs separated
¼ tsp. salt
¼ cup sugar
1 cup scalded milk
1 cup whipping cream, whipped
½ tsp. vanilla

Soak gelatine in cold water. Beat egg yolks and add sugar and salt. Add hot milk and vanilla and gradually cook over low heat until gelatine is dissolved. Chill until gelatine begins to thicken. Beat egg whites until they hold soft peaks and add 1 T. sugar and beat a few seconds. Carefully fold egg whites into gelatin mixture and then fold in whipped cream. Mold in individual molds that have been rinsed in cold water.

MELBA SAUCE

1 lb. frozen raspberries
½ cup sugar
1 T. currant jelly
a pinch of salt

Cook raspberries and sugar until berries are soft. Remove from fire and run through a fine sieve to remove seeds. Be sure to get all the pulp. Return to fire and add jelly and salt. Bring to a boil and cook 10 to 15 min.

FROZEN LEMON ANGEL
(Serves 6)

3 egg yolks
½ cup sugar
1 T. lemon rind
Juice of 1 lemon
1 tsp. vanilla
3 egg whites
1 cup heavy cream, whipped
¾ cup macaroon crumbs

Cook 3 egg yolks slightly beaten with ½ cup sugar in double boiler until it coats the spoon. Remove from heat and add lemon juice, rind and vanilla. When cool add 3 stiffly beaten egg whites, then fold in the whipped cream. Sprinkle ½ the crumbs on bottom of 8 inch pan. Pour in the mixture and sprinkle remaining crumbs on top. Make the night before and freeze.

BAKED PEAR SABAYON
(Serves 6)

4 egg yolks beaten
⅛ tsp. salt
½ cup sugar
2¼ tsp. lemon juice
½ cup sherry
1 tsp. brandy
½ cup cream whipped
6 pear halves

Combine beaten egg yolks, salt, sugar, and lemon juice and beat until light. Cook in double boiler stirring constantly until mixture thickens. Gradually add sherry and brandy blending well. Cook 2 min. longer and remove from heat and cool. (This may be done the day before). Heat pears. Just before serving fold whipped cream into sauce and pour over pears.

COLD CHOCOLATE SOUFFLE   (Serves 6-8)

1 T. gelatin
¼ cup cold water
2 sqs. unsweetened chocolate
½ cup hot water
¼ tsp salt
4 eggs separated
1 tsp vanilla
¾ cup sugar
Orange curacao

Dissolve gelatin in cold water. Mix ¼ cup sugar
in beaten yolks. Melt chocolate in hot water in
double boiler. Add beaten yolks with sugar. Beat
egg whites until stiff and add ½ cup sugar slowly
beating until peaks form. Cool chocolate mixture
and fold in beaten whites. Mold in a damp mold.
After unmolded, sprinkle with orange curacao.
Serve with whipped cream and grated chocolate.

BAKED CUSTARD   (Serves 12)

6 whole eggs
1¼ qts. coffee cream
2 T. sugar
⅛ tsp. salt
1 tsp vanilla

Beat whole eggs slightly, add sugar, salt, vanilla
and coffee cream. Strain—pour into custard cups
and bake in a water bath at 300 degrees for 45 to 60
min. Test with silver knife. If it does not stick to
knife it is done. Do not over bake because it will
become watery. Serve with caramel sauce.

BAKED ORANGE ALASKA

Procedure for 1 large orange:
Wash orange to remove oil. Cut top off orange leaving about ¾ of orange. With a grapefruit knife cut around the orange to remove the meat intact and leave shell clean. Section the orange and reserve the sections and any juice.

Brandied orange sauce:
Remove the white from the top part of the orange. Cook the top in water until tender, changing the water a couple of times. Cool. Cut orange rind into thin strips. Take juice left from orange and add enough water to make ¾ cup liquid. Add 1 / 3 cup sugar and cook until dissolved. Add the cooked orange rind and cook until glazed. Add 2 tablespoons brandy.

Take orange sections and place in bottom of orange shell. Place a scoop of vanilla ice cream in orange shell. Cover ice cream with brandied orange sauce. Clean orange so there is no sauce on outside of shell. Place in freezer while you prepare meringue.

For each orange use 1 egg white and 2 tablespoons sugar and a pinch salt. Add the sugar a little at a time, beating egg white until stiff.

Remove orange from freezer. Fill pastry bag with meringue using a star tube. Start from outside edge of cut orange working your way in an upward spiral. Be sure that ice cream is covered. You may spoon meringue on if you do not have a pastry tube. Meringue should have an uneven surface as it is pretty when browned. Return to freezer until ready to use. Bake on paper covered board in a 450 degree oven until golden brown 10 to 15 minutes. Serve on Galex leaf.

Notes

SECTION II

Hors d'Oeuvres and Appetizers

ANNA'S CHEESE COOKIES

½ lb. butter
½ lb. grated N.Y. sharp cheese
2 cups flour
dash red pepper

Cream butter and cheese together. Slowly add flour and pepper. Roll into "tubes" with wax paper. Put into icebox for an hour or so, then cut off in thin slices and brush with beaten egg white. Bake in 350 degree oven until light golden brown. Sprinkle with salt while still hot.

Mrs. Allan Bulley, Jr.

CHEESE BALL

3 oz. blue cheese
8 oz. wedge of Wispride cheese
4 oz. cream cheese

Have cheese at room temperature. Place blue cheese in bowl and mash thoroughly with fork. Add Wispride and mix thoroughly. Add cream cheese and mix. Place bowl in refrigerator until mix is firm enough to handle.

Place ingredients on foil and roll into a ball. Roll pecans or walnuts on outside. Keep ball in foil (in refrigerator) until ready for use.

Mrs. James L. Taylor

OLIVES STUFFED WITH FOIE GRAS

Stuff extra large black pitted olives with foie gras which has been mixed with grilled chopped almonds and a touch of brandy. Garnish with paprika and parsley. To make them stand well, cut a little bit of the lower end off.

WEIRD AND WONDERFUL WEINERS

2 pkg. Vienna Cocktail weiners
1 8-oz. jar red currant jelly
1 6-oz. jar French's mustard
1 onion sliced very thin
4 good shakes soy sauce

Mix the ingredients together. Cut ends off of weiners and place them in a pyrex baking dish. Pour the sauce over the weiners. Bake 3 hours in a 250 degree oven. Stir occasionally. **Serve in chafing dish with toothpicks.**

PINK SHRIMP SAUCE

Blend together:

1 cup mayonnaise
½ cup catsup
1½ T. lemon juice
Tabasco—a few drops
Salt to taste

Refrigerate until ready to use and serve in a bowl surrounded by shrimp.

CANAPES VELOUTES

White bread, no crust
Lipton's dry onion soup, chopped well
Sour cream and cream cheese
Curry to taste
Mustard to taste
Salt and pepper to taste
Butter to saute bread rounds

Saute round pieces of bread until yellow-gold on both sides. Make a mixture of all ingredients and spread over toast pieces. Mixture should be very smooth but care should be taken not to make it drippy. Serve hot or cold with parsley garnish.

HOT SAUCE FOR AVOCADOS

4 T. catsup
4 T. vinegar
4 T. sugar
4 T. Worcestershire sauce
4 T. butter

Mix thoroughly and heat just before using. Double or triple if necessary.

Mrs. W. Homer Harts

ONION 'CAKE'   *(12 Servings)*

This recipe is good for an after-the-football game Hors de'Oeuvres.

Gently mix together:
2 cups flour
1 cup soft butter
¼ cup milk
pinch each salt and sugar

Chill dough until it can be handled. Divide in half. Roll dough into circles to fit two 8 inch pie tins. Bake at 350 degrees for 10 minutes.

Dice 6 strips bacon, fry until crisp. Remove bacon. Fry 4 large onions, diced, in the bacon fat until tender but not brown. Drain off fat. Beat together 2 whole eggs and an extra yolk. Add to onions. Stir in cooked bacon.

Blend in
¾ cup sour cream
1 tsp. chopped chives
Salt and pepper
Pour into the half baked pie crusts. Sprinkle a generous pinch of caraway seed over the tops.

Bake at 350 degrees for 12-14 minutes. Serve warm, cut into wedges.

Mrs. Charles A. Nixon

CEVICHE
(Serves 8)

Delicious appetizer from Mexico City.

2-1 / 3 lbs. of whitefish cut into cubes
2 cups of lemon or lime juice

Marinate fish in juice 6 hours or overnight in refrigerator.

Make sauce of following:

2 cups chopped onion
½ cup tomato puree
½ cup tomato juice
1 T. salt
12 green olives, chopped
2 T. Worcestershire sauce
1 tsp. Tabasco
2 small green chilies, chopped
3 firm tomatoes, chopped
parsley, chopped

Pour off half of the lemon juice, add sauce, and refrigerate overnight. If too dry, add more of the marinade.

Mrs. Robert A. Maher

MUSHROOMS ON TOAST   (4-6 servings)

A delicious first course

2 lbs. fresh white mushrooms
butter
salt and pepper
1/3 cup Madeira wine
3 egg yolks
1 cup heavy cream

Stem mushrooms. Wash and dry. Saute in butter, a few at a time. Keep warm in oven. After mushrooms are sauted, add 1/3 cup wine to skillet plus combined egg yolks and cream whipped together. Pour liquid, after it's thickened, over toast. Lay mushrooms neatly over toast points.

Mrs. Don H. Reuben

SHRIMP DIP

2 8-oz. packages cream cheese
½ cup chili sauce
1 T. horseradish
1 T. worcestershire sauce
¼ tsp. garlic powder
dash salt
1 8-oz. bag shrimp,
    cooked and cut up.

Combine above ingredients except shrimp and beat until smooth. Fold in shrimp and chill four hours or more.

Serve with broccoli, cherry tomatoes, cauliflower, celery and carrots.

Mrs. Thomas Moorhead

SEAFOOD DIP

½ cup mayonnaise
½ cup sour cream
¼ tsp. hot mustard
¼ tsp. garlic powder
2 tsp. instant minced onion
1 T. white tarragon wine vinegar
Dash cayenne pepper
1 tsp. old hickory smoked salt

Blend mayonnaise and sourcream. Add other ingredients. Chill. Serve with shrimp or crab fingers. Makes one cup.

Makes one cup.

Mrs. Albert D. Williams, Jr.

CHUTNEY DIP OR SPREAD

1 8-oz. package cream cheese
1 / 3 cup chutney, chopped fine
½ tsp. lemon juice
½ tsp. curry powder
salt, to taste
milk may be added if a softer consistency is needed

Combine ingredients and spread on crackers.

Mary Porter Snyder

CHEESE AND SHRIMP PATE   (Serves 6-8)

1 lg. size can prawns
1 lg. pkg. Cream Cheese
1 can Cross & Blackwell Consomme
1 tsp. powdered gelatin

Drain prawns after squeezing fresh lemon juice over them. Liquidize cheese in ½ cup hot consomme. Melt gelatin in the remaining soup and add ½ of the mixture to cheese. Mix well and cool.

Arrange prawns on the bottom of a flat serving dish. Place cheese mixture on top and chill. Finally pour layer of remaining consomme over top to glaze. Chill thoroughly.

MOLDED BLUE CHEESE SPREAD

2 egg yolks
½ cup light cream
1 envelope (1 T) unflavored gelatin
½ cup cold water
8 oz. blue cheese
2 egg whites stiffly beaten
1 cup whipping cream whipped

In saucepan combine egg yolks and cream. Stir constantly over low heat till mixture thickens slightly. Remove from heat immediately. Soften gelatin in cold water. Dissolve blue cheese. Gently fold in egg whites and whipped cream. Pour into oiled 1 quart mold. Chill several hours or until firm. Unmold. Garnish with watercress.

Pass with assorted crackers and melba toast.

Mrs. Thomas B. Hunter III

CHEESE-OLIVE SURPRISE

This next one is an Hors d'Oeuvres that you make
on a rainy day with the children, freeze, and then
bake as needed.

Mix as for pastry:

2 cups grated sharp cheese
½ cup soft butter
1 cup sifted flour
½ tsp. salt
Worcestershire sauce & garlic to taste
1 tsp. paprika

Drain thoroughly:

1 jar of 48 pimento-stuffed olives

Place a small amount of dough in the palm of the
hand, flattened to the size of a large silver dollar.
Put olive in center, wrap dough around it and roll
into a ball. Place on cookie sheet and put into
freezer. When frozen pour into plastic bag and
seal. When ready for use take out as many as
needed and bake in 400 degree oven for 15 min.
Serve hot.

Mrs. Thomas Stratton

CONTINENTAL EGGS

6 Hard boiled eggs
4 slices crisp crumbled bacon
2 T. chopped chutney
¼ tsp. salt
Mayonnaise to moisten

Mrs. William G. Dubinsky

CHEESE AND BACON ROUNDS

1 loaf Pepperidge Farm salty rye—party loaf
1 wheel gouda cheese
½ lb. bacon
Worcestershire sauce
mayonnaise

Grate gouda cheese. Fry bacon until crisp. Crumble and mix with cheese. Add mayonnaise to moisten and worcestershire to taste. Spread on rounds of rye and broil until cheese is melted.

Mrs. Richard Siragusa

HOT CHEESE TARTLETTES

This is a popular Canadian recipe.

Prepare three dozen tiny pastry shells. Preheat oven to 450 degrees. Fill shells with the following mixture:
3 egg whites slightly beaten
½ tsp. salt
1 T. minced onion
2 tsp. Worcestershire sauce
1 tsp. paprika
1 tsp. dry mustard
1½ cups of shredded Canadian cheddar cheese

Bake until puffy and golden

Mrs. John Timmerman

CRESCENT ROLL PIZZA

1 sm. can tomato paste
3 T. water
½ tsp. each: worcestershire, garlic powder, salt
¼ tsp. each: basil, thyme
pinch oregano

Combine above ingredients and set aside. Divide one package crescent rolls into 8 pieces. Roll or press each about 4 inches round. Top with 1 lb. ground beef divided equally among the rounds. Cut 1 6 oz. pkg. mozzarella cheese into ¼ inch squares. Put on each. Bake at 400 degrees for 15 minutes.

Mrs. F. T. Kelsey

CUCUMBER-CREAM CHEESE DIP (OR SPREAD)

Puree cucumber and mix with cream cheese until right consistency. Add beau monde seasoning to taste.

Use as a dip or spread on party rye or crackers.

Mrs. James L. Taylor

POOR MAN'S CAVIAR

1 large eggplant
1 large onion
1 green pepper
1 clove garlic
dash Worcestershire Sauce
2 fresh tomatoes
½ cup olive oil
salt & pepper
¼ cup dry red wine

Bake eggplant whole at 350 degrees until soft. While cooking, peel and chop onion, green pepper and garlic. Simmer these in hot oil until tender. Chop tomatoes, and when eggplant is done and cool, peel it, chop finely, and mix with tomatoes. Add this mixture, along with salt, pepper, and wine to the skillet with onion, etc. Mix thoroughly and cook until the mixture is fairly thick.

Serve well chilled on unsalted crackers. It keeps a very long time in the refrigerator.

Mrs. George Caspari

MARY'S EGGPLANT DIP

Keep this dip handy for snacks. It can also be frozen. The sesame seed oil (also called tahini) can be obtained at specialty food stores or imported food stores or health food stores. Olive oil can be substituted. Recipe from Middle East friend of Lebanese origin.

1 med. eggplant
1 clove garlic
salt to taste
3 T. sesame oil (tahini)
juice of two lemons
2 T. finely chopped parsley

Broil eggplant with skin on, turning frequently. Remove skin under cold water. Mash eggplant, using mixer, fork, or blender.

Pound garlic with salt. Add lemon juice, oil, and mix, with eggplant puree. Put in bowl and garnish with pine nuts and parsley. Chill and use as a dip with raw vegetables or crackers.

"It's very good and good for you"

Mrs. Orville Carl Beattie

HOT CHIPPED BEEF

1 8 oz. package cream cheese
2 T. milk
1 pkg. dried beef, finely chopped
½ c. sour cream
4 T. chopped green pepper
4 chopped scallions
¼ tsp. garlic salt
freshly ground pepper

Mix above ingredients. Top with ½ cup chopped
pecans which have been sauteed in 2 T. butter and
½ tsp. salt. Bake at 350 degrees for 20 min. Serve
with triscuits.

Mrs. William G. Dubinsky

COCKTAIL-MUSHROOMS-FOR-CHAFING-DISH

3 T. marjoram
3 tsp. chives
2 lbs. large fresh mushrooms
1 cup butter, melted
1 cup chicken bouillon
½ cup dry wine (I prefer Chablis)
salt to taste
1½ tsp. pepper freshly ground

Saute washed and dried mushrooms in butter.
Add other ingredients. Stir. Cover. Bake at 350
degrees for 20 min.

Mrs. Edward R. Blomquist

ANCHOVY HORS D'OEUVRES

¼ lb. butter, soft
1 8 oz. pkg. cream cheese
1 cup flour
1 tube anchovy paste

Mix well, roll out. Cut in small rounds. Put a little anchovy paste on one edge. Fold in half. Bake at 350 degrees until lightly browned.

Mrs. William Murray

NACHOS

Tortillas (buy frozen)
Montery Jack cheese
Taco cheese (buy seasoned & grated in package)
mild green chili peppers—chopped (canned)

Cut tortillas into eight pie sections. Fry in hot oil (350 degrees) until crisp. Remove and drain. Place pie sections on cookie sheet. And top with grated cheese. Garnish each with green chili peppers. Bake at 350 degrees until cheese is melted.

Mrs. Richard D. Siragusa

TANGY RAW VEGETABLE DIP   (½ serves 12)

½ cup mayonnaise
½ pt. sour half & half
2 T. dried dill weed
2 T. dried parsley
2 tsp. green onion (dry)
1 T. beau monde

Good with raw vegetables or crackers.

Naomi Williams

CURRY DILL DIP

1 cup sour cream
1 cup mayonnaise
1 T. dried parsley flakes
1 T. dried green onion
2 tsp. dill weed
1 tsp. curry powder
1 tsp. seasoned salt

Combine and chill for at least an hour. Serve with raw vegetables.

Mrs. F. Richard Meyer III

VEGETABLE DIP

1 cup mayonnaise
1 tsp. terragon vinegar
dash pepper
½ tsp. salt
⅛ tsp. thyme
¼ tsp. curry powder
½ small onion, grated
2 T. chili sauce

Mix and chill well in advance. Serve with carrot sticks, celery sticks, cherry tomatoes, cauliflower, sliced zucchini, etc.

TAPFER'S PALM SPRINGS DIP

1 can crabmeat (6½ oz.)
1 can water chestnuts (chopped)
1 cup mayonnaise
1 tsp. soy sauce
1 tsp. chives

Mix and let stand one hour before serving.

Mrs. Joseph A. Rawlins

SEAFOOD DIP

1 can lobster, cut up and drained
1 can crabmeat
1 tsp. drained capers
dash of lemon juice
½ tsp. worcestershire sauce
1 tsp. chives or onion
salt to taste
Mayonnaise—enough to make dip spreadable

Mrs. Benjamin W. Perks

CHEESE PUFFS

This must be frozen before it is baked.

1 loaf Pepperidge Farm sandwich bread
½ lb. grated Black Diamond chedder cheese (if
    not available, 2 pkgs. of the ¼ lb. each shredded
    chedder cheese will do)
1 cup mayonnaise
1 sm. onion, grated
2 tsp. Worcestershire sauce
1 pkg. slivered or sliced almonds (optional)
6 slices *crisp* bacon, crumbled

Cut bread in squares, removing crusts. Combine
ingredients and spread on bread squares. Freeze.
When ready to use, remove number needed from
freezer. Place them in a frozen state in a preheated 400 degree oven and bake for approximately 10 minutes.

Mary Porter Snyder

WHISKEY DOGS

Recipe can be prepared several days in advance.

1 cup brown sugar
1 cup ketchup
1 cup bourbon
1 pkg. frankfurters

Cut up frankfurters into bite size pieces and
marinate in liquid. Heat over low flame before
serving.

Mrs. R. Thomas Howell, Jr.

CHILI-PARMESAN APPETIZERS

8 slices bread
1½ cups grated parmesan cheese
1½ tsp. chili powder
1 cup (2 sticks) butter

Remove crusts from bread and cut in uniform strips (about 5 or 6 to a slice). Place on cookie sheet and bake at 400 degrees for about 5 minutes (turning once) until lightly browned.

Melt butter. Mix chili powder with parmesan. Dunk browned bread strips in butter, then roll in chili-parmesan mixture. Store in refrigerator or freezer (may be frozen for several weeks).

When ready to use, place strips on cookie sheet and bake in preheated 400 degree oven for 5 minutes.

Terry Geiger

HOT SHRIMP TEMPTER   (Serves 12)

¼ cup butter
½ cup thinly sliced green onions
½ lb. fresh mushrooms, washed and sliced
3 T. flour
1 cup half and half
2 T. chopped parsley
toast rounds
¼ cup Madeira wine or sherry
1 tsp. salt
⅛ tsp. pepper
1½ lbs. cooked, shelled and deveined shrimp

Heat butter in blazer pan of chafing dish over direct high flame. Add onions; cook, stirring constantly until limp. Add mushrooms, lower flame and cook until tender, about 5 minutes, stirring often. Sprinkle flour evenly over mushrooms; mix. Stir in half and half and wine, if desired; cook until thickened. Season with salt and pepper. Fold in shrimp and heat, stirring often. Sprinkle chopped parsley over top. Place pan in water jacket for serving.

Serve on buttered or plain toast rounds.

Mrs. Barry J. Carroll

Soups

TOMATO BOUILLON SUPREME   (Serves 4)

1 can plum tomatoes (1 lb. 4 oz. size)
1 large onion, sliced
2 T. butter
1 clove garlic
1 can bouillon (beef)
½ cup fresh orange juice
1 cup tomato juice
1 bay leaf

Simmer tomatoes, onion, butter and garlic covered for 45 minutes. Rub through strainer or use Foley Food Mill to puree the mixture and return puree to pan.

Add can of bouillon, orange juice, and tomato juice, and bay leaf. Simmer ½ hour or so. Discard bay leaf.

Serve hot or cold with sprinkle of shredded orange peel on top.

FROZEN TOMATO COB SOUP   (Serves 6)

4 cups peeled and finely chopped tomatoes
2 / 3 medium onion, grated
½ cup lemon juice
2 / 3 tsp. vinegar
2 / 3 tsp. celery seed
salt
sugar
4 T. mayonnaise
curry powder
chopped parsley

Mix tomatoes, lemon juice, onion, vinegar, celery seed, salt, and sugar. (Be careful adding onion — add just a little at a time and taste before adding more. Add sugar to taste, usually about a teaspoon or two.)
Freeze in a tray until mushy — usually about 1 hour.
Serve half-frozen with curry mayonnaise on top.

This is pretty in glass soup cups or mugs.

Mrs. Samuel S. Crocker

COLD TOMATO SOUP (Serves 2-4)

2 cups fresh chopped tomatoes
1 cup milk
½ cup chopped onion
¼ cup chopped celery
1 T. dill
½ tsp. salt
¼ tsp. pepper

Place all ingredients in blender. Blend for 10 seconds. Add 1 cup of cracked ice and blend for 10 more seconds.

Chill and serve.

Mrs. David O. MacKenzie

CURRIED CORN SOUP (Serves 3-4)

2 T. butter
1 onion, finely chopped
1 apple — peel and slice
2 T. curry
2 T. flour
3 jars baby food corn
2 cups strong chicken stock
1½ cups half & half
salt & pepper
shredded coconut

Saute onion and apple in butter until soft but not brown. Mix together curry and flour and add to onion mixture; cook slowly for 5 minutes. Slowly stir corn, chicken stock, half & half and seasonings into flour paste; blend carefully. Add shredded coconut.

Mrs. Richard Lydy

CURRIED BEETROOT SOUP   (Serves 4)

1 raw beetroot (or 1 jar cooked beets)
1 apple
1 onion
2-3 tomatoes
½ oz. flour
1 oz. butter
1 tsp. curry powder
salt
pepper
1 bay leaf
1½ pints stock
¼ pint milk

Peel beet, apple, onion and tomatoes. Chop very
small. Fry lightly, without browning, in hot
butter. Add curry powder, seasoning, bayleaf and
stock. Bring to boil, and simmer gently until well-
cooked. Remove bay leaf, cool slightly, and blend.
Work in flour with the milk. Return soup to pan
and stir in the flour / milk mixture. Reboil and
simmer a few minutes before serving. Garnish
with dab of sour cream.

JELLIED MUSHROOM CONSOMME   (Serves 6)

1¼ lbs. mushrooms, finely chopped
2 cans (10½ ounces each) consomme
2 tsp. Angostura bitters
2 tsp. lemon juice
sour cream

Chop mushrooms. Add to consomme in saucepan.
Simmer 10 minutes, remove from heat, add
bitters and lemon juice. Pour into soup cups, chill
at least 4 hours. Garnish each serving with a dab
of sour cream.

Mrs. John Alexander

GAZPACHO   (Serves 4)

Chill 3 cans Crosse and Blackwell Gazpacho

Puree about 5 peeled, seeded tomatoes

1½ cups cubed white bread, toasted
1 T. salt
1½ tsp. cumin
3 T. oil (olive oil if you wish)
a touch of tabasco
2-4 T. vinegar

Add to the canned soup and chill again.

Serve with chopped green peppers, green onions, celery, cucumbers and cubed bread sauteed in butter and oil.

Ann McCarty

CURRIED CHUTNEY SOUP   (Serves 6)

2 onions chopped
1 large apple chopped
¼ cup butter
¾ cup chopped chutney
1-2 T. curry powder
1 large can tomatoes
1 pt. consomme—undiluted

Saute onions and apple in butter until soft. Add chutney and curry powder and cook for a few minutes. Add tomatoes and cook about ½ hour. Place mixture in blender and slowly add consomme. Serve hot with dash of unsweetened whipped cream on top.

Mrs. Thomas D. Hodgkins

COLD OR HOT SPINACH OR SWISS CHARD SOUP

(Serves 4)

1 pkg. frozen chopped spinach or chard
4 cups light cream
4 chicken bouillon cubes
¼ cup dry vermouth
1 tsp. grated lemon rind
½ tsp. ground mace
2 hard boiled eggs, chopped

Cook spinach or chard; puree in blender. Dissolve bouillon cubes in cream and bring to a boil. Stir until dissolved. Stir in spinach, wine, lemon rind and mace. Serve with chopped eggs on top.

Mrs. James McAlvin

QUICK SQUASH BISQUE

(Serves 2)

1 pkg. frozen cooked squash
3 T. butter
3 T. flour
1 cup chicken broth
1 cup half & half
salt, pepper, onion salt
allspice
nutmeg

Defrost package of squash. Reserve juice. Melt butter, add flour and thicken over low heat. Add 1 cup liquid (squash juice plus chicken stock or bouillon). Season with salt, pepper and onion salt. Cook for a few minutes, and add defrosted squash and 1 cup half & half. Season again with dash of allspice and nutmeg. Serve with garnish of sour cream or whipped cream.

Mrs. A. W. Phelps

CUCUMBER SOUP   (Serves 3-4)

2 cucumbers (peeled and chopped, but leave a bit
of skin for color)
1 pint sour cream
parsley
salt
pepper
nutmeg
½ onion, chopped
1 can chicken broth

Mix in blender to taste and chill.

Mrs. Christopher G. Janus

CORN CHOWDER   (Serves 6-8)

6 slices bacon, diced
½ cup chopped onion
1½ cups potatoes, diced (red or salad)
2 cups corn cut off cob (approximately 6 ears)
water
milk (skimmed if you wish)
salt, pepper to taste

Put bacon in deep pan. Fry until crisp. Add onion,
cook 5 minutes or until soft, stirring often. Add
diced potatoes, barely cover with water. Cook
until potatoes are tender (15-20 minutes). Add
corn, cook 5 minutes. Add milk to cover, or to
consistency desired. Cover, turn off heat.

This is best when prepared in advance, cooled,
then reheated slowly to serve. Do not boil.

Mrs. John McKinlay

JOSIE'S PEA SOUP
(Serves 4)

1 cup peas, fresh or frozen
1 onion
1 carrot
1 stalk celery
1 medium potato
1 clove garlic
2 cups chicken stock
1 cup cream
1 tsp. salt
1 tsp. curry

Place chopped vegetables, seasonings and 1 cup stock in saucepan. Bring to boil, cover, simmer 15 minutes. Put in blender, blend until smooth, and add remaining stock and 1 cup cream.

A delicious soup which may be varied:

When cooking omit the 1 tsp. curry. Instead soak 1 T. curry in 1½ oz. sherry, add just before serving.

-or-

Add: an equal amount of tomato soup

and / or

Add: chopped chicken, shrimp, or crabmeat

The soup may be served cold, though additional stock should be added to desired consistency. Top with chopped fresh mint.

Mrs. Wrigley Offield

GREEN PEA SOUP   (Serves 3-4)

½ cup shredded lettuce
1 medium size onion diced
2 T. butter
1 pkg. frozen peas, defrosted
1½ cups chicken broth
½ cup of half and half

Saute lettuce and onion in butter until onions are softened. Add peas and chicken broth. Bring liquid to boil; reduce heat and simmer for 15 minutes. Put mixture in blender and puree. Add half and half. When ready to serve, reheat and decorate with croutons.

Mrs. Franklin Lyons

SPECIAL SPINACH SOUP OR LIQUID LEFTOVERS   (Serves 4)

1 pk. frozen chopped spinach
1 can golden mushroom soup
½ can cream of celery soup
1 can milk
1 tsp. curry powder

Puree all of the above in blender. Heat.

All kinds of additions and substitutions are possible. For instance: Add 1 pint sour cream, ½ cup lemon juice, 1 can chicken broth — now it serves 6.

If you have any brocolli or cabbage (green) or cauliflower, etc. leftover in refrigerator — use instead of celery soup. Soggy salad in dressing is a great addition. *Any* leftover that can be pureed might be a delicious addition.

Mrs. Jack I. Westrich

CORN OYSTER STEW

1 T. butter
¾ cup sliced celery
2 cans (10 oz.) oysters and liquid
1 can cream style corn
1 cup milk
2 eggs lightly beaten
⅛ tsp. nutmeg

Saute celery in butter. Add liquid from oysters and milk. Heat until hot but do not boil (double boiler is the best way). Add corn, and then oysters. Pour this mixture over the beaten eggs in a tureen and serve at once.

This is a recipe from the east coast of Canada, where Malpeque oysters can be bought fresh most of the year but canned ones do just as well.

Mrs. John Timmerman

SHORT CUT POTAGE MONGOLE   (Serves 4)

1 can tomato soup
1 can green pea soup
1 can consomme
½ cup water
1 cup cream
½ tsp. curry powder
2 T. water
Sherry to taste
Parsley

Heat first 5 ingredients, adding curry, which has been mixed with 2 T. water, sherry and finely chopped parsley after heating.

Mrs. Gordon D. Shorney

CREAM OF MUSHROOM SOUP   (Serves 4)

½ lb. fresh mushroom caps or stems from 1 lb.
4 cups milk
4 tsp. instant chicken stock base or
4 bouillon cubes — dissolved in a little boiling
water
2 small slices onion
6 T. butter
2 T. flour
1 cup cream or top milk
white pepper to taste
little salt

Melt butter in top of double boiler. Add onion and mushrooms, *chopped fine.* Cook slowly 15 minutes stirring as needed. Add flour and stir well. Add dissolved chicken broth to heated milk and add slowly to mushroom mixture. Bring to boiling point and cook slowly 20 minutes. Just before serving, add cream and reheat. Garnish with whipped cream and parsley.

Mrs. Gordon D. Shorney

BEAN SOUP

(Serves 8-10)

2 cups navy pea-beans
Pick over and soak overnight in water to cover.
Drain.

1 hambone
¾ cup diced celery
½ cup diced carrots
1 bay leaf
3 qts. of water
2 T. butter
¾ cup minced onion
1 cup diced cooked ham
2 T. flour
1 tsp. brown sugar
¼ tsp. pepper
1 cup canned stewed tomatoes

Simmer hambone, celery, carrots, bay leaf and water over low heat for 4 hours with beans. Stir now and then.

Remove ham from bone—discard bone and fat. Dice ham.

Saute onion and ham in butter until onion is golden.

Blend flour brown sugar, and pepper into onion-bean mixture. Then stir in tomatoes. Cook and stir until thickened.

Add all to soup and mix thoroughly—adjust seasonings.

Mrs. Richard Lydy

CREAMED CONSOMME   (Serves 2-3)

2 cans consomme (about 2½ cups in all)
1 small apple (grated or chopped)
1 small onion (grated or chopped)
1 cup cream
salt
paprika
curry powder

Place contents of 2 cans consomme in pan. Add apple and onion. Cook until apple and onion are very tender.

Put these through a strainer and add cream.

Season the soup as desired with salt, paprika and curry powder.

Reheat but *do not* permit it to boil. Serve with game dinner.

Lulu H. Ingersoll

Breads, Coffee Cakes, Pancakes

PUMPKIN BREAD

This is easy and different—an old recipe from a friend.

2 / 3 cup shortening
2 2 / 3 cups sugar
4 eggs
pumpkin (1 pound can)
2 / 3 cup water
3 1 / 3 cups flour
2 tsp. soda
1 tsp. cinnamon
1 tsp. cloves
½ tsp. baking powder
1½ tsp. salt
1 cup nuts
1 cup raisins or cut up dates

Cream together shortening and sugar. Add eggs, pumpkin and water to sugar mixture. Sift together and add flour, soda, cinnamon, cloves, baking powder and salt. Stir in nuts and raisins.

Pour into 2 greased loaf pans or 3 one pound coffee cans. Bake at 350 degrees for one hour.

Julia Baillet

MOLASSES HOT BREAD

Sift together:
1 cup flour
1½ cups whole wheat flour
1 tsp. salt
1 tsp. soda (heaping)

1/3 cup sugar
1 egg
1½ cups buttermilk
1/3 cup molasses
3 T. melted butter

Combine ingredients and bake in 350 degree oven for about 45 minutes in bread pan.

Mrs. Charles Sailor

BANANA BREAD

2 cups sugar
1 cup shortening
6 ripe mashed bananas
4 eggs
2½ cups cake flour
1 tsp. salt
1 tsp. baking soda

Cream sugar and shortening. Add mashed bananas and four well beaten eggs.

In another bowl, sift 2½ cups cake flour, salt, and baking soda. Next blend dry and liquid ingredients together. Be sure not to over mix.

Bake in two greased loaf pans at 350 degree oven for 45-50 minutes.

Mrs. Thomas D. Hodgkins

ORANGE BREAD

3 orange rinds cut in thin strips
1/3 cup water
1 cup sugar
1 cup milk
1 egg
3 cups flour
4 tsp. baking powder
Pinch salt

Boil orange rinds until tender, about ½ hour. Drain. Add water and sugar and boil until sugar is absorbed. Allow to cool.

Mix milk, egg, flour, baking powder and salt. Add mixture to orange peel and bake slowly (325 degrees) for one hour in greased loaf pan. Nuts may be added if desired.

Mrs. Gordon D. Shorney

HOTEL ROANOKE SPOON BREAD   (about 10 portions)

1½ cups corn meal
⅛ lb. butter
1 tsp. sugar
1 1/3 tsp. salt
5 eggs
2 cups milk
1½ cups boiling water
1 T. baking powder

Mix corn meal, salt and sugar. Scald with boiling water. Add melted butter. Beat eggs and add milk to eggs. Put the two mixtures together, and then add baking powder. Pour into baking pan and bake 30 to 35 minutes in oven at 350 degrees.

Mrs. Gordon D. Shorney

CRANBERRY BREAD

2 cups sifted flour
  (sift once then measure)
1 cup sugar
1½ tsp. baking powder
½ tsp. baking soda
1 egg—2 T. hot water,
  beaten
½ cup orange juice
grated rind of one orange
2 T. melted butter
1 cup raw cranberries
  (halved)
¾ cup chopped nuts

Combine ingredients in order listed. Bake for one hour at 350 degrees or until done.

May be frozen.

Ruth Moderwell

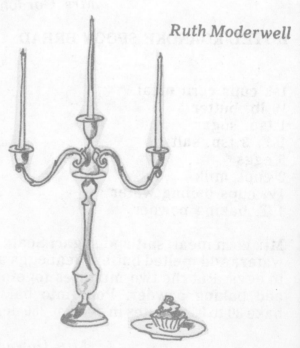

SALLY LUNN BREAD (Williamsburg Inn)

1 cup warm milk
1 cake yeast
4 T. butter
1/3 cup sugar
2 eggs
1½ tsp. salt
3½ cups flour

Dissolve yeast in warm milk. Cream butter and sugar. Add beaten eggs and salt. Mix well. Sift in flour a little at a time along with milk and yeast mixture.

Let rise in warm place until double in bulk. Knead lightly. Rub hands with butter to keep from sticking.

Place dough in well greased angel food cake tin or 10 inch ring mold. Let rise again until double in size.

Bake in preheated 350 degree oven for one hour. Serve warm with generous pats of sweet butter.

Freezes beautifully.

WAFFLES FOR FOUR

3 eggs separated
1 1/8 cups milk
3 tsp. melted butter
1 cup flour
¼ tsp. salt
2 heaping tsp. baking powder

Beat egg yolks, add milk, add sifted dry ingredients, melted butter. Mix thoroughly. Then fold in beaten egg whites. Spoon mixture onto waffle iron and cook until golden.

Mrs. S. Austin Pope

COTTAGE CHEESE PANCAKES

An old family recipe.

3 eggs, separated
¾ cup cottage chesse (large or small curd)
¼ cup milk
¼ cup flour
¼ tsp. salt

Beat egg whites until quite stiff, but not dry. Beat egg yolks with cottage cheese. Add milk and flour and salt. Beat all together. Fold in stiff egg whites, and bake on lightly greased griddle.

Mrs. Karl Tillman Baughman

DAISY CAKES–PANCAKES

8 oz. self-rising flour
1 level tsp. baking soda
1 level tsp. cream of tartar
1 heaping tsp. superfine sugar
good pinch of salt
1 T. olive oil (or substitute)
1 egg
milk

Sift dry ingredients. Add oil, unbeaten egg and enough milk to make a loose batter. Do not beat, merely mix smartly. A beaten batter makes tough pancakes. They should be extremely light and spongy. No time must be lost in proceeding with cooking once the mixing has been done or much of the rising properties will be lost. Use a hot griddle.

Serve with butter and jam, cold or hot with tea.

Also serve hot with syrup at breakfast accompanied by eggs and sausages.

Mrs. Louis C. Duncan

BRAN MUFFIN BATTER

½ box (15 oz.) Post Bran Flakes
1½ cups sugar
2½ cups sifted flour
2½ tsp. soda
1 tsp salt

Mix dry ingredients then add:
1 pt. buttermilk
½ cup Crisco or Wesson Oil
2 beaten eggs

This makes about 1½ quarts of batter. Cover and keep in refrigerator (not freezer). To bake fill greased muffin pans two-thirds full. Bake at 400 degrees for about 15 to 18 minutes, depending on muffin pan size.

Raisins or cut up dates can be added to batter before baking. This batter will keep six weeks to two months.

Mrs. Frank Foss

CINNAMON ROLLS   (Makes 18 rolls)

2 pks. dry yeast (mix with ¼ cup warm water just
before adding to flour)
2 eggs
2 cups milk, scalded
½ cup sugar
½ stick margarine
¼ cup lard
2 tsp. salt
6 or 6½ cups flour
cinnamon & sugar

Beat eggs, add sugar and salt. Put shortening into
hot milk and cool to warm. Pour milk over beaten
eggs and sugar. Add 3 cups flour. Add moistened
yeast and enough remaining flour to make a soft
dough. Add flour by the cup. Let rise until double
(about one hour). Then punch down and let rise
15 minutes more.

Make into rolls:

Take half of the dough, roll out to about ½ inch
thick rectangle. Spread dough with softened
butter, sprinkle on sugar and cinnamon. Roll
from wide end and pinch ends closed. Take string
or thread and cut into rolls.

Place rolls 2 inches apart on ungreased cookie
sheet. Do same with remainder of dough. Bake at
375 degrees for about 20-25 minutes, or until
lightly brown.

Serve warm with butter.

(This recipe can also be used for dinner rolls
without the cinnamon-sugar)

Sue Norell

BISCUITS–SIMPLE, SUPERB, SOUTHERN

1¼ cups flour
2 tsp. baking powder
pinch salt
heaping T. Crisco
little milk (or water) to moisten

Combine ingredients. Do not roll out. Pat together in small biscuit shapes. Bake in hot oven of 425 degrees until brown and done (approx. 12-15 minutes).

These are short, crumbly, and not geometric—but good!

Mrs. Charles Hamilton Davison

SOUR CREAM COFFEE CAKE

1 cup sugar
½ cup butter
2 eggs
1 tsp. vanilla
1 tsp. baking soda
1 tsp. baking powder
¼ tsp. salt
1 cup sour cream

Cream butter and sugar, add eggs and vanilla. Sift dry ingredients and add alternately with sour cream. Layer dough with mixture of ¼ cup brown sugar, 1 tsp. cinnamon, and ½ cup ground nuts.

Place first layer of batter in greased bundt pan. Sprinkle sugar, cinnamon mixture over this. Put rest of batter in pan and bake at 350 degrees for 45 minutes.

Mrs. J. Harry Ramshaw

BUTTERHORN ROLLS

This is a very good roll recipe and easy—all my friends rave over this!

1 yeast cake crumbled
½ cup of sugar
2 eggs
¼ lb. butter
1 cup hot milk
1 tsp. salt
Approx. 4 cups flour

Combine yeast cake and 2 T. of sugar out of the ½ cup of sugar. Mix until liquid. Add rest of ½ cup of sugar. Beat in two eggs one at a time. Add butter dissolved in milk, salt and flour.

Let rise until double in bulk. Roll out and shape in parker house or your desired kind of roll.

Let rise again well

Bake in 375 degree oven until done.

These rolls freeze well and make a large quantity depending upon your needs.

Mrs. H. Earl Hoover

CINNAMON COFFEE CAKE

1 egg
½ cup sugar
½ cup milk
1 cup pancake mix (Bisquick)
3 T. shortening melted (I use butter)

Beat egg until light and fluffy. Add sugar a little at a time, heating continually. Add melted butter, add pancake mix and stir lightly. Pour batter into an 8 inch square cake pan. Sprinkle cinnamon topping, made by combining 2 T. sugar and ½ tsp. cinnamon, over batter.

Bake in preheated 400 degree oven for about 20 minutes.

Cut into squares.

Mrs. Harold T. Martin

GINGER MUFFINS

1 T. butter
1 cup sugar
2 eggs
½ cup molasses
1 cup milk
2½ cups flour
1 tsp. cinnamon
½ tsp. ginger
½ tsp. cloves
3 tsp. baking powder

Bake 15 to 20 minutes in 350 degree oven in greased muffin tins.

GRAHAM NUT BREAD

3 cups graham flour
1 cup white flour
1 cup sugar
1 tsp. baking powder
1 tsp. soda
1 tsp. salt
2 cups buttermilk
1 cup nut meats
1 cup raisins

Mix dry ingredients, add buttermilk and bake in
loaf pan for 1 hour in 350 degree oven.

FEATHER CORNBREAD

1½ cups white flour
1 cup cornmeal
5 tsp. baking powder
4 T. sugar
1 egg
1½ cups milk
3 T. shortening

Sift dry ingredients. Add unbeaten egg, milk and
melted shortening. Mix thoroughly and quickly
keeping spoon on bottom of bowl and stirring in
widening circles. Pour into well greased shallow
pan and bake in 375 degree oven for 35 to 40
minutes.

DUMPLINGS THAT CANNOT FAIL   (Serves 4)

1 egg
1½ cups flour
1 tsp. salt
½ cup milk
1 heaping tsp. baking powder
1 T. butter

Sift flour, salt and baking powder twice. Work in butter (with hands), add egg and milk. Drop batter in pot from tablespoon, but first set pot off burner. Never drop dough in while water is boiling.

Have meat or chicken barely covered, so that the dumplings do not settle in liquid. Put pot back on fire, cover tightly and *do not disturb* for 20 minutes (low fire).

Mrs. William F. Murray

RICE KRISPY MUFFINS

1 egg
1/3 cup honey
3 T. shortening
2 cups Rice Krispies
2 cups flour
4 tsp. baking powder
1 cup milk

Mix all ingredients. Place in greased muffin tins and bake in 400 degree oven for 20 minutes.

APPLE YORKSHIRE PUDDING   (Serves 6)

6 T. butter
½ cup light brown sugar
2½ cups peeled, cooked and sliced apples or
1 can pie sliced apples, well drained
1½ cups sifted flour
¾ tsp. salt
3 eggs
1½ cups milk
cinnamon

Preheat oven to 450 degrees. Melt butter in 9x13"
shallow pan. Sprinkle brown sugar and cinnamon
evenly over butter; arrange apples over sugar.
Sift flour and salt together. Beat eggs until thick
and light in color. Add flour and ½ cup of the milk
until well blended. Gradually add the last cup of
milk and beat until smooth. Pour gently over
apples and bake 25-30 minutes. Serve at once.
Delicious with roast pork.

Mrs. William G. Dubinsky

SPOON BREAD

¼ lb. butter
2½ cups water
2 cups buttermilk
½ tsp. baking soda
¼ tsp. salt
2 cups yellow corn meal
2 eggs
½ tsp. baking powder

Take the 2½ cups water, ¼ lb. butter and ½ tsp. salt and bring to boiling point. Add only 1¾ cups of the cornmeal. Mix well. Add the 2 eggs. Add only 1¾ cups of buttermilk. With the last ¼ cup mix the ½ tsp. baking soda; stir it well and add to the main mixture. To the last ¼ cup of corn meal, add the ½ tsp. baking powder. Mix well and add that to the entire mixture. Pour in a very well-buttered dish, the butter just sticking in thick lumps. Bake in slow oven around 300 degrees for 45 minutes. Time varies with oven as well as with container in which it is baked. Turn oven high for the last few minutes to brown the top if necessary. I have used aluminum, pyrex, crockery ware. Most important point is not to over bake. Just before serving, pour over the spoon bread ¼ lb. of melted butter.

Mrs. E.F. Burch, Jr.

Luncheon Dishes

CRAB AND SHRIMP STUFFED ZUCCHINI
(Serves 8)

8 zucchini
6 medium tomatoes, peeled, seeded and chopped
4 T. butter
1 large shallot, chopped
1 tsp. paprika
pinch of salt
dash of pepper
¼ lb. cooked shrimp
¼ lb. cooked crab
4 T. parmesan cheese

Trim each end of zucchini. Place in boiling salted water for five minutes. Remove and plunge in cold water. Cut a strip from each zucchini and scoop out pulp and chop.

Melt butter and cook shallot until soft but not brown. Add paprika, chopped zucchini pulp and tomatoes. Season with salt and pepper and cook for four minutes. Stir in shrimp and crab meat.

Arrange zucchini in a buttered baking dish and fill with shrimp and crab mixture. Cover with Miss Rhunsberger's Mornay sauce.

Top with parmesan cheese. Bake at 425 degrees for 10 minutes or until brown.

Mrs. A. C. Neilsen

SHRIMP MOLD   (Serves 12-16)

2 pkgs. lemon gelatin
1 cup hot water
1 can tomato soup
3 pkgs. (3 oz.) cream cheese
1 cup mayonnaise
1 cup chopped celery
1 small onion, chopped
1 small green pepper, chopped
1 cup canned green peas
1 lb. shrimp, cooked and cleaned

Dissolve gelatin in hot water and cool. Soften cream cheese and blend with mayonnaise. Add tomato soup, chopped celery, chopped onion, pepper and peas. Add gelatin, then shrimp. Pour into two 6 cup oiled molds, or one large fish mold plus one 6 cup mold. Chill overnight.

Sue Norell

SHRIMP OR SALMON MOUSSE   (Serves 6)

1 envelope of gelatin
1 can tomato soup (not diluted)
2 pkgs. cream cheese
½ tsp. Worcestershire
1 cup mayonnaise
2 cups flaked salmon or shrimp
1½ cups celery, parsley, onion—chopped together

Heat soup to boiling point. Add cheese and gelatin (dissolved in a little cold water). Let mixture cool. Then add remaining ingredients. Pour into greased mold and refrigerate.

This can be made the day before. If you use salmon, serve with green mayonnaise.

Mrs. Harold Grumhaus

SALMON MOUSSE   (Serves 4)
(serves 8 as first course)

1 envelope gelatin
2 T. lemon juice
1 small slice onion
½ cup boiling water
½ cup mayonnaise
1 lb. can drained salmon
¼ tsp. paprika
1 tsp. dill weed (dry)
1 cup heavy cream
Salt to taste

Empty gelatin into blender. Add lemon juice, onion, boiling water. Cover and blend on high for 40 seconds. Add mayonnaise, salmon, paprika, and dill. Cover and turn on high. Remove cover and gradually pour in heavy cream. Blend for only 30 seconds. Pour into four cup ring mold and chill. Serve garnished with watercress and the following sauce.

Sauce:
½ part mayonnaise
½ part sour cream
dill to taste
lemon juice to taste
onion salt to taste

Cucumber, dill and sour cream is also good with this combined to make a sauce.

Mrs. Philip W. Hummer

COULIBIAC

(Serves 5)

Brioche dough
3 hard cooked eggs, chopped fine
½ pint of sour cream
½ lb. smoked salmon, sliced very thin
1½ cups cooked shrimp (very small)
½ lb. sliced mushrooms, sauteed in butter
Lots of fresh chopped dill
Beaten egg yolk to brush dough

To make brioche dough, put 1½ cups flour in a
bowl and add 3 large eggs which have been well-
beaten...2 tsp. sugar, and ½ tsp. salt. Work to a
dough and beat on a board until light. Mix in 5 oz.
of creamed butter and 1 pkg. yeast which has
been dissolved in ¼ cup of warm water. Then mix
in ½ cup more flour and let stand until dough
rises.

Place mixture in a lightly greased and floured
bowl, cover with a cloth, and allow to stand at
room temperature until it rises to double its size.
Chill overnight in the refrigerator, or for one hour
in the deep freeze.

Remove and roll out to ½ inch thickness on a
floured board. Brush with melted butter and
sprinkle with a few browned breadcrumbs.

Put a layer of finely chopped egg on top of the
dough and dot with sour cream. On top of this put
thin slices of salmon, thin slices of shrimp and
sprinkle with dill. Dot with more sour cream and
roll up like a jelly roll. Put in a well greased bread

tin, cover with a cloth, and put in a warm place to rise for ¼ hour. Brush with beaten egg yolk and bake in a 425 degree oven for 30 minutes.

Remove from oven, turn out of tin and serve with melted clarified butter.

This dish looks especially impressive or special if you line one of the various shaped French pate molds with removable sides with the brioche dough. Line the bottom and sides of mold with dough and then layer the mixture. Finally place the top piece of dough in place and decorate with a few pastry cutouts. Beef Wellington can also be made with this dough.

Mrs. H. Alexander Vance, Jr.

SHRIMP RICE SALAD   (Serves 4-6)

3 cups cooked rice (dry)
1½ cups cut up cooked shrimp
1 pkg. (10 oz) frozen petit or tiny peas, cooked, drained. (Do not over cook and lose bright green color)
1 cup Italian dressing (Wishbone)
¾ cup sliced celery
2 T. chopped onion
½ tsp. salt
dash pepper

Combine all ingredients. Leave in refrigerator an hour or more before serving to let flavors blend.

Serve on salad greens. Use for buffet or summer luncheon.

Mrs. John McKinlay

TUNA ELEGANTE
(Serves 6)

3 green onions chopped fine
4 T. butter
4 oz. fresh chopped mushrooms
1- 10½ oz. can cream of chicken soup
2 T. grated parmesan cheese
1/3 cup bread crumbs
½ cup dry vermouth
white pepper to taste
2-3 T. chopped parsley
2- 7 oz. cans white meat tuna (Three Diamond or Chicken of the Sea), drained and broken into chunks

Preheat oven to 450 degrees. Brown onions and mushrooms in 3 tablespoons butter until tender. Remove from heat. Combine soup and vermouth and bring to a boil. Add half of the sauce to onion-mushroom mixture. Spoon equally into buttered sea shells or ramekins. Top with parsley and chunks of tuna. Spoon on the remainder of the sauce. Combine cheese and bread crumbs and sprinkle over each serving. (Refrigerate until ready to serve.) Drizzle a small amount of melted butter over crumbs. Heat in oven ten minutes or until browned.

A marvelous luncheon dish. Try serving it with an English muffin and a green salad.

Mrs. Dennis Muckermann

SHRIMP OR CHICKEN A LA SARIPICO

Cream cheese
Roquefort cheese
(about 3 small cream to one small Roquefort.
Roquefort cheese gets stronger when heated.)
Moisten with champagne or substitute wine. (I
sometimes use milk.) Also, use a little mushroom
juice.

To taste: (chopped fine)

pimento
mushrooms
poppy seeds
garlic
caraway seeds
ripe olives
celery salt
fresh onion juice and
grated pulp
sesame seed

Mix in cooked shrimp or chicken in quantity
desired and to taste. Put in broiler until cheese is
bubbly and brown.

Mrs. E. F. Burch, Jr.

SEAFOOD MOLD
(Serves 8)

2 T. gelatin
¼ cup cold water
1 cup tomato soup
1 large pkg. cream cheese
1 cup mayonnaise
1/3 cup chopped celery
1/3 cup chopped onions
1/3 cup chopped cucumber
1 large can salmon and
1 small can tuna
    or
1 lb. shrimp and 1 lb. crabmeat (or lobster)

Moisten gelatin in cold water and dissolve in hot soup. Melt cream cheese in soup. Mix together mayonnaise, celery, onions, and cucumber and add to soup mixture. Cut up meat and add to above. Pour into well greased mold. Chill. Serve with mayonnaise. Add 1/3 cup chopped cucumbers, if you like.

Mrs. Herbert Watts

SEAFOOD LUNCHEON CASSEROLE (Serves 6)

1 can cream of tomato soup
1 can cream of pea soup
1 can (13 oz.) evaporated milk
1 T. sherry
½ tsp. curry powder
¼ tsp. cayenne pepper
1 lb. cooked shrimp or crab and shrimp

Combine soups and milk. Mix until smooth and add sherry and seasonings. Add shrimp and (or crab). Pour into buttered casserole and bake at 350 degrees for about 35 minutes.

Serve with rice or noodles.

Mrs. Gordon D. Shorney

CRAB CASSEROLE (Serves 4-6)

1 cup chopped celery
2 T. minced onion
½ tsp. salt
⅛ tsp. pepper
1 tsp Worcestershire sauce
1 can water chestnuts, sliced
1 jar button mushrooms
2 pkgs. Wakefield King Crab
1 cup Hellman's mayonnaise

Squeeze out excess moisture from defrosted crab with paper towels. Mix all ingredients in large bowl. Place mixture in flat casserole making contents about 1½ inches high. Cover with bread crumbs. Bake at 350 degrees for 30 minutes.

Mrs. Odette Whipple

CURRIED EGGS AND SHRIMP EN CASSEROLE
(Serves 8)

8 whole eggs deviled
16 shrimp (optional)

Sauce:
3 T. flour
2 T. butter
1 can shrimp soup
1 can milk
½ cup cheese, grated
parsley

Devil eggs, using ½ tsp. curry, ½ tsp. mustard and mayonnaise. Place halves in casserole with shrimp. Make sauce of butter, flour, soup and milk, blending well.

Pour sauce over eggs. Sprinkle with cheese and parsley. Bake at 300-350 degrees until done.

Mrs. George B. Milnor

TOMATO ARTICHOKE SURPRISE

Spread Holland rusks lightly with Hellman's mayonnaise. Top each with a tomato slice, salt, pepper, and one tsp. of chopped salad onions. Place on tomato one drained artichoke heart (Pride of Spain not marinated). Coat with Hellman's mayonnaise to which has been added grated sharp cheese or Parmesan. Bake until brown at 400 degrees for about 15 minutes.

Mrs. Odette A. Whipple

CHICKEN SALAD   (serves 6-8)

4 cups cooked chicken breasts (cut up)
2 cups celery (diced)
½ cup almonds, toasted
1 tsp. salt
2 cups Hellman's mayonnaise
½ cup whipped cream, added to mayonnaise
½ cup cut up green onions
2 cans water chestnuts (drained and sliced)
2 medium pieces candied ginger cut up very fine

Mix together above ingredients except almonds.
Serve on lettuce leaf. Sprinkle nuts on top. Half of
canned peach cut in half may be placed on each
side of salad for color.

Mrs. Harold T. Martin

LUNCHEON MUSHROOMS   (Serves 6)

1 cup medium white sauce
1 can cream of mushroom soup
1 tsp. Worcestershire sauce
dash of tabasco
½ tsp. salt
¼ tsp. pepper
2 cups small mushrooms, sauteed

Combine and cook in a double boiler. When hot,
add 2 T. sherry and ½ lb. grated sharp cheddar
cheese. Heat and serve on toast or English
muffins.

Mrs. W. F. Crawford

HAM AND ASPARAGUS ROLL WITH CHEESE SAUCE
                                        (Serves 4)

1 can (1 lb. 3 oz.) asparagus stalks, drained
4 slices baked or boiled ham, 1/16" thick
2 T. sliced green onions or mushrooms
2 T. butter or margarine
¼ tsp. salt
1 tsp. Worcestershire sauce
2 T. flour
1 cup milk
½ cup shredded cheddar cheese
paprika

Divide asparagus into four equal portions (4 to 5 stalks each). Roll each portion in a slice of ham. Place, seam side down, in a 6x10 inch baking pan. Set aside.

Saute onions in butter. Add salt, Worcestershire sauce and flour. Stir to blend. Add milk. Cook and stir until thickened. Add cheese and stir until melted. Pour over ham rolls. Sprinkle with paprika. Bake at 350 degrees for 20 to 30 minutes or until bubbly.

Mrs. Nancy Elich

CHEESE SOUFFLE   (Serves 6)

12 slices bread
12 slices American cheese
3 eggs
2½ cups milk
Salt & pepper to taste

Make 6 cheese sandwiches (butter bread and use 2 slices of cheese per sandwich.) Arrange very close together in a buttered baking pan. Beat 3 eggs and milk together. Salt and pepper to taste. Pour egg mixture over sandwiches. Let stand 45 minutes or overnight in refrigerator. Bake in preheated oven (350 degrees) for 40-50 minutes until brown and puffed.

Sauce:
Heat in double boiler and serve with souffle: 1 can mushroom soup diluted with ½ cup milk, 1 can butter mushrooms.

Note: This is great for a luncheon served with pickled peaches. It is very easy to make and can be done the night before.

Sue Norell

OMELET–THAT ISN'T!

(Serves 2)

4 eggs seperated
4 T. flour
1 tsp. cream of tartar
1 cup whipping cream
salt and pepper to taste
pinch of cayenne

Beat egg whites with cream of tartar until stiff but not dry. Using same beater, whip cream until very stiff. Still using same beater, beat egg yolks, adding flour and seasoning. Fold whipping cream into egg yolks, gently fold in egg whites.

Pour into hot, well greased casserole and bake in preheated 325 degree oven for 25-30 minutes.

Serve with crisp bacon, cold sliced tomatoes and hot, toasted, buttered English muffins.

GLORIFIED MACARONI AND CHEESE CASSEROLE   (Serves 4)

2 cups uncooked elbow macaroni
1 lb. bulk sausage (I use Jones)
3 large fresh tomatoes
1 pkg. sharp cheddar cheese (8 or 9 oz. pkg.)
1½ cups medium white sauce, seasoned
Sliced or grated cheddar cheese for topping.

Cook macaroni in at least one quart of salted, boiling water for five minutes. Drain and put into a 2½ quart oven casserole dish. Cook sausage until brown and crumbly. Reserve 2 T. of fat for white sauce. Drain rest of fat from sausage meat and add sausage to cooked macaroni in casserole. Mix. Make white sauce with 2 T. of sausage fat, 2¼ T. of flour, and 1½ cups of milk. Cook until thickened. Cut cheese into small pieces and add to white sauce. Stir until blended and season to taste with salt and pepper. Cut tomatoes into small pieces and salt slightly. Add to casserole. Pour cheese sauce over and mix well. Top with shredded cheddar cheese or cheese slices. Bake in 350 degree oven for about 30 minutes or until hot and bubbly.

Mrs. O. Hosmer Morse

QUICHE LORRAINE   (Serves 6)

1 9-inch pie crust
4 eggs
¼ lb. sliced boiled ham
2 egg yolks
½ cup cream
4 T. grated parmesan cheese
½ tsp. salt
A grind of black pepper

Bake crust 5 minutes in a 475 degree oven. Shred ham and line bottom of pie crust. Combine rest of ingredients in a bowl. Beat with wire whisk. Pour in pie crust. Bake in 300 degree oven for 40 minutes. Cut like a pie. Serve at once.

Variation: Substitute ¼ lb. drained crumbled bacon for ham; add one sauteed, chopped onion and one box cooked frozen chopped spinach.

Mrs. John L. Haverkampf

CLUB SANDWICHES FOR TWELVE
(WITHOUT HAVING A NERVOUS BREAKDOWN)

This is a great summer luncheon or Sunday night supper. Can be prepared ahead of time, only add bacon and toast at last minute. I arrange the platter, cover it with Saran wrap and keep it in the refrigerator for 3 or 4 hours.

6 frying chicken breasts cooked (I simmer mine in Campbells chicken broth, but they may be baked.)
36 slices of bacon (if baked in a 350 degree oven they won't need watching).
4-6 heads bibb lettuce
Dish of pickles, olives (black and green), radishes, and anything else that comes to mind.
18-20 tomatoes peeled and sliced (not too thin)
24 slices of white bread, toasted and buttered, served in a basket
Separate bowl of mayonnaise (home-made if possible but you can get by with Hellman's)

Take one huge platter or two big ones. Arrange chicken breasts in slices, bacon, lettuce and tomatoes in rows lengthwise.

If you use two platters, have chicken and bacon on one and lettuce and tomatoes on the other. Have basket of hot toast on buffet and olives, pickles etc. alongside bowl of mayonnaise.

Everyone does their own thing from here on.

Helen Hecht

HOT STUFFED AVOCADOS   (Serves 6)

3 avocados
2 cups medium thick cream sauce
1 large (13 oz.) can crabmeat
2 eggs, hard-cooked
½ tsp. Worcestershire sauce
½ tsp. prepared mustard
2 T. finely chopped onion
4 T. finely chopped green pepper
2 T. finely chopped pimento
Salt and pepper to taste
Grated parmesan cheese

Cut avocados in half, remove stone but do not
peel. Place in flat baking dish. Pour water into
dish to depth of ¼ inch. Spoon creamed mixture
over avocados and sprinkle grated cheese on top.
Heat in 350 degree oven for about 15 minutes.

Mrs. Thomas C. Ratchford

ART FAIR EGGS   (Serves 6)

12 hard boiled eggs
½ tsp. curry powder
½ cup chopped mushrooms
½ tsp. salt
2 cans cream of celery soup (undiluted)
paprika

Peel eggs and halve. Remove and mash egg
yolks. Add curry, mushrooms, salt and enough of
the soup to make a smooth filling. Spoon mixture
into egg halves, and put halves together to make
whole eggs. Spoon soup over eggs and sprinkle
with paprika. Bake in 325 degree oven for 20
minutes.

Mrs. Richard A. Dimberg

Salads and Salad Dressings

COTE D'AZUR SALADE   (Serves 6)

1 package rice (4 cups cooked)

I use brown rice but any kind, even instant will do. Cook as directed but be careful not to overcook. It is better to have the rice just a little crunchy than too soft. Rinse in cold water.

½ cup mayonnaise
½ cup sour cream
3 T. curry powder
1 pkg. frozen crabmeat, thawed
1 pkg. small frozen shrimp

Mix mayonnaise, sour cream, curry powder. Mix crabmeat and shrimp, after rinsing in cold water, with the dressing and add to rice.

A variety of other things may be added. The original recipe called for 1 cup of diced apple sauteed in ¼ cup peanut oil but I have added slice green grapes or artichoke hearts and ripe olives instead of the apple. I usually put the finished mixture in a lightly oiled fish mold and decorate with a few sliced olives and pimentos after unmolding on a bed of lettuce. Try serving this salad with a marinated leg of lamb a melange of summer fruits in kirsch, Florentines for dessert, and a chilled rose for a summer buffet.

Mrs. Gordon R. Ewing

TWENTY-FOUR HOUR SALAD

1 large head lettuce
¼ cup onion, sliced or chopped fine
¼ cup celery, sliced thin
2 cups plus Hellman's mayonnaise
3 tsp. sugar
Romano-parmesan chesse, grated
4 tomatoes, wedges or cherry
parsley
1-6 oz. can sliced water chestnuts
1 pkg. frozen peas (not cooked or thawed)
¾ lb. bacon, fried & crumbled
2 hard cooked eggs, wedges or sliced

Shred lettuce in a large flat serving dish or a shallow large bowl. Sprinkle over the top the onion and celery in layers. Break frozen peas apart and sprinkle over the salad. Spread the mayonnaise like frosting over the top. Seal to edge and cover completely. Sprinkle on sugar and enough of the grated cheese to completely cover the top. Cover and refrigerate overnight. Before serving, top with crumbled bacon. Decorate with tomatoes, hardcooked eggs, and parsley.

DO NOT TOSS THIS SALAD. Each serving should go to the bottom of the bowl to get the full effect of all the layers. The most superb do ahead salad. You won't believe it until you try it.

Mrs. Dennis Muckermann

SHRIMP SALAD   (Serves 6)

1 pkg. lemon Jello
2 cups tomato cocktail
4 T. Piccalilli
Worcestershire sauce
salt and pepper
1 lb. fresh shrimp cooked
1 stalk celery cut fine
1 grated onion
2 hard boiled eggs

Heat tomato cocktail, add Jello and seasonings.
Place ½ egg and a few shrimp in each mold. Pour
Jello mixture over egg and shrimp.

Mrs. William J. Ryan

SPINACH SALAD–"A LA STEAMBOAT
SPRINGS"   (Serves 4)

1 lb. fresh spinach—washed & de-stemmed
2 hard boiled eggs, chopped
6 slices cooked bacon, crumbled
½ small red onion, diced
4 oz. Muenster cheese, cubed
clear French or Italian dressing

Mix all ingredients except eggs, and toss well.
Sprinkle eggs on top.

Julia Baillet

GRANDMOTHER'S SALAD WITH SOUR DRESSING

1 T. butter
2 T. flour
½ tsp. dry mustard
salt
paprika
1/3 cup vinegar
2/3 cup water
2 eggs, hard-boiled
1 cup whipped cream

Mix together butter, flour, mustard. Add dash of salt & paprika, 1/3 cup vinegar and water. Cook in top of double boiler until thickened, stirring constantly. Cool and refrigerate.

Hard boil 2 eggs and refrigerate. When ready to serve, fold in cup of whipped cream and hard boiled eggs cut in small pieces. Spoon onto lettuce wedges.

Mrs. Lawrence O. Holmberg

RAW MUSHROOM SALAD   (Serves 4)

½ lb. fresh mushrooms, sliced
2 tsp. lemon juice
¼ cup thinly sliced scallion greens
3 T. oil
½ tsp. salt

In a serving bowl toss the mushrooms with the lemon juice until the slices are lightly moistened. Then add the scallion greens, oil and salt. Toss again. Chill before serving for hors d'Oeuvres or for salad. Garnish with watercress.

Mrs. James D. Piper

TONY SALAD   (Serves 6-8)

1 head lettuce
1 Bermuda onion
1 green pepper
¼ lb. ham or salami
¼ lb. Swiss cheese
grated Romano cheese
1 cucumber (optional)
1 tomato, cut in chunks
salt
pepper
oregano
8 green and 8 ripe olives (optional)

Dressing:

1 oz. wine vinegar (red)
2 oz. olive oil
juice of 1 lemon or lime

Rub wooden salad bowl with oil, using 1 T. for each 6 people. Pile lettuce lightly in bowl. Slice onion and green pepper on top, tomatoes around edge. Add cheese strips, ham or salami and salt and pepper. Drizzle olive oil first, then wine vinegar, lime juice, pinch of oregano, and grated Romano cheese. Toss. Taste for salt—seems to need quite a bit.

Mrs. Ben W. Perks

CUCUMBERS IN SOUR CREAM   (Serves 8)

6 medium sized cucumbers
salt
garlic
2 T. white cider vinegar
paprika
1¼ cups of sour cream (approx.)

Slice cucumbers very thin with a vegetable slicer.
They may be done by hand but it is much harder
and slower.

Cover each cucumber, when sliced into bowl,
generously with salt. Let stand overnight or at
least 8 hours.

Squeeze as dry as possible with your hands. Add
one garlic bud chopped fine, paprika, white
cider vinegar, and sour cream. Mix
well. Taste, and if more seasoning is desired, add
according to your taste.

Let stand in refrigerator at least 2 hours before
serving. It will keep well for several days.

1 Mrs. William S. Covington

ASPARAGUS VINAIGRETTE

For one can of asparagus, combine 1 T. of
vinegar, 3 T. of oil and 1 tsp. each of Dijon
mustard, chopped parsley and chives. Add salt
and black pepper to taste. Serve as salad on
lettuce with tomatoes, black olives and hard
boiled eggs.

Mrs. James D. Piper

TOMATO ROUNDS

4-½" slices ripe tomatoes
2 large carrots, finely shredded
mayonnaise
worcestershire sauce
dried tarragon

Cover ½ inch slices of unpeeled tomatoes with a generous mixture of mayonnaise and worcestershire sauce (to taste).

Then place a thick covering of shredded carrots over the mayonnaise, and top with a sprinkling of dried tarragon.

Mrs. William F. Regnery

TOMATO ASPIC   (Serves 6)

1 pkg. lemon gelatin
2 cups tomato juice
1 T. tarragon vinegar
1 grated onion
2 avocados cubed
1 can artichoke hearts

Dissolve gelatin in hot tomato juice. Add vinegar and onion. Chill. Allow to partially set. Fold in avocados.

Line an oiled mold with artichokes. Add aspic and chill again.

Serve with 3 T. mayonnaise with a tsp. of curry or a T. of horseradish.

Mrs. George B. Milnor

TOMATO ASPIC   Serves 4 (2 cups)

1¾ cups tomato juice
¼ tsp. celery salt
1 tsp. grated onion
3 whole cloves
1 small package lemon jello
2 T. vinegar (1 white and 1 tarragon)

Simmer tomato juice, celery salt, onion and
cloves 10 minutes. Strain and add to jello. Add
vinegar. Put in individual jello type molds (If you
prefer to use one large mold, add ¼ envelope
gelatin per recipe.).

Dressing: Blend ½ pint sour cream with several
tablespoons mayonnaise. Slice 1 small bunch
green oinions including some green tops. Mix all
together and serve over aspic.

Mrs. Christopher Brown

MANDARIN ORANGE SALAD

1 pkg. orange Jello (add 1 T. Knox plain gelatin)
1 cup liquid (use juice from the mandarin oranges
plus water for 1 cup)
1 pint orange sherbet
1 can mandarin oranges

Heat liquid to boil and add to the orange jello.
When jello is slightly congealed in ice box, add
sherbet and beat well. Add oranges and pour into
the mold and chill overnight in ice box.

Mrs. Henry C. Woods

APRICOT CHEESE DELIGHT   (Serves 8-10)

1 large can apricots drained, prefer peeled type
1 large can crushed pineapple drained
Juice from apricots and pineapple
2 packages orange jello

To Jello add 2 cups hot water and 1 cup fruit juice.
Chill until partially set. Add fruit, place in large
pan 13 by 9" or in 2 pyrex pie plates. Cover with
topping of miniature marshmallows. Make cheese
topping before serving and spread on salad.

Cheese Topping:

½ cup sugar
3 T. flour
1 egg, slightly beaten
1 cup fruit juice

Mix well, cook over low heat until thick. Cool.

Fold in 1 cup heavy cream, whipped. Spread over
salad. Sprinkle about 1 cup grated sharp cheddar
cheese over top.

Attractive when cut in pie shaped wedges.

Mrs. Odette A. Whipple

MOCK VINAIGRETTE

1 cup mayonnaise
red wine garlic vinegar

Mix ingredients. (Add vinegar to taste.) Chill.
Serve over white asparagus. May add ½ tsp. dill.

Mrs. Albert D. Williams, Jr.

SPECIAL PEAR SALAD   (Serves 6)

4 fresh pears
¾ cup orange juice
1 / 3 cup Sauterne or Chablis
¾ cup water, divided
1 tsp. mixed pickling spice
1 envelope unflavored gelatin
lettuce
1 bay leaf
1 stick cinnamon
2 T. lemon juice
1 / 3 cup sugar
1 / 16 tsp. salt
mayonnaise

Combine orange juice, wine, ½ cup water, spices, lemon juice, sugar & salt in skillet. Simmer 5 minutes. Pare, halve & core pears. Cut in small, lengthwise slices. Add syrup and simmer 2 minutes. Lift from syrup and arrange in 8 inch round cake pan.

Strain syrup, discarding spices. Measure. It should be 1½ cups, if less, add wine or orange juice to 1½ cup level. Soften gelatin in remaining ¼ cup water. Add to hot syrup and stir to dissolve. (Reheat if necessary.) Cool syrup. When it begins to thicken, carefully pour over pears in pan.

Chill until firm. Unmold salad onto a serving plate lined with lettuce. Serve with mayonnaise.

Marian Braddock

BING CHERRY SALAD   (Serves 6)

1 can dark seeded cherries
1 pkg. black cherry Jello
pecans

Heat juice of cherries and add enough water to make 2 cups of liquid for Jello. Let set until partially gelled. Meanwhile stuff each cherry with half a pecan. Add to Jello and chill until firm.

Dressing:

1 small pkg. of Philadelphia cream cheese
2 heaping T. currant jelly

Blend these two ingredients thoroughly. Whip ¼ pt. of whipping cream and fold into the cheese and jelly mixture.

Put a dab on top of each serving.

Mrs. R. Thomas Howell, Jr.

CHRISTMAS CRANBERRY JELLY
                    (8 inch mold—makes about 1 qt.)

1 qt. cranberries (1 pkg.)
1¼ cups cold water
2 cups sugar

Cook berries in cold water slowly until all berries have burst. Press through a colander. Add sugar to the mixture and bring to boil again for 2 minutes stirring gently.

Pour into 8 inch mold. (May be frozen.)

Mrs. George B. Milnor

SALAD DRESSING FOR FRUIT SALAD

2 / 3 cup sugar
1 tsp. celery seed
1 tsp. dry mustard
2 tsp. salt
2 tsp. paprika
1 tsp. onion juice
8 T. vinegar
2 cups Mazola oil

Mix dry ingredients. Add a little vinegar. Then alternate oil and vinegar slowly. Beat well with electric beater until very thick.

Mrs. Charles M. Sailor

A SPECIAL FRUIT SALAD DRESSING

1¼ cups sugar
½ tsp. dry mustard
1 tsp. salt
5-6 tsp. paprika

Mix together. Then add

1¼ cups olive oil
1¼ cups lime juice.

Stir. Pour into jar.

Mrs. Karl Tillman Baughman

FRUIT SALAD DRESSING

1 small pkg. raspberry gelatin
1 cup hot water
½ pint sour cream
1 lb. can whole cranberries

Mix and chill gelatin and water until firm but not set.

When it starts to set, whip until frothy in electric mixer. Add the cranberries and cream.

Mix until creamy. Pour into molds and refrigerate until set. Unmold on dark green lettuce leaves. Very eye-appealing and yummy, too.

Mrs. Thomas Stratton

"HAWAIIAN" SALAD DRESSING

1½ cups sugar
2 tsp. dry mustard
2 tsp. salt
3 T. dried onion
¾ cup cider vinegar
½ tsp. garlic salt
1 cup olive oil
3 T. poppy seeds

Put all ingredients in blender and blend until creamy and serve over fruit.

Mrs. Thomas Stratton

HONEY SALAD DRESSING

2/3 cup sugar
1 tsp. dry mustard
1 tsp. paprika
1 tsp. celery seed
1/3 cup strained honey
5 T. white vinegar
1 T. lemon juice
1 cup salad oil
¼ tsp. salt
1 tsp. grated onion

Mix dry ingredients. Add onion, honey, vinegar, and lemon juice. Pour oil in slowly, beating continually.

I do this with a mix-master and get a nice thick dressing.

Mrs. Harold T. Martin

NAOMI'S SALAD DRESSING

3 T. finely chopped anchovies
3 T. chives (or a little green onion)
1 clove garlic, grated
1 T. lemon juice
½ cup sour cream
3 T. tarragon wine vinegar
⅛ cup chopped parsley
salt & pepper to taste
1 cup mayonnaise

Beat well with egg beater or electric blender.

Chill and serve on mixed greens. Pass pepper mill and let guests grind their own pepper over the salad dressing.

Mrs. Thomas A. Kelly

FRENCH DRESSING

1 cup Crisco Oil
½ cup vinegar
1 T. Worcestershire sauce
1 can tomato soup
1 cup sugar
1½ tsp. salt
1 tsp. dry mustard
½ tsp. paprika
½ tsp. garlic salt
½ tsp. minced onion

Combine all ingredients in quart jar. Chill. Shake well before serving.

GREEN GODDESS SALAD DRESSING (OR DIP)

8 fillets of anchovies (imported, 2 cans)
1 bunch green onions (or grated Bermuda)
Parsley, tarragon leaf and chives, chopped

Mash fillets to a pulp and add to above ingredients (all finely chopped). Mix together thoroughly, then add to 3 cups of mayonnaise. One tablespoon of garlic-flavored oil and a little tarragon vinegar may be added if needed or desired.

Use this dressing on mixed greens such as Bibb or Boston lettuce, watercress, romaine, French endive, chicory, etc. (all broken and cut into 2-inch lengths).

'May also be used as a dip with cherry tomatoes, cauliflower buds, endive, carrot sticks, etc.

Mrs. Don H. Reuben

CANADIAN MUSTARD SALAD DRESSING

1½ cups water
½ cup cider vinegar
¾ cup white sugar
3 eggs
1 dessert spoon dry mustard
1 tsp. salt
2 T. flour
1 tsp. butter
½ pint heavy cream, whipped

Mix all dry ingredients together.

Beat three eggs. Add above dry ingredients to beaten eggs—and then combine with vinegar and water in top of double boiler. Stir constantly over hot water until mixture thickens and bubbles. Add butter while dressing is cooking. When dressing is cooked, cool it.

Before serving, fold in ½ pint whipped cream.

Celery seed may be added, if desired.

Store in refrigerator.

Mrs. J. Hayden Macdonald

Entrees

STEAK AU VIN   (Serves 6-8)

2½ - 3 lbs. beef (round steak cut 1 inch thick)
½ cup flour
1½ tsp. steak seasoning
¼ cup butter
1 can (10½ oz.) beef consomme
1 cup red table wine
2 / 3 cup coarsely diced green pepper
2 cups celery cut into 1 inch pieces
1½ cups thinly sliced carrots

Dredge steak in mixture of the flour and seasoning blend. (Set aside any remaining.) Pound the seasoned flour into both sides of the steak and cut into 6 or 8 equal portions. Brown in butter. Add consomme, cover, and simmer gently 2 hours or until meat is almost tender.
Remove from pan, combine wine with the remaining flour, and stir into cooking liquid. Add vegetables and steak. Cover and cook gently for another 30 minutes or until both vegetables and meat are tender.

Serve with steamed rice.

Mrs. Thomas A. Kelly

SPECIAL STEAK FARCI

(Serves 4)

1 sirloin steak about 1½ inch thick
1 T. corn oil

Farci:

½ oz. butter
1 shallot
2 oz. mushrooms
1 oz. ham
1/3 cup fresh white bread crumbs
1 small tin pate de fois gras
salt
pepper

SAUCE:

¾ oz. butter, melted
good squeeze of lemon juice
2 T. chopped fresh parsley
watercress

First prepare the farci. Finely chop the shallot
and soften in the butter over low heat. Wash the
mushrooms, chop finely, and add to the pan.
Cover and cook 4-5 minutes. Chop the ham and
add to the mixture with the bread crumbs, off the
heat. Season with salt and pepper and turn out on
a plate to cool.

Cut the steak on one side horizontally to form a
pocket. Add the pate de fois gras to the farci, mix
well, and fill the pocket. Sew up with a poultry
needle and string or fasten with poultry pins.

Brush the steak with oil and grill 4-5 minutes on
each side. Serve with sauce.

Mrs. Richard Senior

CHERRY GLAZED SPARERIBS   (Serves 6)

3 lbs. spareribs (lean
  baby back ribs)
1½ tsp. salt
¼ tsp. pepper
¼ cup honey
¼ cup lime juice
1 cup orange juice
½ tsp. dry mustard
¼ tsp. tabasco sauce
½ tsp. salt
1 can pitted dark sweet
  cherries

Season spareribs with salt and pepper. Bake in
shallow pan at 425 degrees for 45 minutes. Turn
ribs once while baking. Drain off excess fat. Mix
remaining ingredients, except cherries, and pour
over meat. Lower heat to 375 degrees and bake
one hour longer. Baste several times and add
cherries for last 15 minutes of cooking time.

Mrs. Charles M. Dykema

CLOUTIERS FRENCH CHRISTMAS PIE

1 uncooked 12 inch pie shell and dough for top
½ lb. ground pork
1 lb. ground beef
3-4 potatoes, medium large
¼ tsp. allspice
⅛ tsp. cinnamon
¼ tsp. poultry seasoning
salt & pepper
whole milk
butter

Boil potatoes and mash with milk, salt, butter to taste, and add onions. Mix. Cook meat in skillet until grayish in color, do not overcook. Add salt and pepper. At this point I have always had excess fat and therefore drain slightly. My mother *never* has this excess, so you'll have to judge this for yourself.

Mix potatoes and meat together with seasonings in same skillet and cook over very low heat, stirring occasionally for 15 minutes. Mixture should be quite mushy.

Pour into uncooked pie shell, cover with pie crust and bake approximately 1 hour at 375 degrees. Traditionally our family serves this along with the turkey dinner on Christmas day and also eat it constantly throughout the holidays with just celery. Because the pies can be frozen when partially cooked (½ hour), it is a very convenient late supper dish.

Note: This was a word of mouth recipe for three generations starting in France until I finally cornered my mother with pencil in hand. Mother always makes 6-8 pies at a time so the measurements vary. Therefore, after you cook this once, you may wish to alter some quantity to your own taste, or even add ½ lb. lamb and only ½ lb. beef, as is occasionally done.

Mrs. James Schulz

DELECTABLE POT ROAST   (Serves 4)

For this you'll need a 3½-4½ pound round or blade bone chuck roast. Season both sides of meat with fine herbes, garlic salt and crushed pepper. Brown quickly in a minimum amount of oil over high flame. Lower flame to a simmer.

Add quartered onions, ¼ cup red wine, ¼ cup water. Cover and cook over low flame for two hours. Add more wine (or water if you must) as necessary.

The idea is to let the liquid slowly cook off. It leaves a delectable looking pot roast that should serve more than four but it won't because you'll find people wanting more.

Mrs. John K. Diederichs

CZARIST RUSSIAN STROGANOFF   (Serves 4-6)

2 lbs. beef tenderloin or top grade sirloin
3 T. butter
1 T. olive oil
4 T. flour
2 cups warm sour cream
pinch or two of mace or ginger
salt & pepper
¾ cup extra dry vermouth

Have butcher remove all fat and cut the meat *across* the grain into pencil thin strips about 2 inches long.

Heat butter and oil in heavy skillet and when hot and bubbly add beef and saute long enough to sear but be sure to keep on the rare side.

Remove to platter and keep warm. Add more butter to skillet and blend in flour and seasonings. Brown well. Stir in vermouth and heat through. Add warm sour cream. Do not let it boil. Add beef strips. (If necessary, keep warm in double boiler).

Serve the dish with thin slices of dark rye bread generously spread with sweet butter.

Mushrooms and tomato paste may be added. These ingredients, however, change the delicate flavor of the Czarist Russian stroganoff.

PICADILLO   (Serves 4)

1 green pepper, chopped
2 to 4 cloves garlic, finely chopped
1 T. lard
1 bay leaf
1 T. poppy seeds
2 T. capers
1 to 1¼ tsp. olive brine
salt
1 large onion, chopped
1-1 lb. can tomatoes
½ cup raisins
1 T. sesame seeds
2 T. chopped olives
1¼ lb. ground beef

Cook green pepper, onion and garlic in fat until soft. Add tomatoes and bay leaf. Simmer about 15 minutes. Add raisins, poppy and sesame seeds, capers, olives and olive brine. Simmer a few minutes. Add beef and simmer 20-30 minutes. Serve over white, wild, or saffron rice. (Saffron rice preferred).

Note: You can vary seasonings as to your personal liking—such as: caraway seed, oregano, etc.

Mrs. E. F. Burch, Jr.

FAVORITE MEATBALLS   (Serves 4)

1½ lbs. ground round
½ cup cornflake crumbs
dash oregano
¼ cup red wine
1 egg
5 T. Girard's clear French dressing
1 can onion soup
salt & pepper

Combine and mix all ingredients except soup.
Form into small meatballs and brown in ½ inch
bacon fat. Drain and place in buttered casserole.
Pour undiluted soup over meatballs and bake at
300 degrees for 30 minutes.

Mrs. William G. Dubinsky

MEAT SOUFFLE   (Serves 4-5)

Season 2 cups white sauce with chopped parsley
and onion juice.

Stir 2 cups diced, cooked meat (chicken, veal,
beef, or lamb) into sauce and heat. When hot, add
four beaten egg yolks.

Cool. Add four beaten egg whites. Bake in buttered baking dish at 350 degrees for about 30
minutes.

Good meat stretcher.

Mrs. Charles Sailor

GROUND BEEF EGGPLANT CASSEROLE
(Serves 4)

1 large eggplant
1¼ tsp. salt
1 cup salad oil
1 clove garlic
1 lb. cooked ground beef
¾ cup chopped mozzarella chesse
2 cups Italian flavored tomato sauce
¾ cup freshly grated parmesan cheese

Peel eggplant cut into ¼" slices. Sprinkle with salt. Let drain for ½ hour. Heat oil in large skillet. Add garlic. Cook one minute and remove. Pat eggplant dry. Fry, a few slices at a time, until golden on both sides. Drain on absorbent paper.

Arrange one layer of eggplant in a deep casserole dish. Sprinkly with some of meat, mozzarella cheese, tomato sauce and parmesan cheese. Repeat until all eggplant is used, ending with a layer of tomato sauce and a sprinkling of parmesan chees. Bake uncovered at 400 degrees for 20 minutes.

Mrs. H. Earl Hoover

HUNGARIAN GOULASH   (Serves 6)

A recipe from a Hungarian cook.

1½ lbs. pork cubed (1 inch x 1 inch)
1½ lbs. veal cubed
⅛ lb. butter or bacon fat
2 medium size onions, chopped
finely chopped large "toe" of garlic
salt
pepper
1 large can of sauerkraut
1 pint sour cream

Saute the onions in butter until transparent. Add the large "toe" of garlic, and immediately add the meat. Season with salt and pepper. Cover and cook over medium heat for one hour. Stir occasionally. Should not get brown.

At the end of one hour cover the meat with a large can of sauerkraut. Do not stir. Cover the pan again and cook for ½ hour. Then stir sauerkraut in and cook another ½ hour. Remove from stove, mix in 1 pint of sour cream and serve.

May be kept warm on low flame but do not cook any more.

Accompaniments: mashed potatoes and golden fried onions, fried in butter, mixed together. Use water the potatoes are cooked in instead of milk for the mashed potatoes. Green beans are very good with the goulash as well as the potatoes.

Mrs. William S. Covington

AUNT CHRISTINE'S CORNED BEEF

Bring water with brisket of beef in it to a boil. Pour out water.

In large pot place beef and the following ingredients:

1 T. honey
1 T. cider vinegar
3 or 4 bay leaves
1 T. mixed pickling spices
1 clove garlic
A little green pepper
A little celery
1 T. dried mushrooms

Cook at high simmer *one hour per pound*. Add following to broth when removing beef after cooking:

1 T. honey
1 T. cider vinegar
1 T. baking soda
½ tsp. caraway seeds

Add cabbage and cook. Slice beef after one half hour.

Mrs. Peter Economou

LASAGNE   (Serves 8)

1. Make tomato sauce:

½ cup chopped onion
1 clove garlic, minced
3 T. olive oil
2 cans (1 lb. 4 oz. each) Italian tomatoes, rubbed
through sieve
1 can (8 oz.) tomato sauce
1 can (6 oz.) tomato paste
1 cup water
1 tsp. basil
2 T. fresh minced parsley
2 tsp. salt
¼ tsp. pepper

Saute onion and garlic in oil. Add rest of
ingredients. Simmer over low heat for one hour.

2. Prepare meat to add to above sauce. 1 and 2
then should simmer a good 1½ to 2 hours.

¾ lb. ground beef
¼ lb. ground pork
1 cup fine dry bread crumbs
½ cup Parmesan (grated) cheese
1 T. minced parsley
1 clove garlic, cut fine
½ cup milk
2 eggs, beaten
1½ tsp. salt
⅛ tsp. pepper

Mix above ingredients together. Brown meat in
hot fat. Add to above sauce.

3. Prepare cheeses:

Grate 1 lb. Mozzarella. Mix 1 lb. Ricotta with 1

T. parsley and 1 tsp. oregano. Grate ¾ cup Parmesan.

4. Cook lasagne noodles according to package directions. (Need ½ lb.)

Place the following ingredients in layers in oblong pan 13 x 9½ x 2 inches in order listed, beginning and ending with the sauce. Repeat until all ingredients are used up.

Tomato Meat Sauce
Single layer of noodles
Ricotta mixture
Parmesan
Mozarella

Bake 30 min. at 350 degrees. Let stand 15 minutes. Cut and serve. Will last in refrigerator for one week and can be easily frozen. Just reheat with a cover for 20-25 min. at 350 degrees. Important: must be at room temperature for reheating.

Mrs. H. Alexander Vance, Jr.

CANTONESE SPARERIBS   (Serves 4)

2 sides pork spare ribs
2 cups Chinese soy sauce
1 cup sugar
2 tsp. salt
2-3 T. catsup

Trim ribs and marinate for *at least* one hour in mixture of soy sauce, sugar, salt and catsup. Roast for 30 minutes in 400 degree oven. Baste often. Reduce heat to 300 degrees and roast for 2 hours basting often.

Mrs. Thomas D. Hodgkins

MODIFIED PHILADELPHIA SCRAPPLE

1 pkg. chop suey meat
1 tsp. salt
¼ tsp. pepper
5 cups cold water
1½ to 2 cups golden corn meal
4 T. poultry seasoning
  (perhaps more)

Simmer meat in salt-pepper-water mixture until meat is tender. Shred meat with a fork. Add corn meal with whisk or fork and poultry seasoning.

Cook slowly, stirring constantly until mixture is thick enough to pour into bread pan. Chill over night. Turn out on floured bread board, cut into ½ inch slices. Dip in flour and saute quickly in butter.

Serve with catsup.

Mrs. John Grace, Jr.

FAMILY BEEF STEW   (Serves 6)

3 lbs. stewing meat cut in 1½ inch cubes
carrots
parsnips
celery
2 med. size onions
Seasonings
2 cans (1 lb. 4 oz) Hunt's Tomato sauce
3 T. Minute tapioca

Do not brown meat. Put meat in bottom of a
covered roaster that has been greased with Pam.
Add vegetables, which have been cut the same
size as the meat. Add chopped onions, and
seasonings to taste. Add two cans of tomato sauce
and one can of water. Stir in Minute Tapioca.

Bake in a preheated oven at 300 degrees for 2½
hours. Then open the roaster and taste for
seasoning and add more if needed. Also, check for
thickening, and add more tapioca if needed.

At this time, if you wish to serve this as a pretty
main course for a buffet, add frozen peas for color
on top of the other vegetables.

Bake covered for another hour, or until the additional frozen vegetables are done.

Mrs. Clyde E. Hamilton

HAM LOAF

1 lb. ground ham
1 lb. ground pork
1 cup seasoned bread crumbs
chopped celery stalks
chopped onion
½ cup milk
2 eggs
salt, pepper, onion salt

Combine ingredients and cook at 350 degrees one hour. Serve with mustard sauce.

MUSTARD SAUCE

½ cup sugar
1 tsp. flour
½ cup mustard (not powder)
½ cup water
3 yolks
¼ cup butter

Beat well. Cook for ½ hour in double boiler.

Mr. Peter Grumhaus

HUNGARIAN PORK FILLET (Serves 4-6)

2 pork fillets
1 oz. clarified butter
2 shallots
1 T. paprika
1 T. flour
¼ cup sherry
5 oz. jellied stock
¼ lb. mushrooms
¼ to ½ cup sour cream

Chop the shallots finely. Cut the pork fillets into nice-sized pieces. Saute quickly in the butter. Add the shallots and paprika and cook slowly for 2 to 3 minutes. Stir in the flour, add the sherry and stock, and bring to a boil. Simmer gently 30-40 minutes. Saute the mushrooms in butter for 3-4 minutes and add them to the pork. Pour in the sour cream, adjust the seasoning and serve with boiled rice.

Mrs. Richard Senior

212

Entrees (Meats)

PORK CHOPS WITH CURRY
AND APRICOT SAUCE

(Serves 4)

4 loin pork chops
4 oz. mushrooms
3 oz. butter
1 can strained halved
   apricots
salt and pepper

Chop the mushrooms and saute them in the butter
for a few minutes, until brown, but still firm.
Remove them with slotted spoon, and set aside.

Saute pork chops in the same pan, until browned
on both sides. Place the chops in fireproof dish,
and put one apricot half on top of each chop.
Scatter the mushrooms over the top. Set dish
aside.

SAUCE:

2 onions, finely chopped
1½ oz. butter
1 T. flour
1 T. curry powder
generous ¼ pint of stock
juice from canned apricots
2 T. apricot jam
¼ pint single cream

Saute the onions in the butter until tender and
golden. Sprinkle with the flour, then add curry
powder. Cook 1-2 minutes, stirring well. Then add
the stock, juice from the can, salt and pepper. Add
the apricot jam, stir well, bring to a boil, and then
lower heat and simmer for 30 minutes. Strain.
Add the cream, stirring well. Adjust seasoning.

Pour the sauce over the chops in a fireproof

dish. Bake, covered, at 350 degrees for one hour.

The chops and sauce can be prepared ahead and baked before serving time.

Mrs. Ralph Daniel

PORK TENDERLOIN TOWERS   (Serves 4)

4 one inch thick pork tenderloin slices
salt & pepper
4 slices onion, cut ½ inch thick
4 slices tomato, cut in ½ inch slices
8 slices bacon

Wrap all ingredients in bacon, 2 slices around each tower and hold together with tooth picks.

Place in covered baking dish. Bake at 350 degrees for 1 hour. Uncover and broil until bacon is crisp.

Mrs. F. T. Kelsey

PORK TENDERLOINS IN WINE

(Basic recipe for any amount)

pork tenderloins
flour
salt & peper
dash garlic powder
¼ cup Soy Sauce
¾ cup sherry wine
jar boiled onions

In brown paper bag, mix flour, salt, pepper and small dash of garlic powder. Shake port tenderloins in mixture until each has a light coat of seasoned flour. Place tenderloins in pyrex dish either flat or rolled up, depending on size of tenderloins.

Using a combination of soy sauce and wine, pour over tenderloins until they are half covered.

Bake in 350 degree oven uncovered for at least 2 hours. During last 15 minutes of baking add a jar of **boiled onions**. Turn **once** or twice.

                                        Mrs. A. W. Phelps

PORK CHOPS CALIFORNIA   (Serves 6)

6 pork chops, ¾ inch thick
6 thin lemon slices
2 T. brown sugar
2 / 3 cup catsup
1 / 3 cup water

Brown chops in skillet. Drain off excess fat. Place
in baking dish. Combine brown sugar, catsup and
water and pour over chops. Place lemon slice on
each chop.

Bake in 325 degree oven for 1½ hours, covered.

Mrs. Vincent D. Sill

PORK SAUSAGE

¼ lb. pork fat ground
¾ lb. lean pork meat ground
1 tsp. ground sage
1 tsp. ground thyme
1 tsp. salt
⅛ tsp. fresh ground pepper
1 dash cayenne peper (opt.)

Have your butcher mix the pork fat and meat
together or do it yourself. Have the meat mixture
at room temperature and add all of the remaining
ingredients. Mix well with a wooden fork or spoon
after each addition so that the spices are evenly
distributed.

This sausage has very little fat and therefore will
not shrink when cooked. Make the meat sausage
into patties and broil as you would a hamburger.

Mrs. Charles A. Comiskey II

ORANGE-GLAZED PORK CHOPS   (Serves 4)

4 loin pork chops (thick)
6 T. water
5 T. sugar
1½ tsp. cornstarch
¼ tsp. salt
¼ tsp. cinnamon
salt, pepper, paprika
10 whole cloves
2 tsp. grated orange rind
¼ cup orange juice
4 orange slices

Trim fat from pork chops and put in skillet to coat. Sprinkle chops with salt, pepper and paprika on both sides. Brown chops well on both sides over high heat. Then add 6 T. of water, cover, and cook one hour or more until very tender, over low heat. The chops may need turning serveral times. Add water if necessary.

Twenty minutes before chops are done, combine sugar, cornstarch, salt, cinnamon, cloves, orange rind and orange juice.

Cook over medium heat, stirring constantly, until thickened and clear. Arrange chops on platter, pour orange sauce over them. Decorate with orange slices—mandarin oranges can be used. This recipe can easily be doubled or tripled.

Mrs. H. H. Kittleman

PORK CHOPS WITH GLAZED CHERRIES

Saute medium thick pork chops until brown on each side. Then cover with water and add a sauteed onion. Cover the pan and bake or simmer until chops are tender. Season and thicken the gravy slightly.

Pour 1 cup of juice from a can of sour pitted cherries into a sauce or frying pan. Add 1 cup sugar. Cook until juice is reduced by ½.

Add the cherries and simmer until nearly all the juice is cooked away and the cherries are glazed.

Place the chops on a warm platter and pour the glazed cherries over them.

Mrs. Burton W. Hales

CEYLON PORK CHOP BAKE   (Serves 6)

6 pork loin chops cut 1 inch thick
salt
lemon pepper
1 T. vegetable oil
½ cup white wine
1 tsp. instant tea powder
2 T. ketchup

Sprinkle chops with salt and lemon pepper. Then brown them quickly on both sides in the heated oil in a large skillet.

In a small saucepan, heat the wine, add tea and ketchup. Pour off any grease in skillet. Pour wine mixture over browned chops. Cover pan and bake in a preheated 350 degree oven for about 40 minutes.

Mary Porter Snyder

OVEN LAMB CURRY

(Serves 4)

2 lbs. lean lamb stew
   meat, cut into 1½ to
   2 inch squares
1 can cream of celery
   soup, undiluted
½ soup can of white
   wine or water
¼ cup dry onion soup mix
curry powder to taste
   (about 1 T.)
¼ cup chopped celery
   (optional)
1 medium onion, chopped
   (optional)

Mix all ingredients in an oven dish with tight cover or a pot with tight cover. It is not necessary to brown the meat first. Cook in a 350 degree oven for 3 to 3½ hours, checking occasionally and adding more water if necessary.

Serve over hot steamed rice with curry side dishes such as crumbled bacon, chopped peanuts, minced green onions, shredded coconut, raisins and chutney.

Mrs. James P. Canepa

BARBECUE LAMB SHANKS WITH VERMOUTH
(Serves 6)

6 lamb shanks
1 cup dry vermouth
1 cup oil
1 T. lemon juice
3 shallots, chopped
2 garlic cloves, minced
1 tsp. chopped tarragon
1 tsp. chopped basil
1 tsp. salt
10 pepper corns, crushed

Marinate lamb shanks in vermouth, oil, lemon juice, shallots, garlic, herbs, salt and pepper. Let stand at room temperature for at least four hours. Turn lamb shanks once or twice and spoon marinade over.

Broil lamb for about 30 minutes, turning frequently and basting with the marinade.

Mary Jane Hardwicke

MARINATED LEG OF LAMB   (Serves 10-12)

7 to 8 lb leg of lamb—boned and flattened. Have
your butcher give the meat several hearty swacks
with the broadside of the cleaver so that the meat
will be more or less of an even thickness.

Mix one bottle of mint sauce (Cross & Blackwell
or any other brand. I make my own in the summer
but use a commercial brand in the winter when
fresh mint is not available), with one small bottle
of soy sauce.

Put the meat in a 9x12 glass baking dish (actually
you can marinate in any flat dish that will hold the
meat and marinade comfortably but confined),
fat side down. Pour on mixture of mint and soy
sauce. Put this in the refrigerator covered with
wax paper or Saran wrap. Start the whole
proceeding at least 24 hours before you plan on
serving the meat and after the first six hours, turn
the meat.

Many of the mint leaves will cling to the meaty
side. Let them, but using a fork, pierce the fat in
several places. Using a spoon or baster, dribble
the marinade over the lamb, repeating at in-
tervals until cooking time.

The lamb may be cooked two ways:

1. With a grill—drain the meat, reserving the
marinade, and pat dry with paper towels. Cook
the lamb the same way you would a steak of equal
thickness and "doneness," remembering that
lamb will dry out a little more than steak, as it is
not a marbled meat. Put on a serving tray and cut
in diagonal slices about ½ inch thick. Heat the
marinade and serve it in a side dish with the
lamb. I always add the pan juices to the

marinade, heating them in the pan with a little hot water or white wine added to make sure you get all the crusty brown pieces which will flavor the sauce. Add any additional seasoning you feel necessary.

2. Oven roasting—Follow the same procedure in draining, reserving marinade, etc. Roast the lamb for 45 minutes in a 325 degree oven. (We like our lamb on the very pink side, so add a few minutes of time if you prefer more well done). Use the same procedure for serving the lamb and sauce.

I use the grill method in the summer and the oven method in the winter when charcoal grilling is not so practical. Both have proved very satisfactory.

Mrs. Gordon R. Ewing

BONELESS ROLLED LEG OF LAMB
(Serves 8-10)

Marinate overnight one boneless rolled leg of lamb in 2 cups red wine and 1 small bottle Wishbone Italian style dressing.

Bake in marinade at 350 degrees for about three hours or until done.

Slices best when cold. May be reheated in foil packages.

Mrs. Thomas A. Kelly

SHISH KEBABS   (Serves 6)

Make the following marinade:

½ cup Wesson oil
¼ cup soy sauce
¼ cup Worcestershire sauce
2 T. dry mustard
2½ tsp. salt
1 T. freshly ground pepper
½ cup wine vinegar
1 / 3 cup fresh lemon juice
½ tsp. basil
½ tsp. oregano
½ tsp. thyme
small crushed clove garlic
  (optional)

Mix all of these ingredients.

Have your butcher cut up 3 lbs. leg of lamb meat
into 1½ inch cubes, with all fat removed.

Put the meat in a large bowl, pour the marinade
over it and stir thoroughly. Place in refrigerator
for several hours, stirring once. (Can be
marinated overnight).

Prepare the following:

Green pepper cut into
  1 inch squares
1 box cherry tomatoes
1 lb. large mushrooms, cleaned
1 inch squares fresh onion
1 inch squares bacon(½ lb.)

On skewers alternate the marinated lamb with
the above ingredients until each skewer is full.

Place the skewers in a shallow roasting pan and brush all with the marinade until ready to barbecue.

Have a medium-hot fire ready. Barbecue the kebabs 3 to 4 inches above the fire, turning and basting often. It will take about 15 minutes. The lamb should be slightly pink inside and the vegetables cooked, but crunchy.

Serve with parsleyed rice.

Spicy but very good!

Mrs. Rudy L. Ruggles

LEMON BROILED LAMB

Even lamb-haters like this one. It will take a 4-5 pound boned and rolled leg of lamb to serve 10. However, you can use these steps with any leg of lamb.

Using a sharp knife, make 7 or 8 slits down into the meat about 2 inches apart. Fill each slit with finely chopped garlic, a pinch each of powdered ginger and cracked black pepper. Juice 2 lemons and generously rub the surface of the lamb with the juice. Save extra juice for later. Place the lamb on a rack in an open pan and brown under a preheated broiler.

Then roast in a slow oven (300 degrees) brushing occasionally with more lemon juice. Allow two hours depending upon how pink you like your lamb.

Mrs. John K. Diederichs

RAGOUT OF LAMB   (Serves 6)

3 lb. very lean lamb (from the leg) cut in to 1 inch cubes
¼ cup flour
2 tsp. salt (use half when dredging)
¼ tsp. freshly ground pepper
¼ cup olive oil
1¼ cups chicken broth
½ cup dry sherry
2 cloves minced garlic
¼ tsp. marjoram
¼ tsp. savory
2 T. chopped parsley
1 T. lemon juice
½ T. grated lemon rind

Dredge lamb in seasoned flour. Heat oil and brown lamb. Add broth, garlic, marjoram, savory and 1 tsp. salt. Cover and bake at 350 degrees one hour or until tender. Remove from oven and skim off fat. Reduce gravy to 1 cup. Just before serving, stir in parsley, lemon juice, and rind. Garnish with clusters of tiny cooked carrots, whole onions, and sprigs of watercress. Serve with rice.

Mrs. William G. Dubinsky

SAUSAGE STUFFED LEG OF LAMB
(Serves 8-10)

7 lb. leg of lamb, boned
lemon juice
salt
peper

STUFFING:

1½ lbs. sausage meat
1 8 oz. pkg. stuffing mix
3 T. fresh mint, chopped finely
1 minced garlic clove
1 small onion, chopped
½ cup raisins
¼ cup melted butter
6 T. rose wine

SAUCE:
2 cups rose wine
½ cup soy sauce
½ tsp. oregano

Rub leg of lamb with lemon, salt and pepper. Brown sausage. Do not drain. Combine it with next seven ingredients.

Mix and scoop into cavity of leg. Tie together with string. To make the sauce combine rose wine, soy sauce and oregano. Simmer 2 minutes.

Bake at 350 degrees for 2½ hours, basting frequently with the sauce.

Mrs. Albert D. Williams, Jr.

VEAL, MUSHROOMS AND WHITE WINE
(Serves 4)

2 lbs. veal, cut in
  thin scallops
flour
salt & pepper
dash of paprika
6 T. butter
3 or 4 shallots
1 cup mushrooms, sliced
½ cup white wine
1 T. chopped parsley
Few leaves of tarragon

Dredge scallops with seasoned flour. Saute slowly in butter. When brown, remove and keep warm in casserole. Saute onions in butter for 2 minutes. Add mushrooms. Add ¼ cup white wine and allow to cook down a few minutes. Add parsley and tarragon. Finally add ¼ cup more white wine and allow to boil up for 1 or 2 minutes before pouring over the scallops.

Mrs. Albert D. Williams Jr.

VEAL MARENGO IN TOAST BOXES   (Serves 4)

2 lbs. veal shank cubed
½ lb. boiling onions, chopped
¼ lb. mushrooms
3 T. olive oil
1½ T. flour (increase
  according to wine required)
Cover with white wine
  (approx. 3 cups)
1 bouquet garni
Salt, pepper, garlic,
  basil
Parsley
4 fresh tomatoes

Dry veal on a towel, brown slowly in hot oil. When well-browned, add onions and brown them. Then add salt, pepper, bouquet garni, garlic, basil, and wine. Cover the pan and cook for 45 minutes. Remove bouquet garni and serve spooned into and over toast boxes. Top with chopped parsley.

Slice off all crusts from 12 inch long loaf of unsliced white bread. Then slice cross-wise into cubes about 2 inch square. To shape each box, lay each cube flat on a board. Cut around inside of cube, ¼ inch from sides and ¼ inch from bottom. Then slip knife through only one side of box ¼ inch up from bottom and cut across to release center piece of bread. Lift out and discard.

Dip bread boxes in ½ cup melted butter. Bake in a 350 degree oven 10 to 15 minutes. Makes 6 toast boxes.

Mrs. H. Alexander Vance, Jr.

ROAST VEAL BECHAMEL   (Serves 6)

About 3 pounds of meat. When cooking veal, it is important to remember that of all the meats, veal is the one that shrinks the most in cooking.

6-8 slices baked or boiled ham
2 to 3 cups of Bechamel sauce (the roast should be well covered)
Marjoram or oregano for the meat
Breadcrumbs for the dish
Butter for the dish
Chopped parsley for garnish

Rub veal roast with salt. pepper, marjoram or oregano, and place the garlic clove (which has been cut into 2 or 3 pieces) at each end of the roast. Place in a pan (with or without a rack) with about one inch of water. Dot well with butter. Cook in a 300-325 degree oven. Cook for a minimum of 25 minutes per pound, depending upon the quality of the meat and the oven. Baste often. When roast is cooked, let it cool, as it will be easier to slice. Veal is not supposed to be sliced too thinly.

Place butter and breadcrumbs around an ovenware serving dish. Reassemble roast alternating veal and ham being sure to start and finish with a slice of veal. Keep all the edges straight.

Pour the Bechamel sauce (see p. 263) generously over the top. Sprinkle with breadcrumbs, dot with butter, then sprinkle with chopped parsley and place in oven. When completely reheated, place under broiler until the top is golden brown.

Grated Parmesan or Gruyere cheese may be added.

Mrs. H. Alexander Vance, Jr.

VEAL PICCATA   (Serves 2)

1 lb. veal cutlets
 pounded *very* thin
½ cup butter
½ cup chicken broth
2 tsp. lemon juice
¼ cup finely chopped parsley
1 lemon sliced thin

After cutlets are pounded, dredge in ½ cup flour
plus 1 tsp. salt. Saute in butter—add stock and
reduce. Add lemon juice, lemon and parsley—
Shake pan until cutlets are covered and the lemon
is hot. Serve at once with pasta or rice.

Mrs. Richard D. Siragusa

CALVES LIVER WITH AVOCADO   (Serves 4-6)

8-10 slices calves liver
2 large avocados
flour seasoned with salt and pepper
1 cup butter
juice of 2 lemons
½ cup beef stock
½ tsp. thyme

Dredge calves liver and avocado in seasoned
flour. Heat ½ cup of the butter and saute the liver
and avocado quickly until done. Prepare the
sauce by heating the remaining ½ cup butter in a
saucepan until lightly browned. Add lemon juice,
stock and thyme. When hot, pour over liver and
avocado.

Mrs. William Glenn Dubinsky

CHICKEN BREAST GRAND MARNIER (Serves 4)

2 large chicken breasts—boned, skinned and cut in half. Lightly salt and flour. Fry in peanut oil until nicely browned. Remove chicken to platter and after pouring off all oil in pan, Add:
1 T butter
3 T brown sugar
Juice of ½ sunkist orange
Simmer, stirring until smooth. Replace chicken breasts. Add:
½ sunkist orange sliced
2 nectarines, peeled and halved (or canned peaches)
¼ cup Grand Marnier
Simmer and baste for 5 minutes. Arrange chicken and fruit on platter. Top with toasted almonds.

Mrs. Franklin Lyons

GLAZED CHICKEN WITH GRAPES (Serves 6-8)

4 large boned chicken breasts cut in ½ inch strips
2 T. orange marmalade
2-3 cans of seedless grapes
6 T. margarine or butter
1 cup flour
¼ tsp. salt
¼ tsp. nutmeg

Add salt and nutmeg to flour. Mix together. Dip the chicken strips in flour mixture. Brown chicken lightly in 6 T. butter or margarine in 300 degree oven. After chicken is cooked, push strips to one side and add grapes. Heat grapes thoroughly. Add 2 T. marmalade. Mix all together and serve with plain or wild rice.

Evelyn P. Aiken

CHICKEN BREASTS IN ORANGE
SAUCE   (Serves 6)

Can be cooked ahead—a *very* easy company dish.

3 large chicken breasts
 (boned and halved
¼ cup butter or
 margarine
2 T. flour
2 T. sugar
¼ tsp. dry mustard
¼ tsp. cinnamon
⅛ tsp. ginger
1 tsp. salt
1 can frozen orange
 juice plus enough water to
 make 1½ cups liquid

Sprinkle chicken breasts with ½ tsp. salt and
brown in butter in frying pan. Remove. Add flour,
sugar, spices and remaining ½ tsp. salt to drippings in pan. Stir to smooth paste. Gradually stir
in orange juice. Cook, stirring constantly, until
mixture thickens and comes to a boil. Add chicken
breasts.

Cover. Simmer over low heat until chicken is
tender, 20-30 minutes. Can be cooked ahead.

Julia Baillet

CURRY GLAZED CHICKEN   (Serves 8)

Curry glaze (2 cups):

6 slices chopped bacon
2 / 3 cup chopped onions
2 T. flour
1 T. curry powder
1 T. sugar
2 T. catsup
1 can condensed beef
 broth
3 T. flaked coconut
2 T. applesauce
2 T. lemon juice

Combine all ingredients in saucepan. Heat to boiling and stir frequently until thickened.

Chicken:

2 broiler fryers (3 lbs
 each) quartered
6 T. flour
1½ tsp. salt
1 tsp. ground ginger
6 T. butter(melted)

Cut away back bones and rib bones. Shake chicken in flour-salt-ginger mixture in a paper bag. Roll in melted butter and arrange skin side up in a baking dish. Bake at 400 degrees for 20 minutes or until it turns golden. Spoon half of curry glaze over chicken to make a thick coating. Bake 20 minutes longer.

Serve with rice. Garnish with lemon cups filled with pepper relish.

Mrs. Arthur T. Moulding

TROPICAL CHICKEN (Serves 6)

3 fresh pineapples
3 T. butter or margarine
4 T. flour
1 cup chicken broth
1 cup milk
½ tsp. salt
½ tsp. paprika
⅛ tsp. pepper
1 tsp. finely grated
  onion
1½ cups diced cooked
  chicken
½ cup diced fresh
  pineapple
½ cup slivered almonds
Grated fairly sharp cheese

Cut pineapples lengthwise, keeping the leaves intact. Hollow out halves about ½ inch from exterior skin.

Melt butter, add flour and stir over low heat until blended. Add cold broth and milk stirring constantly until thickened. Then put pan in hot water. Add seasonings and chicken. Heat thoroughly. Blend in diced pineapple. Fill pineapple halves with chicken mixture. Top with almonds and grated cheese. Broil until top is slightly brown.

Serve with rice.

Mrs. George B. Milnor

CHICKEN MADRAS

(Serves 4)

This recipe is relatively quick, produces a decidedly gourmet effect and makes a splendid single dish party meal when served with fluffy rice.

1 chicken (fryer)
 cut up
6 T. butter
Seasoned salt and
 coarse ground pepper
1 med. onion or 1 T.
 dried onion
½ cup dry white wine
1 T. Madras curry
 powder
¾ cup of half and half

Dry pieces of chicken carefully and season with coarse ground pepper and seasoned salt. Place in skillets in which butter has been melted. (Two sizeable skillets will be needed for one chicken). Brown pieces well on both sides. Add ¼ cup of wine and continue cooking for about 10 minutes. Then add onions. Mix the curry powder with remainder of wine and pour over chicken. Cover and cook for fifteen to twenty minutes or until tender.

Then remove chicken to one skillet, sauce from this having been combined with sauce in other skillet. Cover the chicken. It will keep warm while sauce is completed.

Add the half and half slowly to the sauce, stirring constantly. If a slightly thicker sauce is desired, make a roux, combining 2 T. sauce with 1 T. flour and add this carefully to the sauce.

Two important notes: Do Not Skimp on Wine. Use the Very Best Imported Curry Powder.

Anne P. Nicholson

CHICKEN BOMBAY   (Serves 2)

Brown 2 lbs. chicken in Wesson Oil. Pour off fat. Add one can Campbell's Tomato Soup mixed with 1 / 3 cup water, curry powder, parsley, green onions (sliced), lemon-pepper marinade, and Lawry's Salt. (Add spices to taste).

Simmer for 45 minutes. Serve topped with Chow Mein noodles and chopped almonds, lightly browned.

Margo C. Moss

CHICKEN CACCIATORE WITH ARTICHOKE HEARTS
(Serves 4-6)

1 jar marinated artichoke hearts
2 T. olive oil
3 split, boned chicken breasts, floured
1 clove garlic (or more), minced
1¼ tsp. salt
1 tsp. Accent
½ tsp. basil
½ tsp. oregano
½ tsp. pepper
1 T. parsley
½ lb. sliced mushrooms
½ cup dry sherry (more if necessary)

Drain artichoke hearts and combine liquid with oil in a skillet. Brown chicken and put in casserole. Mix next 8 ingredients well in sauce from skillet. Pour this over chicken and cover. Bake at 350 degrees (covered) for 1 hour or until tender. Add sherry and artichoke hearts and bake for another 10 minutes. May be assembled early in the day.

Terry Geiger

CHICKEN FANTASTIC   (Serves 3)

1½ T. butter or margerine
1 frying chicken cut up
1 cup bottled sweet and sour sauce
1 can mandarin oranges, drained
Onion salt & pepper

Heat oven to 350 degrees. Melt butter in 9x12 pan.
Pour ½ cup sauce in pan. Dip chicken in sauce,
turn over and place upside down in pan. Season
with onion salt and pepper and place in oven on
top shelf and bake about 45 minutes. Baste with
remaining sauce occasionally and turn when
necessary. Have skin side up last 15 minutes.

5 minutes before serving, add mandarin oranges
and finish baking.

Serve, garnish with watercress.

Instead of sweet and sour sauce and oranges, you
may use one cup bottled barbecue sauce or:
½ cup fresh lemon juice
¼ cup olive oil
1 tsp. onion salt
2 tsp. oregano

Mrs. Peter Fazio

FAMILY CHICKEN AND NOODLES   (Serves 4)

1 cut up frying chicken simmered until tender in at least 4 cups water, seasoned generously with salt, freshly ground pepper, celery seed, chopped onion.

Cook 8 oz. package egg noodles. Drain and blanch with cold water. Return to pan and mix in 2 or 3 T. butter and salt to taste.

Sauce: In saucepan melt over medium heat 4 T. butter or margarine. Stir in and mix thoroughly ¼ cup flour. Stir in gradually 2 cups of the hot strained broth from the chicken. Stir until smooth and glossy—should be slightly thickened. Add more liquid if desired.

Noodles, chicken and sauce may be served separately or combined in a casserole.

Mrs. Charles G. Rummel

LEFT OVER TURKEY (Serves 8)

4 cups diced turkey
1½ cups soft bread crumbs
2 slightly beaten eggs
1 6 oz. can evaporated milk
1 / 3 cup chicken broth (use chicken boillon cubes)
2 / 3 cup diced celery
¼ cup diced pimento
1¼ tsp. salt
Dash pepper
Dash rosemary
Dash marjoram
Dash nutmeg

Mix together all ingredients. Pour into large greased mold lined with foil. Bake at 350 degrees for one hour. Serve it with a sauce of undiluted mushroom soup.

This can be cooked and put into freezer for future use. Just pour a little broth over mold and reheat.

Mrs. Harold Grumhaus

TURKEY IN PAPER BAG

20 lb. turkey with your own stuffing
1 or 2 large brown paper bags
½ lb. butter broken into small pieces

Rub soft butter all over the outside of turkey.
Place the ½ lb. of broken pieces of butter over
bottom of paper bag. Place the turkey in the bag
and seal very tightly. I staple the end of the bag
closed. If sealed well the turkey will be very moist
and beautifully browned. Place the bag on a high
rack over 1½ inches of water in a roasting pan.
Be sure that the seam side of the bag is away from
the water as the steam might cause it to open. Add
more water from time to time if necessary. Roast
for 23 minutes per pound in a 325 degree oven.
Strain off gravy and if time permits put in
refrigerator to degrease. Make a roux and add
strained gravy. Add brandy and sherry to taste.

Mrs. H. Alexander Vance, Jr.

COHO SALMON   (serves 4)

1 salmon (4 lb.)
¼ lb. butter
4 tsp. orange marmalade
salt & pepper
½ lemon

Place cleaned whole fish on broiler rack. Season with salt and pepper to taste. Put stick of butter in cavity. Spread marmalade generously all over fish. Squeeze lemon juice over fish. Broil in preheated oven about eight minutes on each side.

Mrs. Jack I. Westrich

SALMON LOAF   (serves 4)

Old family recipe of four generations.

1 can salmon (squeezed dry and rubbed with 2 T. butter)
2 eggs beaten lightly
¾ cup crumbled crackers
¼ cup cream
1 T. finely chopped celery
pinch of cayenne pepper
½ tsp. salt

Line top of buttered double boiler with wax paper. Combine above ingredients, and pack mixture lightly into double boiler. Cover and steam for one hour.

Sauce:
2 T. butter melted
add 2 T. flour
¼ tsp. salt
1 cup milk (add all at once)

Cook sauce over low flame stirring constantly until thickened. Remove from flame. Add 4 T. ketchup.

Unmold salmon loaf on warm platter. Pour sauce over it and garnish with parsley.

Mrs. Allen P. Stults

BAKED TROUT   (serves 6)

6 trout washed and wiped dry
salt & ground pepper
1 tsp. parsley
1 tsp. minced onion
1 T. chives
1 tsp. dill
3 T. chopped mushrooms
1 tsp. taragon leaves
2 T. melted butter
4 egg yolks
1 ounce brandy
5 T. bread crumbs
5 T. grated Gruyere cheese
paprika

Season trout with salt and pepper. Line a buttered baking dish with parsley, onion, chives, dill, mushrooms, and tarragon. Place fish on top and pour melted butter over them. Cover with foil and bake at 400 degrees for 12 minutes. Beat egg yolks with brandy.

Remove foil from fish and pour egg-brandy mixture over the fish. Sprinkle with bread crumbs, cheese, and paprika. Return to oven and bake till golden brown.

Serve in baking dish.

Mrs. David O. MacKenzie

HADDOCK CASSEROLE   (serves 6-8)

2¼ or 3 lbs. haddock fillets
3 cups milk (1 cup should be evaporated milk)
Ritz cracker crumbs
3 T. butter or margerine
3 T. flour
2 large onions
handful of small pieces of parsley

Steam fish 20 minutes *or less* on a perforated base
that can be set in a strainer in a kettle with gently
boiling water.

Bring the milk to a boil with thick pieces of onions
and parsley for one minute. Strain out onions and
parsley. Add melted butter and flour. Cook for a
few minutes and season.

Mix crumbs with a little butter in the top of a
double boiler. Then put a thin layer of crumbs in
the bottom of a casserole. Add layer of chunks of
haddock. Season with salt and pepper. Cover with
a layer of crumbs, then a layer of fish, then pour
the milk over all. Scatter buttered crumbs on top.
Heat in 375 degree oven for 20 minutes. Garnish
with slices of lemon and parsley.

(Preparation may be done two days ahead.)

Mrs. Burton W. Hales

SOLE AU CHAMBERTIN

Season the sole and poach it on a buttered dish with 1/3 pint of Chambertin or any good Burgundy wine.

As soon as it is poached, drain it, place on platter, and keep warm. Reduce the cooking liquor to half, add a little freshly ground pepper and 2 or 3 drops of lemon juice. Thicken with a lump of creamed butter and flour the size of a walnut, and finish the sauce with 1 or 2 ounces of plain butter.

Cover the sole with the sauce; set to glaze quickly and garnish both sides of the dish with a little heap of julienne filleted sole, seasoned and tossed in butter at the last moment, so that it is very crisp.

Mrs. Charles A. Nixon

SEAFOOD CASSEROLE   (Serves 4-6)

¾ cup chopped green pepper
¾ cup chopped onion
1 cup diced celery
1 can crab meat flaked
1 can shrimp

½ tsp. salt
1 cup mayonnaise
1 tsp. worcestershire
1 cup bread crumbs
2 T. melted butter

Saute vegetables in butter. Mix in crab and shrimp. Add mayonnaise and worcestershire sauce and put in greased casserole dish or shells.

Top with bread crumbs mixed with 2 T. melted butter. Bake at 350 degrees for 15-20 minutes. If using shells, place on cookie sheet to bake.

Barbara Pontius

SOLE A LA ST. CROIX   (Serves 4-6)

2 lbs. small sole fillets
3 T. lemon juice
3 T. butter
salt & pepper to taste
1½ tsp. curry powder

1 cup half & half
3 T. flour
3 T. shredded parmesan cheese
½ lb. small cooked shrimp
   (frozen & thawed)

Fold each piece of sole in half and arrange side by side in casserole. Sprinkle fish lightly with salt and pepper, lemon juice. Dot with 1 tablespoon of the butter. Cover and bake in 425 degree oven for 20 minutes.

Remove casserole from oven and let stand until slightly cool. Drain juices into measuring cup and add enough half and half to make 1¾ cup total.

Melt 2 tablespoons of butter, blend in flour, gradually add liquid from measuring cup, blend. Add cheese and curry powder, cook, stirring until boiling. Remove from heat, correct seasoning, cover.

Both fish and sauce can be refrigerated (covered) overnight.

When ready to reheat, mound shrimp on sole pieces and spoon sauce on top. Sprinkle with more cheese and bake at 475 degrees till bubbly. About 20 minutes. I also arrange tomato halves around fish and bake at the same time. The color adds and it's always an easy second vegetable.

Mrs. James Schulz

LOBSTER SAUCE

2 cups chicken stock
1½ cups whipping cream
4 T. butter
8 T. flour
Bouquet garni with chervil
2 to 3 cups lobster, shrimp,
  or crab
4 T. grated parmesan cheese
(Excellent served it toast boxes.)

salt and pepper to taste
½ tsp. curry
⅛ tsp. mace
6 T. dry sherry
1 T. brandy
¾ cup mushrooms (measure
  after sauteed)

Make a roux. Cook it five minutes so flour is not
raw. Add chicken stock mixed with cream slowly.
Add curry, salt, pepper, mace and bouquet garni,
and cook 5 minutes. Put sauteed mushrooms in
and cook 2 minutes. Add sauteed lobster (crab,
shrimp). Add cheese and when melted add sherry
and brandy. (Men like this recipe and it freezes
well.)

Mrs. Christopher Brown

SWEET & SOUR SHRIMP   (Serves 6-8)

2 lbs. cleaned, cooked shrimp

Sauce:
1 small green pepper
½ onion, red
12 sliced water chestnuts
1 lb. mushrooms

Arrowroot or cornstarch
salt, pepper, garlic salt
3 T. butter
2 bottles Reese Sweet 'n
   Tart Sauce

Saute in butter thinly sliced red onion and green
pepper for about 10 minutes. Add cleaned, sliced
fresh mushrooms. Continue to cook for 3 minutes.
Add sliced water chestnuts. Season with dash salt,
pepper, garlic powder. Add 2 bottles sweet 'n tart
sauce and thicken with cornstarch or arrowroot.
Add shrimp and heat.

Serve on bed of rice or chinese noodles.

Mrs. A. W. Phelps

SHRIMP-LOBSTER DELIGHT

1 part lobster (1 lb.)
2 parts shrimp (3 lbs.)
10 whole blanched almonds
   per person
10 button mushrooms
   per person
5 ripe pitted olives per
   person (sliced in half)

Sauce:
white sauce
pinch of thyme
lemon juice
paprika
grated sharp cheddar cheese
   (at least 16 or 18 oz.)
garlic salt

Cook shrimp and lobster separately, adding "shrimp boil spice" to water. Cut lobster and shrimp into medium size pieces, and add fish, almonds, mushrooms, and olives to the sauce.

Place mixture in large sea shells. Sprinkle with bread crumbs (roll dry bread and saute in garlic butter). Place shells on cookie sheet and bake 15 minutes in a 375 degree oven.

Sauce may be made thinner and then served over rice.

Mrs. J. Carter Miller, Sr.

SHRIMP BAIANA   (Serves 4-6)

2½ lbs. large raw shrimp
5 or 6 ripe tomatoes,
  peeled and seeded
1 med. onion, grated in
  the largest section of
  a grater
2 cloves garlic, crushed
1 bay leaf
small bunch parsley, tied
green onions

1 cup coconut milk
pinch each of coriander,
  sweet basil and marjoram
2 or 3 hot red peppers
juice of one lemon
oil
salt and black pepper

Peel and clean shrimp. Marinate for one hour in juice of one lemon, crushed garlic and a little black pepper.

Saute onion (green onions can be sauteed with grated onion) in one tablespoon oil for a bit. Add

tomatoes and all herbs tied together (for easy removal if fresh herbs are used). If fresh herbs are not used, add only parsley and bay leaf. Dried coriander, sweet basil and marjoram should be added after the shrimp. Allow to simmer until the tomatoes are "un-done" into a nice sauce.

Add shrimp plus marinade. Add the red peppers and a bit more oil (if you like). When the shrimp are done, remove parsley and herbs (fresh ones). Add coconut milk, taste and correct seasoning. Stir and heat, but don't boil or coconut milk will "cut."

Serve with boiled rice.

This is a true shrimp dish from Bahia given to me by a friend living in Sao Paulo, Brazil. She said this is a hot dish in Bahia but, in restaurants, a hot sauce of red peppers in oil is served separately.

Mrs. A. Norman Freeman

NAOMI'S CRAB CAKES   (Serves 2)

In a bowl combine 1 cup crumbled day-old bread with ¼ cup mayonnaise (*Gourmet*, May, 1969). Add two tsp. prepared mustard, a dash each of red and black pepper, and salt to taste. Work in gently one pound back fin crab meat, being careful not to flake it, and shape the mixture into cakes.

Heat a skillet coated with shortening and add the crab cakes. Saute them for 3 to 5 minutes, or until they are hot and golden brown on both sides.

Serve the crab cakes hot (with a salad of Bibb lettuce and a chilled bottle of dry white wine!).

Mrs. Christopher Stack

PHEASANT-BELL RANCH

This recipe may also be used for Partridge.

2 pheasants
2 apples
½ cup dry Vermouth
1 T. butter
1 T. currant jelly

½ tsp. garlic powder
½ cup heavy cream
1 T. flour
pinch curry powder

Core and quarter apples. Stuff in cavities of birds. Salt and pepper birds. Roast them on a rack at 450 degrees for 45 minutes. While roasting, baste every 15 minutes with drippings and ½ cup watered down vermouth. This is important as it will prevent birds from drying out. Serve with vermouth sauce.

VERMOUTH SAUCE

Melt 1 T. butter and 1 T. currant jelly in an iron skillet. Add garlic, curry powders, cream, and ¼ cup dry vermouth. Stir in ½ cup of drippings. Thicken with flour. Cook the sauce over a low flame until thick. Salt and pepper to taste.

Mrs. Allan Bulley, Jr.

PHEASANT CASSEROLE

1 pheasant quartered and boned
4 small onions
5 celery stalks (whole)
2 pinches thyme
2 pinches marjoram

½-¼ cup butter
½ cup red wine
½ cup consomme
Parsley

Put flour, salt and pepper in paper bag. Shake
pheasant in this. Put pheasant in deep dish and
cover with celery, thyme, onions, and marjoram.
Strew ½ cup parsley over top. Pour previously
mixed wine, consomme, and butter mixture over
all.

Cover with lid and bake in over at 500 degrees for
½ hour, then lower temp. to 300 degrees and bake
for an additional 2 hours. Baste every ½ hour.

If it isn't brown, put under broiler for a few
minutes.

Mrs. Peter D. Grumhaus

RABBIT IN WHITE WINE SAUCE   (Serves 3)

Do not pass this recipe by. If you didn't know it
was rabbit or you don't mention it to your guests,
all will think they are being served chicken. There
are several rabbit farms in the Chicago area
where fresh rabbit is available.

1 rabbit (2½ lbs.)
¼ lb. salt pork
3 shallots
3 T. butter
Graves white wine to cover rabbit

1 bouquet garni
¼ lb. small mushrooms
Salt and pepper
Chopped parsley

Cut rind off salt pork. Cut in small pieces and
blanche 10 minutes in boiling water. Cut rabbit
into serving pieces. Brown rabbit and salt pork in
butter. Add flour to frying pan and cook briefly.
Add white wine to almost cover rabbit, chopped
shallots, bouquet garni, mushrooms, salt and
pepper to taste. Simmer for 1 hour. Brown rabbit
liver and add to the pan before simmering.
Sprinkle chopped parsley on dish before serving.

Mrs. H. Alexander Vance, Jr.

SAUCES FOR BEEF FONDUE

BERNAISE SAUCE

1 cup sour cream
juice of one lemon
2 egg yolks
½ tsp. salt
½ tsp. horseradish

¼ tsp. paprika
¼ tsp. parsley
¼ tsp. tarragon
¼ tsp. onion powder or garlic

Mix all ingredients together and cook 5 minutes in
top of double boiler.

VINAIGRETTE SAUCE

1/3 cup wine vinegar
1 tsp. salt
dash pepper
¼ tsp. chives
¼ tsp. chevril
¼ tsp. parsley

½ tsp. dry mustard
1 chopped onion
1 stalk celery
1 cup salad oil

Put vinegar and seasonings in blender. Let stand
10 minutes. Add onion and celery. Start blender
and add oil, 1/3 at a time.

CAPER SAUCE

¼ cup drained chopped
   sour pickles
2 T. drained chopped
   capers
1 cup mayonnaise

1½ tsp. mustard
1½ tsp. dried parsley

Mix all ingredients together.

CURRY SAUCE

2 T. butter
2 T. flour
1 tsp. curry

1 cup milk
1 tsp. minced onion
1 tsp. lemon juice

Melt butter and flour in top of double boiler over
boiling water. Add milk slowly. Then mix in
onion, curry and lemon juice. Cook until
thickened. A little salt may be added.

Mrs. A. Norman Freeman

CHEESE FONDUE   4 servings

1 lb. grated Swiss cheese
12 oz. can beer
3 T. flour
¼ tsp. salt

¼ tsp. Tabasco
dash of nutmeg
1 loaf French bread

Heat beer in fondue pot. Combine cheese and flour. When beer is heated, gradually add cheese mixture in small amounts, stirring until each addition is melted. When mixture starts bubbling, add salt and Tabasco, and sprinkle with nutmeg. Cut French bread into bite-size chunks. If fondue thickens, stir in small amount of warm beer.

Mrs. Richard A. Dimberg

SAUCE LILI

½ cup mayonnaise (or Miracle Whip)
1 T. tarragon vinegar
1 tsp. malt vinegar

1 tsp. catsup
1 tsp. chili sauce
paprika, salt, & pepper

Mix thoroughly, serve with cold lamb; excellent for avocado or sea food cocktail; very good with shrimp. This will keep in refrigerator.

Margo C. Moss

SAUCE FOR LAMB
(for leftover lamb)

Heat in a skillet:
¼ cup tarragon vinegar
¼ cup currant jelly
½ cup catsup
1 T. butter
1 tsp. Worcestershire sauce
salt and pepper

Cook slices of leftover lamb for 20 minutes in sauce.

Mrs. Allan Bulley, Jr.

CHUTNEY SAUCE FOR LAMB

1 cup chutney, chopped
2 T. lemon juice
2 tsp. curry powder

1 tsp. ginger
½ cup butter
a little water

Combine all ingredients in saucepan, cook slowly over low heat for about 10 minutes.

Mrs. Allan Bulley, Jr.

SAUCE FOR COLD SALMON

GREEN MAYONNAISE   for either cold salmon mold or cold salmon.

1 cup chopped spinach—cooked and well drained
1 T. each chopped parsley, tarragon,
    and chives
2 cups Hellman's mayonnaise
1 tsp. Dijon mustard
Salt to taste

Chop spinach real fine—add chopped herbs. Fold in mayonnaise. Let stand at least 2 hours. Makes 3 cups.

Can be made the day before.

Mrs. Harold Grumhaus

MUSTARD SAUCE

1 cup cream
¼ cup sugar
2 T. dry mustard
2 egg yolks beaten with ¼ tsp. salt
¼ cup vinegar

Heat cream, add sugar, then add mustard mixed with a little cream. Add egg yolks beaten with salt and stir constantly over low fire for 2 minutes. Add vinegar and stir until blended.

Serve with ham—may be frozen.

Mrs. Christopher G. Janus

SAUCE FOR BAKED HAM

8 oz. crabapple jelly
1 tsp. dry mustard
½ tsp. ground cloves
½ tsp. cinnamon
2 tbsp. vinegar

Slowly dissolve jelly—add spices and vinegar—
serve warm.

Naome Williams

TED'S TERIYAKI

(Marinade for any meat or fish—the longer you
marinate, the better the flavor.)

¾ cup soy sauce
1 cup brown sugar
5 cloves garlic
5 T. catsup
¼ cup olive oil
1 T. paprika
1 T. powdered mustard
1 T. parsley
1 tsp. pepper
¾ cup Saki wine

I especially like to marinate a de-boned (or
"butterflied") leg of lamb (for at least 6-8 hours).
Grill on barbecue for about 45 minutes; slice like
steak and serve with additional marinade.

Mrs. Thomas D. Hodgkins

RAISIN SAUCE FOR HAM

1 large orange cut into very thin slivers
2 cups sugar
¼ cup tarragon vinegar
½ tsp. salt
4 T. Grand Marnier
2 cups fruit juice (such as pear or peach)
8 crushed ginger snaps
1 cup water
1 cup raisins

Cut the rind of one large orange into very thin slivers. Avoid getting any of the white skin underneath.

In a sauce pan add sugar, tarragon vinegar, salt, & fruit juice. Slowly bring these ingredients to a boil and add crushed ginger snaps. Stir continually until all the ginger snaps are dissolved. If sauce is thin just add a few more ginger snaps. Add the orange rind slivers and boil very slowly.

In another sauce pan place water with raisins and boil these slowly until the water has been absorbed. Add the raisins to the sauce and just before serving add 4 T. of Grand Marnier that gives it a special flavor.

Keep warm in a double boiler.

Mrs. H. Alexander Vance, Jr.

BECHAMEL SAUCE

(In France there is a saying that a crow, well covered with Bechamel, is superb. This famous French sauce is good with meat, fowl, fish, vegetables and left-overs. Can be prepared in advance and kept in freezer).

4 T. onions, finely chopped
4 T. butter
2 T. flour
2 cups liquid (milk,
  cream, stock or mixed)
Bouquet Garni
Pinch of mace
Salt & pepper
Cheese (optional)

Place half of the butter in a heated pan and saute the onions until yellow-gold. Add the liquid (broth or cream-mixed) which has been heated. Add salt, pepper, mace, and bouquet garni. Cover pan and simmer very slowly for 10 to 15 minutes. Strain, squeezing through all the contents.

Make a roux with flour and remaining butter, add milk mixture slowly, mixing well. Check seasonings for flavor. Cover and simmer for 10 to 12 minutes more. If using with meat, such as the roast of veal, the sauce is now ready to be poured over the meat.

Mrs. H. Alexander Vance, Jr.

Vegetables

GEORGE'S FAVORITE BEANS (Serves 4)

1 pkg. (10 oz.) Italian style green beans, cooked
3 T. fine white bread crumbs, toasted
1 cup sour cream
3 T. grated sharp cheese
⅛ tsp. MSG
Salt and pepper to taste

Prepare green beans according to package directions. To toast bread crumbs, melt 2 T. butter in a skillet add bread crumbs and saute until crumbs cease to bubble and are fairly dry and browned. Remove from skillet and cool.

Mix sour cream, 2 T. toasted crumbs, 2 T. cheese, MSG, salt and pepper. Toss beans evenly through mixture. Turn into buttered baking dish. Top with remaining crumbs mixed with remaining cheese.

Bake at 325 degrees for 20 minutes, or until cheese bubbles on top.

Mrs. George Caspari

BROCCOLI RING WITH BABY CARROTS

(Serves 6)

2 pkgs. chopped frozen broccoli cooked and drained
1 cup consomme
1 pkg. Knox gelatin
2 T. lemon juice
4 tsp. Worcestershire
1 tsp. tabasco sauce
1 tsp. salt
5 chopped hard-cooked eggs
¾ cup mayonnaise

Dissolve gelatin in ¼ cup consomme. Heat remaining consomme and add to gelatin. Mix in lemon juice, Worcestershire sauce, tabasco, salt and broccoli. Cool. Add chopped hard-cooked eggs and mayonnaise. Place mixture in chilled ring mold. Chill for six hours. Unmold and serve with marinated cold canned baby Belgian carrots in the center of the ring.

Mrs. Don H. Reuben

PANNED CARROTS   (Serves 6)

4 cups coarsely shredded carrots
1 cup chopped green pepper
1 cup chopped onion
1 cup chopped parsley
3 T. oil
½ tsp. salt
⅛ tsp. pepper
1 T. Tarragon
3 T. apple cider vinegar

Heat oil in a heavy skillet. Add vegetables, and
season with salt and pepper, stirring constantly.
When well mixed, add Tarragon. Cover and cook
until tender but crisp. Add vinegar, stir and serve.

Mrs. Hubachek Watkins

PARTY CARROTS   (Serves 6-8)

3 or 4 cups carrots (I use frozen, bulk carrot
fingers)
3 T. butter
1/3 cup apricot preserves
¼ tsp. salt
dash nutmeg
¼ tsp. fresh lemon peel, grated
2 tsp. lemon juice

Cook carrots. If using fresh carrots, cut into 2 or
2½ inch pieces. Drain. Melt butter in medium
skillet. Stir in preserves. Add the rest of the
ingredients. Cook briefly until hot, then toss
carrots in sauce.

Mrs. O. Hosmer Morse

CARROT RING   (Serves 6)

4 cups mashed cooked carrots
2 cups half & half
6 T. butter
1 tsp. salt
2 tsp. onion juice
4 eggs, beaten
2 T. flour
½ tsp. paprika

Cook and mash carrots. Add other ingredients
Bake one hour at 350 degrees in a well but
tered ring mold. (Set ring into a pan of hot water
as you would a baked custard.) Unmold onto a
round plate. Serve with fresh peas in center.

Mrs. Henry C. Woods

FAR EAST CELERY   (Serves 6)

Cook four cups one inch celery pieces in water fo
8 minutes. Drain. Add 5 oz. can water chestnut:
drained and thinly sliced. Add 1 can chicken sou
and ¼ cup diced pimento. Place in 1 quar
casserole. Cover with buttered bread crumbs and
sauteed slivered almonds. Bake 35 minutes at 35
degrees.

Mrs. James L. Taylo

CORN CHEESE CASSEROLE   (Serves 4)

Good with turkey or ham.

2 cups corn
3 T. butter
3 T. flour
2 cups scalded milk
1 cup grated cheese
2 eggs, beaten
1 tsp. sugar
1 tsp. minced onion salt & pepper

Melt butter and saute minced onions in it. Scald milk. Add flour to butter. Add milk slowly, scald until thickened. Add spices and grated cheese. Take mixture off stove. Beat eggs and add corn to it. Mix everything together. Either brown bread crumbs in butter or add crumbs with bits of butter on top. Bake one hour at 300 degrees.

EGGPLANT A LA PROVENCE   (Serves 6)

3 medium eggplants
1½ lbs. tomatoes peeled, seeded and cut in fourths
1 generous cup grated cheese
Pinch of sugar
Breadcrumbs
Salt and pepper to taste
Flour for flouring eggplant
Bouquet garni
1 generous T. flour for Roux
2 T. butter for Roux
2 T. butter for buttering sides of dish and top of casserole
¾ cup beef stock
Fat for deep frying
3 medium size onions, chopped well

Peel eggplant, cut in round slices each about ½ inch thick. Sprinkle the slices with salt and let stand at room temperature ½ hour. In the meantime, make the tomato sauce: Make the roux with butter, flour and stock. Add tomatoes, onions, bouquet, sugar, salt and pepper. Cook very slowly in covered saucepan, mixing from time to time, for about 30 minutes. Remove bouquet garni. Pass sauce through blender and check seasonings for flavor.

Run the pieces of eggplant under water to remove excess salt. Dry them well on Scotch towels. Roll in flour. Deep fry them until they are yellow gold. Place again on Scotch towels to remove fat.

Place them in a buttered baking dish, in layers, putting over each layer the tomato sauce, and grated cheese. Sprinkle the top with cheese, breadcrumbs and butter. Heat in oven. Run under the broiler until top is golden brown.

Mrs. H. Alexander Vance, Jr.

STUFFED EGGPLANT   (Serves 2)

1 large eggplant
½ medium onion, chopped
3 T. chopped parsley
1 can condensed cream of mushroom soup
Worcestershire sauce
Garlic powder

Cut eggplant in half. Remove meat, leaving ¼ inch in shells. Parboil meat in salted water until just tender. Saute onion in butter and parsley and mix all with soup. Add cracker crumbs, and a little garlic powder. Mix until the texture of dressing. Cover with cracker crumbs, dot with butter, and bake in 375 degree oven for 30-35 minutes.

This recipe is adapted from a favorite at the Old Stone Inn, one of rural Kentucky's most charming restaurants.

Mrs. C. Gary Gerst

NO FAIL EGGPLANT SOUFFLE   (Serves 6)

1 medium eggplant
8-10 small square soda crackers
2 T. butter
2 beaten eggs
1 8-oz. can pizza sauce
2 tsp. sugar
1 tsp. dried basil leaves
½ tsp. onion salt
2 T. grated parmesan cheese

Heat oven to 400 degrees. Peel, dice and steam
eggplant in 4 cups water until tender. Drain and
mash. Add remaining ingredients except cheese.
Check for seasoning. Pour into buttered flat
baking dish (6x10"). Top with grated cheese.
Bake in 400 degree oven until puffy and brown,
about 20-25 minutes.

Mrs. Peter Fazio

GNOCCHI CASSEROLE   (Serves 8)

1 qt. milk
½ cup butter
1 cup hominy grits (not quick-cooking)
1 tsp. salt
nutmeg
⅛ tsp. pepper

Topping:
1 cup grated imported Swiss or Gruyere cheese
1/3 cup Parmesan cheese, grated
1/3 cup melted butter

Bring milk to a boil. Add butter, stirring until it melts. Then *slowly* stir in grits. Resume boil while stirring constantly; cook until mixture takes on the appearance of cooked farina—i.e., is *very* thick. Remove from heat. Add salt, pepper and nutmeg. Then beat for 5 minutes with an electric mixer until grits take on a creamy appearance.

Pour into a 13x9x2 inch casserole. Allow to set, then cut into rectangular pieces. Place them one over another (like rows of fallen dominoes) in a buttered shallow casserole which may be brought to the table.

Over these pour the 1/3 cup melted butter and sprinkle the grated cheeses.

At serving time, heat in a hot oven (400 degrees) for about 30-35 minutes, and then, if you like, under broiler briefly to obtain light brown crust.

A good party dish—may be made ahead and goes well with roasts.

Mrs. Samuel S. Crocker

SUPER LAZY LIMAS
(Serves 8-10)

3 pkg. frozen lima beans, cooked according to directions
1½ pkg. dry mushroom with beef flavor soup
salt and pepper to taste
bread crumbs
2½ cups sour cream or cottage cheese put in blender
5 med. size yellow onions—2" diameter

Combine all the ingredients. (Except bread crumbs). Put in greased 2 quart casserole. Sprinkle on crumbs. Bake at 350 degrees for about ½ hour—until browned on top and bubbly.

Mrs. James Schulz

MARVELOUS MUSHROOMS
(Serves 3-4)

1 lb. mushrooms, fresh
4 T. butter
1 heaping tsp. garlic juice
1 tsp. flour
½ cup sour cream
1 tsp. lemon juice
salt and pepper

Saute mushrooms (peeled or cleaned and sliced) in butter and garlic juice. Sprinkle flour over mushrooms and stir. Add sour cream and lemon juice and seasonings, still stirring. Serve on toast for brunch or plain as a side dish with steak.

Mrs. Jack I. Westrich

NOODLE-ALMOND CASSEROLE   (Serves 8)

Combine 1 can condensed cream of mushroom soup, 1 cup slivered almonds, ½ cup each cottage cheese and sour cream, ¼ tsp. each garlic powder and oregano.

Cook 1 pkg. (8-oz.) medium noodles until tender. Drain. Add sauce. Turn into casserole. Brown 1 cup fine fresh bread crumbs in ¼ cup butter. Sprinkle crumbs over casserole.

Bake at 350 degrees for 25 minutes.

Can be made in advance.

Mrs. Richard D. Siragusa

GREEN NOODLES   (Serves 6)

1 pkg. green noodles (spinach or artichoke)
3 qts. salted water
2 T. olive oil
1 T. butter
2 T. cream
½ tsp. salt
Dash paprika
1 T. chopped chives
2 T. grated Parmesan cheese

Boil noodles in salted water for 7-10 minutes. Drain thoroughly. Put into a hot casserole and add oil, butter, cream, salt, paprika, chives and cheese. Toss thoroughly and serve with meat sauce and grated Parmesan.

Mary Jane Hardwicke

NOODLES ROQUEFORT   (Serves 6)

1 8-oz. pkg. cream cheese
1 4-oz. pkg. Bleu cheese (leave out of refrigerator to soften)
1 cup sour cream
½ tsp. Worcestershire sauce
1 small onion minced
1 8-oz. pkg. fine noodles
½ cup bread crumbs

Beat cream cheese, bleu cheese, sour cream, Worcestershire sauce and onion together. Cook noodles and add to cheese and sour cream. Stir together and put in shallow baking dish. Sprinkle bread crumbs over top and bake at 350 degrees for ½ hour.

You can make this dish ahead and refrigerate until time to bake it.

Myrtle Rose

ONION PIE   (Serves 6-8)

Biscuit dough made from 2 cups Bisquick and ½
cup water
8-10 thinly sliced medium baking onions
6 T. butter
1 cup sour cream
2 eggs
1 tsp. salt
Pepper

Line an 8 or 9 inch round cake or springform pan
with the Bisquick dough. Chill until ready to use.
Slice onions and saute in butter until clear. When
ready to assemble pie spread onions over dough.
Beat eggs slightly and mix in sour cream and
seasonings until thoroughly blended. Bake at 450
degrees for 10 minutes. Reduce temperature to
350 degrees and bake for 45 minutes longer. Slice
in wedges and serve. This is especially good with
roast pork.

Mrs. H. Alexander Vance, Jr.

HEARTS OF PALM   (Serves 8)

Cut 8 hearts of palm in two lengthwise and saute
in butter very lightly. Place the hearts of palm in
a dish and cover them with the mornay sauce.
Sprinkle with gruyere cheese and bake it for
about 4 minutes at 400 degrees.

Mornay Sauce:
Stir 2 cups of boiling milk into a white roux of 1 oz.
of butter, 2 T. flour, and simmer gently until thick
and creamed. Remove the mixture from the heat
and add 2 T. of grated gruyere cheese and 2 egg
yolks. Add salt, pepper and nutmeg to taste.
Garnish with chopped parsley.

Mrs. James D. Piper

DEEP FRIED PARSLEY

Deep fried parsley is a MUST in haute cuisine
with all breaded dishes. It can be made in advance and reheats very well.

Wash and dry parsley. Cut off thick stems. Drop
sprigs in very hot fat for a few seconds. Place on
paper towel to remove excess fat. Sprinkle with
salt and pepper.

Serve hot.

Mrs. H. Alexander Vance, Jr.

WILD RICE MOLD   (Serves 6-8)

1 cup wild rice
1 tsp. salt
1 clove garlic sliced
4 cups boiling water
¼ cup butter
½ tsp. poultry seasoning
½ tsp. nutmeg
1 cup diced onions
1 cup mushrooms

Add salt and garlic to rice. Steam until tender in 4
cups boiling water and until all water is absorbed.
(About an hour, stirring frequently.)

Melt butter and saute onions and mushrooms.
Add poultry seasoning and nutmeg.

Mix all with rice and place in greased 5 cup mold.
Set in pan of water and bake at 350 degrees about
20 minutes.

Jeanne Bowes

RICE CHINESE STYLE   (Serves 6 generously)

¼ cup butter
¾ cup celery chopped fine
1 small green pepper chopped fine
½ cup green onions chopped fine
4 cups white *cooked* rice (1¼ cups uncooked)
1 tsp. salt *or* 3 T. soy sauce (preferred)
pepper to taste
¾ cup Spanish peanuts

Heat butter in skillet and stir in vegetables and
cook 5 minutes. Add cooked rice and seasonings.
Heat through. Add peanuts just before serving.

Barbara Pontius

SPINACH BALL   (Serves 8-10)

2 boxes frozen chopped spinach
2 cups fine bread crumbs (Don't use store bought.
I use stale bread crusts in the blender).
¼ lb. butter, melted
salt and pepper
3 eggs separated
½ onion grated
1 tsp. parsley cut fine

Sauce:
2 T. butter
2 T. flour
1 cup boiling milk
salt
pepper
small amount of grated onions
2 hard boiled eggs
parsley

Cook frozen spinach in hot water until melted.
Drain in colander. Add crumbs, butter, beaten
egg yolks, salt, pepper, parsley, and onion. Mix
well and fold in egg whites beaten stiff. Tie
mixture in an old napkin or linen tea towel and
boil one hour in water to cover on top of the stove.
When removed from napkin, spinach will be in the
shape of a ball.

While spinach is cooking, hard boil two eggs and
put whites and yolks through a sieve separately.
Also make sauce by melting butter and then
adding flour and allowing to bubble 2 minutes
without browning.

Remove from heat, beat in boiling milk with wire
whip, then return to boil for 1 minute. Remove
from heat and add salt, pepper and grated onion
to taste.

To assemble spinach ball: place ball on a serving platter. Circle with grated egg whites, over which sprinkle yolks. Pour cream sauce over ball and allow to run down sides. Garnish with parsley and serve. A very elegant vegetable!

Mrs. Samuel S. Crocker

SPINACH LOAF   (Serves 6)

4 pkgs. frozen chopped spinach
1 large onion
½ cup chopped celery
1 lb. sausage
3 eggs
1 cup seasoned bread crumbs
Salt & pepper

Partially cook spinach. Drain. Saute chopped onion and chopped celery in butter. Cook separately 1 lb. sausage. Drain and combine with above ingredients.

Add three beaten eggs, one cup of seasoned bread crumbs, salt and pepper. Stir lightly. Place in greased baking dish and bake at 350 degrees for 30 minutes.

I make it early in the day except for eggs and bread crumbs.

Mrs. Albert D. Williams, Jr.

SPINACH CASSEROLE
(Serves 4)

2 boxes frozen chopped spinach
1 pkg. Lipton's onion soup mix
1 8-oz. carton sour cream
bread crumbs
grated Swiss cheese
butter

Cook 2 boxes frozen spinach. Drain well. Mix sour cream and onion soup together and add to spinach. Put in buttered casserole. Cover with about ¾ cup (or more) grated Swiss cheese. Put about ¾ cup pulled bread crumbs on top of this and dot with butter. Bake at 350 degrees for about 20 minutes or until crumbs are browned.

Terry Geiger

SPINACH-CHEESE SQUARES
(Serves 4-6)

1 pkg. frozen chopped spinach
½ cup chopped onion
¼ cup margarine
1 tsp. salt
¼ tsp. pepper
2 eggs slightly beaten
2 cups milk
2 cups cooked rice
1½ cups grated cheddar cheese

Cook spinach. Drain thoroughly. Saute onion in margarine. Add seasonings. Mix spinach, onion and remaining ingredients. Turn into a buttered oblong baking dish about 11x7 inches. Bake at 325 degrees for about one hour and 15 minutes or until custard is set.

SQUASH SOUFFLE   (Serves 6)

2 cups cooked yellow squash
¾ stick butter
2 eggs
1 tsp. salt
pepper
1 cup chopped onions
1 cup grated cheddar cheese
1 cup evaporated milk
2 cups Ritz Cracker crumbs

Mash squash. Add other ingredients. Put in a buttered casserole and bake at 375 degrees for about 40 minutes.

Mrs. C. Gary Gerst

SAUCY SUCCATASH   (Serves 6)

1 16-oz. can whole kernel corn (drained). Fresh corn may be used.
1 10-oz. pkg. frozen lima beans cooked and drained
½ cup (2 oz.) shredded sharp cheddar cheese
¼ cup chopped celery
½ cup chopped onions
½ cup mayonnaise
½ tsp. Worcestershire
1 cup soft bread crumbs
2 T. butter or margarine melted

Combine corn, beans, cheese, celery and onion. Combine mayonnaise and Worcestershire and fold into corn mixture. Turn into 1 qt. casserole. Combine crumbs and butter and sprinkle on top. Bake at 350 degrees for 30 minutes.

Mrs. Robert E. BonDurant

TOMATO PUDDING   (Serves 4)

1 10-oz. can tomato puree
¼ cup boiling water
1 cup light brown sugar
salt
2 cups fresh white bread cut in one inch squares
¼ cup melted butter

Add sugar, salt and water to tomato puree and
boil 5 minutes. Place bread in casserole, pour
melted butter over it, and add tomato mixture.
Bake 30 minutes, covered, at 375 degrees.

Delicious served with fish.

Mrs. Burton W. Hales

BAKED CURRIED TOMATOES   (Serves 6)

6 ripe tomatoes
1 cup tomato sauce
2 tsp. curry powder
2 T. currant jelly
4 T. grated cheddar cheese
3 T. bread crumbs
6 crisp bacon slices

Preheat oven to 450 degrees. Remove skin from
tomatoes and put in baking dish. Combine tomato
sauce, curry powder, and currant jelly and cook 5
minutes. Mix cheese and bread crumbs. Cover
tomatoes with sauce and then crumbs. Bake 15
minutes. Sprinkle with crisp bacon.

Mrs. Herbert Watts

BROILED TOMATOES   (Serves 8)

8 tomatoes (cut slice off stem and chop center.
Invert tomatoes to drain.)
2 / 3 stick butter
½ large or 1 small canned artichoke heart
1 cup chopped onion
¾ tsp. garlic powder
salt & pepper to taste
1 tsp. sugar
6-8 slices of fresh bread, crusts removed

Melt butter. Add onion and garlic powder. Cook
slowly until transparent. Add pulp and cook 5
minutes. Salt and pepper to taste. Add sugar and
enough bread crumbs from fresh bread to soak up
moisture. Insert artichoke heart in bottom of
tomatoes. Add pulp mixture, let cool, and top with
dry bread crumbs. Dot with butter. May be done
day before and kept in refrigerator. Cook at 400
degrees for 15 minutes (no longer).

Mrs. H. B. Erickson

SAUCY MUSTARD TOMATO HALVES (Serves 6)

3 ripe tomatoes
¼ tsp. salt
⅛ tsp. pepper
½ cup dairy sour cream
1½ T. sliced green onions
1½ tsp. prepared mustard.

Heat oven to 500 degrees. Cut tomatoes crosswise
in half. Sprinkle with salt and pepper. Mix sour
cream, onion, and mustard. Spread about 1 T.
mustard mixture on each tomato half. Place
tomatoes on lightly buttered baking sheet. Bake
until tomatoes are tender, 10-12 minutes.

Mrs. Robert E. Molumby

TOMATO AND CAULIFLOWER
CASSEROLE   (Serves 6)

2 pkgs. frozen cauliflower
1 cup grated cheddar cheese
2 medium onions, chopped
2 T. parsley, chopped
3 T. butter
1 No. 2 can tomatoes (2½ cups)
1 bouillon cube
1 T. sugar
1 tsp. salt
½ tsp. pepper
3 T. dried bread crumbs

Cook cauliflower and drain. Mix in ¾ cup cheese. Brown onion and parsley in butter. Add tomatoes, bouillon cube, sugar, salt, pepper and bread crumbs. Simmer 5 minutes. Place half tomato mixture in casserole. Add cauliflower, then remaining tomato mixture. Sprinkle ¼ cup cheese on top. Cover and bake 15 minutes at 350 degrees. Remove cover and bake an additional 15 minutes.

Mrs. Thomas A. Kelly

VEGETABLE CASSEROLE IN CUCUMBERS
OR "RATATOCUMBERS"   (Serves 8-10)

3 cucumbers
8-10 cups any or all of the following: sliced zucchini, (unpeeled); eggplant diced or cubed,
(unpeeled); tomatoes, peeled and seeded;
summer or pancake squash, cubed; onion,
chopped coarsely; cucumber, peeled, seeded, and
cubed

2 cups grated cheddar and or mozzarella cheese

Peel cucumbers. Cut in half lengthwise. Remove
seeds (scrape out with a spoon). Drain on paper
towels (as long as overnight). Line 9x13x2 inch
casserole with drained cucumbers, filling cavities
with butter chunks (1 stick for 6 halves), salt and
pepper, and ½ to ¾ cup grated cheese.

Bake in moderate oven (325 degrees) for ½ hour
or until cucumber is soft and butter and cheese
melted and bubbly. Set aside.

Saute seasoned vegetables in manageable
amounts in ample butter until soft and slightly
browned. Transfer in slotted spoon to top of
"cheesed cukes". Top with remaining cheese.
Heat thoroughly when ready to serve.

Mrs. Jack I. Westrich

YAMS WITH ORANGES AND COGNAC (Serves 8)

Cook 6 sweet potatoes in jackets until not quite tender. Peel and slice in buttered oven proof dish. Thinly slice two oranges and remove rinds. Layer sweet potato slices alternately with orange slices, dotting each layer with butter. Sprinkle with brown sugar.

Pour ½ cup of cognac over all. Sprinkle more brown sugar and dot with butter. Bake at 350 degrees for ½ hour, or until well browned.

Mary Elizabeth Schmidt

SPICED YAMS OR SWEET POTATOES
(Serves 6)

4 cups mashed yams
¼ cup butter or margarine
½ tsp. ground ginger
¼ cup cooking sherry or
2 tsp. sherry extract
½ cup milk
½ cup sugar
½ tsp. salt
½ tsp. ground nutmeg

Combine together. Beat until fluffy. Turn into buttered 1 qt. casserole dish. Bake at 375 degrees for 45 minutes, or until lightly browned.

Mary Elizabeth Schmidt

ZUCCHINI MARSALA   (Serves 4)

4 medium sized zucchini
½ small can of Contadina tomato paste
½ cup tomato juice
¼ cup of marsala wine
parmesan cheese

Wash and peel zucchini. Cut crosswise in thin slices. Arrange in quiche Lorraine dish or if not available in a pyrex pie plate.

In sauce pan, bring to quick boil: tomato paste, tomato juice, and wine. Pour over zucchini and top generously with Parmesan cheese. Bake in 350 degree oven for 40 minutes.

Mrs. Franklin Lyons

ZUCCHINI IN SOUR CREAM   (Serves 4)

Scrub 7 zucchini well. Slice about ½ inch thick and boil about 10 minutes. Drain and lay in an *un*-buttered baking dish in layers. Melt one stick of butter and 1 cup grated cheddar cheese. Add one cup sour cream. Pour mixture over zucchini. Cover with crumbs. Bake 20 minutes at 350 degrees, or prepare a day ahead of time, refrigerate, and bake 40 minutes at 350 degrees.

Mrs. J. C. Miller, Jr.

STUFFED ZUCCHINI   (Serves 12)

Cut 6 medium zucchini in half lengthwise. Parboil in salted water until tender (about 15 minutes). Drain and cool. Scrape out center and chop up pulp. Saute ½ cup chopped onion in ¼ cup butter. Add chopped zucchini. Add 2 cups cooked wild white rice, ¼ cup chopped parsley, ½ tsp. salt, dash of pepper. Toss well. Stir in 1 cup sour cream. Spoon into zucchini shells. Place on greased baking dish. Bake at 375 degrees for 20 minutes. Can be made up to a day in advance.

Mrs. H. B. Erickson.

STUFFED ZUCCHINI AU GRATIN   (Serves 8)

8 zucchini split in two
6 T. butter
½ lb. mushrooms, chopped
4 T. chopped onion
¼ cup grated carrot
½ tsp. salt
¼ tsp. pepper
½ cup grated cheddar cheese
¼ cup water

Remove pulp from zucchini, and saute in butter with onion, carrot, mushrooms, cheese and seasonings. Return to shells. Put in greased baking dish, cover with foil, and bake for 30 minutes at 375 degrees.

Mrs. R. D. Cooper

BAKED MUSHROOMS   (serves 4)

1 lb. mushrooms
2 T. lemon juice
2 T. finely minced onion
2 T. butter
¼ tsp. salt
2 T. minced onion
1 / 3 tsp. freshly ground black pepper
2 tsp. freshly grated parmesan cheese
1 cup heavy cream
2 egg yolks, lightly beaten
2 tsp. fine white bread crumbs

Preheat oven to 400 degrees. Butter a baking dish or four individual ramekins. Wash the mushrooms and cut off the bottoms of the stems. Slice the mushrooms thinly and sprinkle them with the 2 tsp. of lemon juice to prevent discoloration. Simmer the mushrooms in a tightly covered saucepan with the finely minced onion and 2 T. of the butter. Season the mushrooms with salt and pepper. Stir in the freshly grated Parmesan cheese. Cook about three minutes. Place the mushroom mixture in the prepared baking dish or ramekins. Mix the heavy cream and egg yolks together. pour over the mushrooms. Sprinkle with bread crumbs and dot with butter (remaining tablespoon). Bake until golden brown, about 10 minutes. Serve immediately.

Mrs. H. Alexander Vance, Jr.

Cakes, Cookies, Pies

DOUBLE CHOCOLATE CREAM CAKE AU RHUM

1 1/3 cups buttermilk
2 eggs
1 regular size chocolate cake mix
1/3 cup honey
1/3 cup rum
6 T. sugar
⅛ tsp. salt
6 T. cocoa
3 cups whipping cream

Combine buttermilk and eggs with chocolate cake mix. Beat at medium speed in electric mixer about 3 minutes. Pour into two buttered and lightly floured 9 inch cake pans. Bake at 350 degrees for 30 to 35 minutes. Cool in cake pans for 10 minutes. Meanwhile warm honey over low heat: Add rum (preferably dark). Remove cake from pans; spoon syrup over layers. Cool completely. Combine sugar, salt, cocoa and whipping cream. Chill 1 hour or more. Whip until stiff. (three T. of rum may be added if desired.) Frost layers, top and sides. Refrigerate at least 1 hour before serving.

Mrs. Gordon R. Ewing

ORANGE CAKE

1 cup butter
1 cup sugar
1 cup sour milk or buttermilk
2 eggs (beaten)
½ tsp. salt
1 tsp. soda
1 tsp. vinegar
rind of 2 oranges
1 cup nuts (chopped)
1 cup dates (cut up)
1 tsp. baking powder
2½ cups flour
   (sift before measuring)

Sift all dry ingredients together. Cream butter, sugar, and eggs, beat together very well. Sift a little of the flour over nuts and dates. Add orange rind to cream mixture (I usually add rind of 1 orange). Add dry ingredients and buttermilk alternately. Vinegar is added to butter milk. When all is mixed well, add nuts and dates. Batter may be baked in two 9 inch cake pans or one large flat pan. Bake in 350 degree oven until done (when pricked with a toothpick and it comes out clean).

While cake is baking squeeze two oranges and add 1 cup sugar to juice; stir occasionally. When cake is done pour juice over cake. Leave cake in pan until cold.

Cake may be served just as is with powdered sugar sprinkled over it or when baked in layers I make a confectioners sugar frosting to which I add grated orange rind.

Mrs. Harold T. Martin

BANANA NUT CAKE

2/3 cup butter
1½ cups sugar
2 eggs beaten
1 cup mashed bananas
4 T. sour cream
2 cups flour
1 tsp. soda
salt
1 cup nut meats
vanilla

Cream sugar and butter. Add eggs, then mashed bananas and sour cream. Add sifted flour, salt and soda. Save a small amount of flour to sprinkle over nuts before adding them. Bake in a loaf or layer pans at 350 degrees until done.

Caramel Frosting:

1 cup brown sugar
½ cup white sugar

Mix thoroughly with enough cream to make a paste. Boil until soft ball is formed in water. Cool to room temperature. Add ½ tsp. baking powder and 1 tsp. vanilla. Beat until creamy and of the right consistency to spread.

You may use sour cream to make the frosting.

Ellen Ryan
(Mrs. William J.)

DOUBLE FUDGE CAKE

2 cups cake flour
1/3 tsp. salt
4 T. cocoa or 1½ oz. chocolate
½ cup buttermilk
1¼ tsp. soda
½ cup boiling water
¾ cup butter
1½ cups sugar
2 eggs (room temperature)
1 tsp. vanilla

Cream butter and sugar. Add whole eggs and cream again. Add buttermilk, soda, flour and salt. Add flavoring. Last add hot water mixed with cocoa. Pour batter into 3 8-inch cake pans or 2 9-inch pans. Bake at 375 degrees for 25 or 30 minutes.

Ice with fudge frosting.

Mrs. Harold T. Martin

ARMENIAN SOUR CREAM CAKE

2 cups dark brown sugar
2 cups all purpose flour, sifted
½ cup butter
1 beaten egg
1 tsp. nutmeg
1 cup sour cream
1 tsp. soda

Cut together brown sugar, flour, and butter as for pie; put half (about 2½ cups) in bottom of 9x13 inch pan—loosely.

To remainder add egg, nutmeg, and sour cream (to which 1 tsp. soda has been added). Mix well. Pour over crumbly mixture. Bake in preheated 350 degree oven for 40 minutes. Do not open door the first half hour. To glamorize, sprinkle top with cinnamon and nuts before baking. Cut in squares when cool.

Mrs. F. Richard Meyer III

DUTCH POUND CAKE

½ lb. butter
1½ cups cake flour
1 cup sugar
4 eggs
½ tsp. vanilla

Cream butter and sugar. Add flour & beaten eggs one at a time. Add vanilla—bake in a greased loaf pan one hour at 350 degrees.

This is an excellent pound cake recipe given to me by a Dutch cook we had. It is real "squeaky."

Mrs. David Danforth

ALLINE'S CAKE–A DELICIOUS DALLAS DELIGHT

2 cups sugar
2 sticks butter
6 eggs

1-12 oz. pkg. vanilla wafers, crushed
1 cup pecans
1 can Angel Flake Coconut (7 oz.)

Grease tube pan, put waxed paper in the bottom with more butter on top of the paper. Mix in order given. Bake in tube pan at 350 degrees for 1 hour 15 minutes—will keep a long time.

Frances Hooper

PLUM BUNDT CAKE

2 T. cinnamon
2 jars of baby food plums
1 tsp. vanilla
1 cup chopped nuts
2 cups sifted self-rising flour
2 cups sugar, sifted
1 cup salad oil
2 eggs

Sift 3 dry ingredients into large bowl. Add remaining ingredients. Blend. Bake in a Bundt pan for 60 minutes at 350 degrees.

A marvelous coffee-breakfast cake. Delicious at tea time or try it for dessert topped with a little sweetened whipped cream.

Mrs. Dennis Muckermann

QUICK DESSERT CAKE

2 cups Bisquick
2/3 cups milk
2 T. sugar
1 egg
1 pkg. chocolate chips (6 oz.)

Mix Bisquick, sugar, milk and egg. Beat until well blended, about a half a minute. Stir in ½ package of chocolate chips. Turn into a greased 9 inch square pan. Top with chocolate chip topping:

CHOCOLATE CHIP TOPPING

1/3 cup Bisquick
1/3 cup sugar
¼ cup firm butter
½ pkg. chocolate chips

Mix Bisquick and sugar. Cut in butter until crumbly. Stir in chocolate chips. Sprinkle over batter in pan. Bake cake in 400 degree oven for 20 to 25 minutes. Serve warm or cold.

Mrs. O. Hosmer Morse

LEMON FILLING FOR THREE LAYER CAKE

Pare and grate 1 large apple
Add:
1 cup granulated sugar
1 egg
juice and rind of 1 lemon

Beat all together thoroughly. Cook in double boiler until thick or about 5 minutes. When *cold*, spread between layers of cooled cake.

Winifred Marx

FILLING FOR ANGEL FOOD CAKE   (Using 3 layers)

Cream:
½ lb. butter
4 or more cups confectioners sugar

Add:
5 egg yolks (beaten first)
3 squares bitter chocolate (melted)
2 tsp. vanilla

Fold in 5 egg whites, stiffly beaten.

If icing seems too thin, more sugar may be added.

This recipe gives liberal icing for large angel food cake having 3 layers.

Refrigerate at least an hour. Will freeze.

ORANGE CHIFFON CAKE

1 orange chiffon cake cut into 4 layers
1 large can sweetened crushed pineapple
1 T. lemon juice
1 pkg. instant lemon jello pudding

Mix all the above ingredients together and let stand five minutes. Whip 1 pint whipping cream until very stiff. Fold the whipped cream into the pineapple-pudding mixture. Add a generous jigger of Grand Marnier. Spread this mixture between all the layers and the sides and top of the cake. Refrigerate overnight. Remove one hour before serving and decorate with fresh strawberries.

Mrs. Richard Siragusa

BUTTERSCOTCH COOKIES

½ cup butter
1½ cups light brown sugar
2 eggs
2½ cups flour
½ tsp. baking powder
1 tsp. soda
½ tsp. salt
1 cup sour cream
1 tsp. vanilla
2/3 cup chopped pecans

Cream butter then add sugar and mix thoroughly—Beat eggs and add to above. Mix flour, baking powder, soda, and salt together and add to creamed mixture alternately with sour cream. Last add vanilla and nuts. Chill until dough is firm—overnight is best. Drop two inches apart on greased cookie sheet. Bake about 10-12 minutes in a 350 degree oven. While warm frost with burned butter frosting

Burned butter frosting:

¼ lb. "butter"—do not use margarine!
1½ cups confectioners sugar
1 tsp. vanilla
Hot water

Melt butter keeping it over heat until it is very brown (not burned). Watch carefully as it burns and gets black. Remove from heat and blend in confectioners sugar until there are no lumps. Stir in about 4 to 6 tablespoons hot water until icing is right consistency to spread. These cookies freeze beautifully. I have kept them in the freezer in cans for months.

Mrs. Frank Foss

SCREEN DOOR COOKIES

1 cup brown sugar
4 T. butter
1 egg
1 cup English walnuts or
   pecans, chopped
1 large T. of flour

Drop ½ tsp. mixture on teflon (greased) cookie
sheet. Bake at 375 degrees. Remove with spatula
when cookies have cooled a bit.

Mrs. Christopher G. Janus

BUTTER TEA COOKIES (Kourabiethes)

1 lb. sweet butter
½ cup confectioners sugar
½ cup orange juice
1 oz. cognac
6-7 cups cake flour
1 cup chopped nuts (optional)
1 box confectioners sugar for topping

Melt butter and then refrigerate until thickened.
Beat in mixer at medium speed until almost white
(about 15 minutes). Add powdered sugar and
continue beating. Combine cognac and orange
juice and add to mixture. Blend thoroughly. Fold
in flour by hand adding a little flour at a time until
a soft dough is formed that can be easily handled.
Take a teaspoon at a time and roll into a small
ball and place on an ungreased cookie sheet. Bake
at 350 degrees for 15 minutes. When done sprinkle
very liberally with sifted powder sugar while still
hot. Finished cookie should resemble a snowball.

Mrs. Peter Economou

FRENCH LACE COOKIES

½ cup corn syrup
¼ cup butter
¼ cup oleo
2/3 cup brown sugar
dash of salt

Stir all in sauce pan and bring to a brisk boil. Take off fire and add one cup of flour. Drop by spoon (marble size) on teflon cookie sheet. Bake in 350 degree oven, 8-10 minutes. Cool a few minutes on cookie sheet. Then remove and cool. Store in tight tin.

Mrs. James H. McAlvin

SUGAR COOKIES

1 cup soft butter
1 2/3 cups sugar
2 eggs not beaten
3 tsp. vanilla
3½ cups sifted all purpose flour
2½ tsp. baking powder
¾ tsp. salt

Beat together butter and sugar until light and fluffy with wooden spoon. Add eggs and vanilla. Bend well. Sift together in separate bowl, flour, baking powder, and salt. Add to butter mixture. Roll balls size of walnuts between palms of hands and place 2" apart on buttered cookie sheet or teflon. Use bottom of small glass to press out. Butter bottom of glass often, and dip in sugar frequently. Bake at 400 degrees 8 or 10 minutes or until edges are browned.

Eloise Brown

SESAME PRALINE COOKIES

¾ cup butter, melted
1½ cups brown sugar, firmly packed
1 tsp. vanilla
¼ tsp. salt
1 egg beaten
½ cup sesame seeds
1 cup sifted all purpose flour

Mix together butter, sugar, and vanilla. Beat until well blended. Stir in egg, sesame seeds. Add flour and salt; mix thoroughly. Drop by ½ teaspoonsful onto well greased cookie sheet. Bake only 6 or 8 cookies at a time in preheated 350 degree oven for four to five minutes or until lightly browned—cool for 1 or 2 minutes before removing from sheet. Reheat if hard to remove. Cookies will be thin and crisp. Store in closed container to keep crisp— makes about 100 small cookies.

Mrs. Chester Dudley Tripp

PRALINE GRAHAM COOKIES

24 whole graham crackers
1 cup butter
1 cup brown sugar
1 cup chopped pecans

Arrange graham crackers on ungreased cookie sheet. Combine butter and sugar in saucepan; heat to boiling point, stirring constantly. Boil 2 minutes more. Stir in pecans and spoon over crackers. Bake at 350 degrees for 10 minutes. While still warm, cut each cracker in half.

Mrs. Henry C. Woods

PECAN BALLS

1   cup   butter
3 heaping T. powdered sugar
dash salt
2 cups pastry flour (Swansdown), sifted
1 cup chopped pecans
1 tsp. vanilla

Mix above ingredients, roll into balls, bake in 250
oven 25 minutes (may have to adjust temperature
and increase baking time depending upon oven)
till golden brown. Roll balls in powdered sugar
(sifted works best) and again when slightly
cooled. Store in tin box.

Terry Geiger

"SCRATCH MY BACKS"

1 cup of rolled oats
1 cup flour
1½ cups grated coconut
1 cup brown sugar
¾ cup Fluffo
1 egg, well beaten
1 tsp. baking powder
½ tsp. salt
½ cup chopped pecans

Mix all ingredients and bake at 375 degrees for 10-
12 minutes.

This is a Canadian recipe handed down from my
mother and one of the favorites of my children.

Mrs. John Timmerman

OATMEAL COOKIES   (3 dozen)

2 cups oats, uncooked
1½ cups flour
1 cup brown sugar
½ cup wheat germ
2 eggs
1 cup shortening
½ cup sugar
1 tsp. salt
1 tsp. baking soda
1 tsp. vanilla

Preheat oven to 375 degrees. Measure all
ingredients into bowl. Mix for 4 minutes. Drop by
teaspoons onto ungreased baking sheet. Bake for
10 minutes. Remove to wire racks to cool.

Mrs. Richard A. Dimberg

OATMEAL CRISP COOKIES

½ cup butter
½ cup margarine
½ cup fine granulated sugar
1 cup flour
1½ cups quick oatmeal

Mix and chill dough, roll into tiny balls. Flatten
with a glass dipped into sugar. Bake in a 350
degree oven. Cool slightly before removing from
pan. Sprinkle with powdered sugar.

Mrs. Henry C. Woods

NORWEGIAN CHRISTMAS COOKIES

1 cup butter
1 cup sugar
2 cups flour
1 egg yolk
1 tsp. baking soda
1 tsp. vanilla

Mix all ingredients—roll in logs—roll in cinnamon and sugar. Bake in 275 degree oven for 20 minutes. Roll again in cinnamon and sugar.

Mrs. Thomas D. Hodgkins

OLD FASHIONED CHRISTMAS ANIMAL COOKIES

1½ cups sugar
1 cup butter and shortening mixed
1 egg
½ cup buttermilk
1 T. vanilla
4 cups flour
1 tsp. soda dissolved in milk
Generous tsp. freshly grated nutmeg

Cream butter and shortening. Add sugar and beat until light and fluffy. Beat in egg and buttermilk. Gradually add flour, nutmeg, and vanilla. Chill dough for 30 to 40 minutes. Roll out on floured board and cut with cookie cutters. Place on ungreased cookie sheet. Bake at 375 degrees until lightly browned.

Frost and decorate or sprinkle with colored sugar before baking.

EGG NOG COOKIES

1 cup butter
¾ cup sugar
1 egg
1 T. vanilla
2 tsp. rum extract
1¾ cups flour
1 T. freshly ground nutmeg
¼ tsp. salt
Confectioners sugar

Cream butter. Gradually add sugar and beat until light and fluffy. Beat in egg, vanilla and rum extract. Sift together flour, nutmeg and salt. Gradually add to creamed mixture. Chill dough for ease in handling. Shape into 1" balls. Place on ungreased cookie sheet. Bake at 350 degrees for 7 to 10 minutes. Cool and coat with confectioners sugar.

MINCEMEAT COOKIES

½ cup sugar
¼ cup light brown sugar
½ cup butter
2 eggs
½ tsp. vanilla
¾ cup mincemeat
½ cup raisins
½ cup chopped nuts

Sift together:
1½ cups flour
½ tsp. cinnamon
½ tsp. soda
¼ tsp. salt

Cream butter and sugar together. Add the eggs and vanilla. Blend thoroughly. Add sifted dry ingredients next. Beat until blended. Add mincemeat, raisins and nuts last. Place tablespoon size pices of dough on cookie sheet. Bake at 375 degrees for 12 minutes. Makes 32 soft moist cookies.

Mrs. Harold T. Martin

MINCEMEAT REFRIGERATOR COOKIES

¾ cup butter
1 cup sugar
1 egg
3 cups flour
1 tsp. cinnamon
½ tsp. soda
½ tsp. salt
1 T. grated orange peel
1 tsp. vanilla
1 cup drained mincemeat
½ cup chopped nuts
chocolate sprinkles

Cream butter and add sugar. Beat in egg. Sift together flour, cinnamon, soda, and salt. Gradually add to creamed mixture. Add orange peel, vanilla, mincemeat and nuts. Shape into 2 rolls 1½" in diameter. Roll in chocolate sprinkles and wrap in waxed paper. Chill overnight. Slice thin and place on ungreased cookie sheets. Bake at 375 degrees 7 to 10 minutes.

MINT KISSES (Makes a big hit with the ladies.)

2 egg whites—beat until stiff
1/3 cup sugar, gradually added
1 small pkg. mint chocolate chips

Add flavoring and few drops green or yellow food coloring. Fold in 1 small pkg. mint chocolate chips. Drop by teaspoons on greased cookie sheet. Preheat oven to 400 degrees and close door and shut off heat. Leave cookies in oven overnight, or 8 hours. Don't make in hot and humid weather.

Mrs. Henry C. Woods

SNORKY'S FUDGE COOKIES

½ cup butter
1 cup sugar
2 eggs, well beaten
3 squares chocolate, melted
1½ cups flour
2 tsp. baking powder
½ tsp. salt
¾ cup nuts, chopped
¾ cup raisins, chopped
½ tsp. vanilla

Melt butter, stir in sugar. Add eggs, then chocolate. Sift together flour, baking powder, and salt, Add to other ingredients. Add nuts, raisins, and vanilla and drop by spoonsful on greased tins. Bake in 350 degree oven 10 to 15 minutes. Cool and frost.

Frosting:
4 T. melted butter
4 T. Droste cocoa
4 T. boiling water
2½ cups powdered sugar

Combine in double boiler; cook, stirring, until creamy. Frost cooled cookies.

Mrs. Allan E. Bulley

MOIST BROWNIES

3 squares Baker's unsweetened chocolate
½ bar of German sweet chocolate
2 T. white Karo syrup
1 cup butter

Melt above ingredients over hot water until smooth. Cool slightly.

4 eggs
2 cups sugar
1 cup sifted flour
1 tsp. vanilla
1 cup broken nut meats (optional)

Beat eggs until foamy. Gradually add sugar, beating thoroughly after each addition. Blend in chocolate mixture. Then fold in flour. Add vanilla and nuts. Bake in moderate oven—about 325—for about 40 minutes. Cool in pan. Cut in squares with sharp knife. Roll in powdered sugar...if you wish.

Mrs. Hays MacFarland

BLUEBERRY TARTS AU COINTREAU

12 tart shells
1-3¼ oz. package instant vanilla pudding
1 cup milk
1 cup heavy cream
⅛ tsp. salt
1 T. cointreau

Make pudding according to directions, but use milk and cream for liquid. Add salt, then the cointreau. Fill tarts, heap with blueberries, sprinkle with powdered sugar. Serve with whipped cream.

Mrs. R. D. Cooper

NO BAKE CHOCOLATE LAYER COOKIES

2 cups coconut
½ cup chopped nuts
2 cups crushed graham crackers
½ cup margarine
5 T. cocoa
½ cup sugar
1 unbeaten egg
1 tsp. vanilla
dash of salt

Set coconut, nuts, and graham crackers aside in bowl.

Blend margarine, cocoa, sugar, egg, salt and vanilla in double boiler. Pour over mixture in bowl and pat firmly in 9x9 inch pan. Chill.

Frost with:

4 T. instant vanilla pudding mix
6 T. milk
½ cup soft butter
3 cups powdered sugar

Mix and spread over preceding mixture.

melt:

3 squares sweet chocolate
3 T. butter

Spread over top.

Store covered in refrigerator.

Mrs. Thomas D. Hodgkins

COCONUT BARS

½ cup butter
½ cup light brown sugar
1 cup flour

Cream butter and sugar, add flour. Pat into 9x13 inch pan. Bake in 375 degree oven for 12 minutes. Then spread on the following ingredients which have been combined and bake 20 minutes more.

1 cup light brown sugar
¼ cup flour
½ tsp. salt
1 can angel flake coconut
1 tsp. vanilla
2 eggs—slightly beaten
1 cup chopped nuts

Cut into equares when slightly cool.

Mrs. Henry C. Woods

NEVER-FAIL PIE CRUST   (Makes 3 crusts)

3 cups flour
1¼ cups shortening
   (1/3 butter, rest Crisco or lard)
1½ tsp. salt
1 well beaten egg
1 T. vinegar
5 T. water

Mix flour, salt and shortening until crumbly. Beat egg, add vinegar and water, add all to flour mixture and mix with fork—until it forms a ball.

Mrs. Harold T. Martin

CHOCOLATE MOUSSE PIE   (Serves 6-8)

½ cup butter
¾ cup sugar
2 squares unsweetened chocolate
2 eggs
1 carton (4½ oz.) Cool Whip
1 pie shell

Cream butter and sugar. Stir in cooled chocolate. Add eggs, one at a time, beating at high speed for 5 minutes after each addition. After all eggs have been added, fold in whipped topping. Pour into pie shell. Chill until firm. (Approximately 2 hours)

Mrs. Nancy Elich

ANGEL PIE

6 egg whites
⅜ tsp. cream of tartar
1½ cups granulated sugar
½ tsp. vanilla

Beat egg whites until stiff. Beat in cream of tartar and granulated sugar, a spoonful at a time. Beat in vanilla drop by drop. Continue beating. Spread in 2 slightly buttered 9-inch glass pie plates. Bake for 10 minutes at 275 degrees; then 40 minutes at 250 degrees. Cool.

Filling:

Beat: 6 egg yolks, 8 T. sugar, 4 T. lemon juice until fairly thick. Cook in a double boiler until thickened. When cool, mix with whipped cream (½ pint). Put filling between layers and on top of pie. Place pie in refrigerator for a few hours or longer.

When I make this pie for a large group, I use a glass cake plate (13 inch x 8½ inch). For each layer I use the full recipe.

Helpful hints: Have eggs at room temperature for 24 hours. Add each ingredient slowly, especially sugar. Watch the filling and stir constantly. The filling occasionally needs more lemon. *Taste* it.

Mary Elizabeth Schmidt

CHOCOLATE TOFFEE PIE

Pie Shell

¾ cup pecans, chopped fine
¼ cup brown sugar
1 square chocolate, grated
1 tsp. vanilla
4 T. melted butter

Combine ingredients and mix well with 1 T. water. Press into *well-greased* pie plate (9" glass). Bake 15 minutes at 375. Cool.

Filling:

½ cup butter
¾ cup sugar
1 square chocolate melted and cooled
2 tsp. instant coffee (not freeze dried)
2 eggs each beaten for 5 minutes

Mix butter and sugar until light and fluffy. Add chocolate and coffee. Blend well. Add 1 egg beaten for 5 minutes; then add other egg beaten for 5 minutes. Put filling into cooled pie shell, cover and refrigerate overnight.
Topping:

½ pint whipping cream
2½ tsp. coffee(instant)
½ cup confectioners sugar
1 square chocolate grated for curls

Blend cream, coffee and sugar and refrigerate for 1 hour. Then whip. Spread chocolate on top.

CHOCOLATE PECAN PIE

2 eggs
1 cup sugar
½ cup butter, melted
3 to 4 T. bourbon
¼ cup cornstarch
1 cup finely chopped pecans
6 oz. pkg. semi-sweet chocolate chips

Beat eggs slightly. Add sugar gradually. Add melted butter and bourbon and mix well. Blend in cornstarch. Add pecans and chocolate chips. Pour into unbaked 9 inch pastry shell. Bake in a pre-heated 350 degree oven for 45 to 50 minutes. Cool about 1 hour before serving. Serve with mellow whipped cream.

½ cup whipping cream
2 T. confectioners sugar
1 to 2 tsp. bourbon

Whip cream, fold in sugar and bourbon.

Mrs. J. Harry Ramshaw

OPEN FACE PEACH PIE

Boil in a double boiler:

1 cup cream
1 cup sugar
2 T. cornstarch

Boil 15 minutes and pour mixture into unbaked pie shell. Cut peaches and lay on top of custard. Bake 45 minutes to one hour at 350 degrees.

Mrs. Franklin B. Schmick

FUDGE PIE

1 stick butter
2 oz. Baker's chocolate
2 beaten egg yolks
1 cup sugar
2 barely rounded T. flour
1 tsp. vanilla
2 egg whites, beaten stiff
¾ cup broken pecans

Put butter and chocolate in top of a double boiler until melted. Let cool a little. Mix egg yolks, sugar, flour and vanilla and add to the almost cool chocolate mixture. Beat egg whites and fold into chocolate mixture, than add pecans.

Pour into buttered 9 inch pie pan. Bake at 300 degrees for 30 minutes. It will be quite soft in the center. Serve with ice cream or whipped cream.

Dorothy Jane Cook

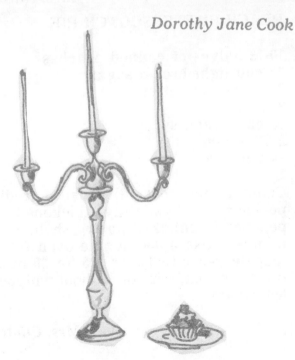

PUMPKIN PIE

3 eggs
1 solidly packed cup light brown sugar
(beat this until nice and fluffy)
1 cup cooked pumpkin
1¼ cup milk (to make a richer pie you can use
1 / 3 to ½ cup of light cream instead of all milk)
1 tsp. cinnamon
¼ tsp. cloves
½ tsp. ginger

After all is mixed together well, pour into unbaked pie shell and bake about 10-15 minutes at
400 degrees, then bake 350 degrees for about 25 to
30 minutes. I usually insert a knife in middle of pie
to see it it is done. If it comes out clean, pie is
baked enough.

Mrs. Harold T. Martin

PEACH BUTTERSCOTCH PIE

10-12 halves of canned peaches
¾ cup light brown sugar
6 T. oleo or butter
3 T. flour
¼ cup peach syrup
2 T. lemon juice
⅛ tsp. mace

Combine and cook all above ingredients except
peaches until slightly thickened. Pour over
peaches in unbaked pastry shell. Bake about 40
minutes. Use a 450 degree oven for 10 minutes,
then decrease to 350 or 325 for 30 minutes. Serve
warm or cold, with or without whipped cream or
ice cream.

Mrs. Clinton O. Dicker

COCONUT CREAM PIE

Prepare pie shell

Filling:

2 cups milk
3 heaping T. coconut
½ tsp. vanilla
2/3 cup sugar
2 T. Cornstarch
2 eggs
2 T. sugar for meringue

Take ½ sugar and heat with milk, coconut and vanilla. Mix cornstarch with other half of sugar. Beat egg yolks. Add yolks to cornstarch and sugar and beat together. Pour half the warm milk into this. When mixed stir into the remaining milk mixture over heat and stir all the time until thick but not stiff.

To make the meringue, beat together 2 egg whites and 2 T. of sugar. Pour custard into pie shell—top with meringue. Bake 10 minutes 400 degrees.

Mrs. Clyde E. Shorey

CHEESE PIE

Make graham cracker crust to fit an 8 inch pie or cake pan.

Crust:
18 graham crackers—crushed
3 T. brown sugar
1 / 3 cup butter

Reserve some crumbs for top.

Filling:

4 small or 1½ large pkg. of cream cheese
2 eggs
¾ cup sugar
2 tsp. vanilla

Bake at 350 degrees for 18-20 minutes. Cool 10 minutes. Put on topping and bake 10 minutes more. Cool and refrigerate.

Topping:

1 carton sour cream
3½ T. sugar
1 tsp. vanilla

Sprinkle crumbs on top. A very rich dessert.

Mary Lou Maher
(Mrs. Robert A.)

COFFEE ICE CREAM PIE

Crust:

2 T. butter
2 squares chocolate
2 T. hot milk
2 / 3 cup confectioners sugar
1½ cups shredded coconut

Butter 9 inch pie plate. Melt butter and chocolate over hot water; blend. Combine milk and sugar, then stir into chocolate mixture, mixing well. Stir in coconut. Press onto bottom and sides of prepared pie plate. Chill in refrigerator.

Filling:

1 qt. vanilla ice cream
2 tsp. instant coffee
¼ cup chopped pecans
8 pecan halves

Stir ice cream to soften, mix thoroughly with instant coffee and chopped pecans. Spread into pie shell, swirling the top. Freeze until firm.

Mrs. J. Harry Ramshaw

GERMAN CREAM PIE   (Serves 6)

Make—don't buy—1 pie crust and line a pie tin. Prick with fork and trim edge.

Into this crust pour ½ cup sugar.

Mix 4 tsp. flour into the sugar using fingers. Dot top with small pieces of butter. Fill crust to the brim with cream and sprinkle lightly with nutmeg. Bake at 300-325 degrees until custard is set. This takes at least an hour.

Insert a silver knife into center of custard—if it comes out clean, your pie is ready. Cool a little before serving.

Mrs. Ernst R. Schmidt

BLUEBERRY PIE

3 cups blueberries
¾ cup sugar
3 T. flour
¼ tsp. salt
1 T. lemon juice
¼ tsp. almond extract
3 eggs, separated
2 T. confectioners sugar

Mix blueberries, sugar, flour, salt, lemon juice, and almond extract. Add egg yolks. Cook in double boiler for 15 minutes or until thick, stirring constantly. Cool slightly. Beat egg whites until stiff. Add confectioners sugar. Pour into baked 9-inch pie shell. Bake in 350 degree oven for 10 minutes. Serve with whipped cream.

C. Bjorkman

TINY PECAN TARTS   (Makes 2 dozen)

1-3oz. pkg. cream cheese
1 stick butter
1 cup flour

Mix above ingredients. Form into 24 balls. Press into tiny muffin pans and fill each with 1 tsp. filling.

Filling:

1 cup chopped pecans
¾ cup brown sugar
1 beaten egg
1 tsp. vanilla
1 T. melted butter

After each tart is filled, bake 12 to 15 minutes at 400 degrees. (Each tart should be size of ½ dollar at bottom of pan.)

Mrs. J. C. Miller, Jr.

GERTRUDE'S BLUEBERRY LAYER PIE

(Can be made a few hours ahead of time—add whipped cream before serving.)

Filling:

1 pint blueberries
1/3 cup water
2/3 cup sugar
¼ tsp. salt
1 T. lemon juice
1 tsp. grated lemon peel
3 T. flour

Combine water, sugar, and salt and bring to a boil. Stir in berries and lemon juice and cook over low heat until a few berries begin to pop their skins. Moisten flour with a little water and stir into berries. Cook about two minutes longer until the mixture is slightly thickened. Add lemon peel and remove from heat. When berries are cool, spread one-half of them over one of the pastry rounds, leaving it in the tin in which it was baked. (A straight sided cake tin is preferable to a pie tin for this.) Place the second round over it and spread with the remaining fruit. Whip ¾ cup of heavy cream, sweeten it with 1 T. of sugar and flavor with ½ teaspoon of vanilla and a little freshly grated nutmeg. Spread over the pie. Cut with a sharp knife. Lift out pieces with a spatula and they will retain their shape.

Helen Hecht

BERMUDA LIME PIE

A century old recipe from the lovely island.

1 pint vanilla ice cream
2 eggs
½ cup sugar
green food coloring
1 cup cream
juice from 3 limes
1½ T. grated lime rind
1 cup ginger snaps or chocolate wafer crumbs
3 T. butter, melted

Beat eggs until thick and lemon-colored. Gradually add sugar to eggs and continue beating until mixture is light and fluffy. Add enough coloring to tint mixture pale green. Stir in cream, lime juice, and 1 T. rind; mix well. Pour into refrigerator tray and freeze until firm. Turn into a bowl; beat until smooth.

Mix crumbs and melted butter and press onto sides and bottom of 9-inch pie pan. Chill. Whip vanilla ice cream until smooth and spread in shell. Top with lime mixture and sprinkle with lime rind. Freeze until firm.

Mrs. Thomas C. Ratchford

RED RASPBERRY PIE   (Serves 6-8)

Crust:

18 graham crackers, crushed
¼ cup sugar
¼ lb. butter, melted

Mix and press into 9-inch pie plate. Bake 8 minutes at 350 degrees.

Filling:

¼ cup light cream
¼ lb. cream cheese
1 cup sugar
3 T. cornstarch
1 cup whipping cream, whipped
4 cups red raspberries (2 pt. boxes)
1 tsp. vanilla
2 T. confectioners sugar

Beat cream cheese and light cream until smooth. Spread over bottom of graham cracker crust. Place 1 cup fresh raspberries over cream cheese. Place remaining berries (1 cup) in a sauce pan and bring to a boil. Mix cornstarch with 1 cup white sugar and add to berries, stirring constantly. Cook over low heat 10 minutes. Cool. Pour over berries in pie plate and chill. Add vanilla and confectioners sugar to whipped cream. Heap on top of pie and serve.

Mrs. David Danforth

LEMONADE PIE

Crust:

1½ cups graham cracker crumbs (about 16 or 17 crackers)
4 T. sugar
½ cup melted margarine (regular, not soft)

Press into pie pan. Save a little to sprinkle on top.

Filling:

1 envelope unflavored gelatin
½ cup sugar
6-oz. can frozen lemonade (thawed)
2 cups Cool Whip

Dissolve 1 envelope unflavored gelatin and sugar in 1 cup boiling water. Mix in frozen lemonade. Chill until slightly thickened. Beat until fluffy and thick. Blend in Cool Whip. Pour into crust. Chill until firm.

Mrs. H. H. Kittleman

LEMON PARFAIT PIE

¼ cup butter
1 cup sugar
2 T. cornstarch
¼ tsp. salt
1 T. lemon peel
1 / 3 cup lemon juice
3 egg yolks
2 pints vanilla ice cream
3 egg whites
¼ tsp. cream of tartar
1 / 3 cup sugar

Melt butter in top of double boiler. Add sugar, cornstarch, and salt. Add lemon peel, lemon juice, and egg yolks. Cook over simmering water, stirring constantly (8-10 minutes or until thick). Cool. Soften 1 pint vanilla ice cream and smooth into baked pie shell. Freeze. Spread ½ of lemon sauce on ice cream. Freeze. Spread on 2nd pint of vanilla ice cream. Freeze. Spread remaining lemon sauce on and freeze. Beat egg whites and cream of tartar to soft peaks. Beat in 1 / 3 cup sugar and continue beating until stiff. Cover frozen pie with meringue

Bake at 475 degrees for 3 minutes. Serve immediately! (Or freeze for later use.)

Suzanne Zeddies

Desserts

ALMOND MACAROON TORTE   (Serves 16)

½ lb. butter
2 cups confectioners sugar
6 eggs separated
1 tsp. almond extract
¾ lb. almond macaroons finely crushed (blender)

Cream butter and sugar until light. Add one egg yolk at a time until all 6 are used. Fold in the almond macaroon crumbs and almond extract. Fold in the beaten egg whites. Line the bottom and sides of a 10 inch angel food cake pan with split lady fingers. Cover the bottom layer of lady fingers with the almond macaroon mixture as you would the filling of a layer cake. Then add another layer of ladyfinger and mixture until the pan is filled to the top. It will take 6 to 7 dozen lady fingers to fill the pan. Place in refrigerator and chill overnight. It also freezes well at this point. When ready to serve unmold torte on large platter and cover the whole torte with one pint of sweetened whipped cream and a can of Angel Flake coconut.

I put the almond macaroons in a slow oven for a few hours to dry them out.

Mrs. H. Alexander Vance, Jr.

HAZELNUT TORTE WITH MELBA SAUCE   (Serves 8)

4 egg whites
1¼ cups superfine sugar
1 tsp. vanilla
½ tsp. vinegar
4½ oz. browned, ground hazelnuts
5 oz. whipping cream
½ lb. raspberries
1/3 cup powedered sugar

Prepare two 8-inch cake tins by rubbing the sides with butter and dusting with flour and lining the bottom with a disc cut out of foil. Set the oven at 375 degrees. Whisk the egg whites until stiff; then gradually beat in the superfine sugar. Continue beating until very stiff, adding the vanilla and vinegar. Lastly fold in the nuts that have been prepared by browning them in the oven, then rubbing off the skins and grinding them up finely. Pour the mixture into the prepared tins and bake for 30-40 minutes. When cool, layer the meringues with whipped cream and dust the top with powdered sugar. Pass the melba sauce separately.

To make the melba sauce, rub the raspberries through a nylon strainer and beat in 1/3 cup of powdered sugar a little at a time, enough to thicken the puree.

Mrs. Richard F. L. Senior

LEMON ANGEL TORTE   (Serves 16)

1 T. plain gelatin
¼ cup cold water
6 egg yolks—beaten until light color
¾ cup sugar
¾ cup lemon juice
2 tsp. grated lemon rind
1 cup sweetened whipped cream
6 egg whites, beaten
¾ cup sugar

Mix gelatin and cold water—soften until ready. Combine egg yolks, sugar, lemon juice, and grated lemon rind on top of double boiler and cook over hot water, stirring until it coats a spoon. Remove custard mixture from heat and add gelatin mixture—stir until dissolved—cool. Beat 6 egg whites until frothy—gradually add ¾ cup sugar—beat until stiff peaks. Fold into cooled custard. Tear into bite size pieces one large angel food cake and arrange a layer of pieces in bottom of oiled large springform pan. Pour enough custard over pieces to cover. Alternate layers ending with custard. Cover—chill until firm. Unmold by loosening sides first with knife. Put on platter and spread with whipped cream.

Mrs. Richard Lydy

COFFEE MOUSSE   (Serves 8)

2 envelopes unflavored gelatin
½ cup water
1 cup confectioners sugar
1 cup milk
4 tsp. instant coffee
1 T. rum
2 egg whites, stiffly beaten
2 cups heavy cream, whipped

Sprinkle gelatin in cold water to soften. Stir together sugar, milk and instant coffee in top of double boiler over boiling water. Cook until the mixture is hot. Add softened gelatin and stir until it dissolves. Set mixture aside to cool to consistency of an unbeaten egg white. Add rum and beat lightly. Fold in beaten egg whites and then the whipped cream. Turn into large mold and chill until firm (about 2 hours).

Sauce:

2 egg yolks
¾ cup powdered sugar
1/3 cup rum
1 cup heavy cream, whipped
½ cup chopped toasted almonds

Beat egg yolks until creamy with the sugar. Add rum. Mix thoroughly. Fold whipped cream into rum mixture. Add chopped almonds. Serve with mousse.

Mrs. Thomas A. Kelly

GRAND MARNIER MOUSSE   (Serves 6)

1 T. gelatin
¼ cup cold milk
3 egg yolks
3 T. granulated sugar
½ cup Grand Marnier or Cointreau
3 egg whites, stiffly beaten
1 cup heavy cream, whipped

Soften gelatin in milk (I use a little more gelatin). Dissolve over hot water. Beat egg yolks and granulated sugar until thick. Add the softened gelatin and Grand Marnier or Cointreau. Fold in stiffly beaten egg whites and heavy cream. Pour into a 1 quart mold. Chill 4 hours or more. Serve with blueberries or strawberries, and mint leaves for decoration.

Jeanne Bowes

FROZEN GRAND MARNIER–MOUSSE WITH
FRUIT SAUCE   (Serves 6)

2 egg whites
pinch salt
6 T. sugar
¼ cup Grand Marnier
1 cup heavy cream

Beat egg whites with salt until peaked. Gradually
add 4 T. sugar until eggs are stiff and shiny. With
same beater, cream should be whipped until stiff
and remainder of sugar beaten in. Blend in Grand
Marnier. Fold in egg whites. Turn nixture into 1
quart mold or individual molds. Freeze until firm,
4 hours or overnight. Unmold on serving plate and
serve with sauce.

Strawberry-Raspberry Sauce:

Defrost 1 package each frozen strawberries and
raspberries. Drain excess juice. Place in blender
until smooth. Strain and add Grand Marnier to
taste. Makes 2 cups.

Mrs. John Alexander

STRAWBERRY MOUSSE   (Serves 4-6)

1 pkg. Jello (strawberry or raspberry)
1 cup boiling water
1 cup cold water
juice of ½ lemon
¼ cup orange juice
1 cup whipping cream

Make Jello as directed on box. Put in icebox about
15 minutes or until slightly gelled. Churn it up in
blender. Add juice of ½ a lemon & ¼ cup orange
juice and beat. Whip 1 cup whipping cream and
fold it into the jello mixture. Put in icebox. Serve
with sweetened strawberries on top of mousse.
Delicious!

Margo C. Moss

CREME BRULEE I
(Serves 6-8)

This is really a rich custard with a hard thin top—
and that takes doing. For six or eight people you
need only five ingredients:

1 quart of heavy cream
2 T. of granulated sugar
8 egg yolks
2 tsp. vanilla
light brown sugar

Heat the cream in a double boiler but do not scald.
Then add, in order, the granulated sugar, stirring
until dissolved, and the well beaten eggs and
vanilla. Mix well and pour into a shallow baking
dish that allows you a custard about 1½ inches
thick. Place in hot water and bake in a slow oven
until set (Preheat oven to 275 degrees.) Put in
refrigerator until thoroughly chilled. Now comes
the harder part. After taking the dish from the
refrigerator, cover the surface with a quarter of
an inch of soft light, not dark brown sugar. Place
the dish under a blazing broiler and watch it like a
child near a pool. The top of the sugar should melt
and run together, leaving a shining caramel top.
When the surface is glazed, put the custard in the
refrigerator for new chilling. The whole thing
must be ice cold. Just before serving, tap the
glaze, shattering it lightly. It's wonderful!

Evelyn McGrath
(Mrs. Arthur W.)

Variation:

Instead of brown sugar glaze, top with 1 quart of
strawberries which has been dipped in 1½ cups
currant jelly (melted).

Mrs. R.D. Cooper

CREME BRULEE II   (Serves 6)

2 cups whipping or heavier cream
4 well beaten eggs
2 T. sugar

Heat in a double boiler until hot 2 cups of whipping
or even heavier cream. Pour it slowly over eggs.
Beat constantly while pouring. Return mixture to
double boiler. Stir in 2 tablespoons sugar. Beat
until eggs thicken and custard coats a spoon
readily.

Brulee Crust:

Cut a piece of aluminum foil the size of the dish in
which you will serve the Brulee. Grease the foil on
one side with butter. Pat onto the buttered side in
lacy disc pattern, about ¼ inch thick brown sugar
(light). Put the sugar covered foil on a cookie
sheet. At this point, give this your full attention.
Put cookie sheet under broiler until sugar is
glazed. Remove it from oven and place on cake
rack to cool. When slightly cool the sugar topping
should peel off the foil like a large praline. Place it
on the custard just before serving so it does not
disintegrate.

Optional: 2 T. orange liqueur and 1 T. grated rind
added to custard.

Mrs. George B. Milnor

CARAMEL DUMPLINGS   (Serves 4-6)

1-½ cups sugar
2 T. butter
2 cups hot water
⅛ tsp. salt

Caramelize ½ cup sugar, add butter and rest of sugar. Add salt and hot water. Cook until smooth.

Dumplings:

2 T. butter, melted
½ cup sugar
1-½ cup flour
2 tsp. baking powder
½ cup milk
½ tsp. vanilla

Sift flour, sugar and baking powder. Add milk, melted butter and vanilla. Drop by spoonfuls into syrup. Keep heavy skillet covered and cook over low flame 30 minutes. Serve with whipped cream.

Mrs. Franklin B. Schmick

COCONUT RING   (Serves 8)

1 T. gelatin
¼ cup cold milk
1 cup milk
¼ tsp. salt
1 cup sugar
2 cups whipping cream
2 cups fresh grated coconut (or 1 can)
1 tsp. vanilla

Dissolve gelatin in ¼ cup cold milk. Set aside.
Heat 1 cup milk and ¼ tsp. salt in double boiler.
When hot, add 1 cup sugar and gelatin. Cool. When
slightly thickened, beat until fluffy. Fold in 2 cups
of heavy cream, whipped, 2 cups freshly grated
coconut (or 1 can), and 1 tsp. vanilla. Pour into 6
cup ring mold. Chill.

Sauce:

1 T. flour
1 cup brown sugar
2/3 cup cream
1 T. butter
1 cup white sugar

Mix ingredients and bring to a boil. Cool sauce to
room temperature before serving.

                                    Mrs. Charles Sailor

POTS DE CREME   (Serves 8)

½ lb. dark sweet chocolate
6 or 7 T. liquid (water or coffee)
2 T. rum or brandy
5 egg yolks
5 beaten egg whites

Break up chocolate and put in pan. Add liquid.
Stir over low heat until dissolved. Stir in rum or
brandy. Add egg yolks. Add beaten egg whites
(not too dry). Mix very well. Pour into small pots
and place in icebox to set (at least 8 hours).

Mrs. Philip W. Hummer

ICE CREAM PUDDING   (Serves 12)

1 stick melted butter
12 squares graham cracker
24 saltine crackers
2 pkg. vanilla pudding
2 cups milk
1 qt. butter pecan ice cream
½ pt. whipping cream
3 crushed Heath bars

Crush crackers and mix with butter. Press into
9x12 inch pyrex pan and place in refrigerator.

Beat together 2 pkg. vanilla pudding and 2 cups
milk. Blend in 1 qt. butter pecan ice cream.
Spread on crumbs; set in refrigerator. One half
hour before serving, top with ½ pt. whipping
cream whipped and sprinkle 3 crushed Heath bars
over all.

Mrs. J. Carter Miller, Sr.

LEMON MAGIC   (Serves 6)

1 full cup of sugar
1 heaping T. flour
pinch of salt
butter (size of walnut)
juice and grated rind of 1 lemon
yolk of 2 eggs
1 cup milk
fold in 2 egg whites—beaten stiff

Pour in buttered baking dish; set in pan of water.
Bake ½ hour in moderate oven (350 degrees).

Patricia Anne Barton

LEMON PUDDING   (Serves 4)

1 cup of sugar
1 T. butter
3 eggs
juice and rind of 1 lemon
2 T. flour
1 cup milk

Cream butter and sugar. Add the yolks of eggs
(well beaten) and the other ingredients in above
order. Fold in egg whites, beaten stiff. Bake for 60
minutes at 350 degrees in baking dish set in pan of
hot water.

This pudding is like lemon jelly with sponge cake
on top.

C. Bjorkman

ELDORA'S BREAD PUDDING   (Serves 6)

5 slices of day old bread
1/3 cup rice, cooked
2 cups cream
¾ cup sugar
2 eggs, beaten well
½ stick butter
1½ T. nutmeg
1½ T. vanilla flavor

Soak bread in milk; mash until bread is soft.
Place in 1½ qt. casserole, add remaining
ingredients and bake about 45 minutes at 400
degrees or until brown. Serve with cream or
vanilla sauce.

Mrs. Allan E. Bulley, Jr.

SUET PUDDING   (Serves 8)

1 cup finely chopped suet
1 cup molasses
1 cup sweet milk
3½ cups flour
1 cup chopped raisins
1 tsp. soda (dissolved in hot water)

Combine in order given. Steam for two hours
without lifting cover.

Sauce:

Cream 1 cup sugar with 1/3 cup butter; then add
yolks of 3 eggs and pinch of salt. Beat well and add
1/3 cup milk. Place dish in basin of hot water and
stir until butter is melted. Flavor with vanilla or
brandy.

RED RASPBERRIES WITH CREAM CUSTARD
(Serves 6)

1 12-oz. jar apricot preserves
2 pints fresh red raspberries
¼ cup Kirsch
4 egg whites
2 cups heavy cream
3 T. sugar
1 tsp. almond extract

Coat berries with preserves and Kirsch mixture and chill until serving time. Scald 1 cup of cream in top of double boiler, add sugar. Combine egg whites with other cup of cream and beat until blended. Add a small amount of the hot cream misture to the egg mixture, then gradually stir egg mixture into hot cream. Continue to cook in double boiler until the custard is thick enough to coat a metal spoon. Chill. Add extract and chill thoroughly. Serve with glazed berries over top.

APRICOT UPSIDE DOWN PUDDING (Serves 6-8)

2 T. butter
1/3 cup brown sugar (firmly packed)
18-20 canned or cooked and sweetened halves of
  apricots
1½ quarts soft bread cubes
18-20 maraschino cherries
2 beaten eggs
1/3 cup *each* white sugar, apricot juice, milk
3 T. melted butter

Heat oven to 350 degrees. Melt butter in 8-inch
round cake pan. Add brown sugar and stir until
dissolved. Center apricot halves with cherries and
place in pan, cut side down. Mix remaining
ingredients, adding bread cubes last. Pour into
prepared pan. Bake about 30-35 minutes in 350
degree oven until lightly browned and knife
comes out clean. Cut into wedges while slightly
warm and serve.

Mrs. Peter Fazio

JELLIED IRISH COFFEE   (Serves 6)

1 envelope (1 T.) unflavored gelatin
1½ cups hot water
¼ cup sugar
1½ T. instant coffee
¼ cup Irish Whiskey
2 T. whipped cream

Put ½ cup cold water in sauce pan. Sprinkle with gelatin, soften. Add 1½ cups hot water. Stir until gelatin is dissolved. Add rest of ingredients. Pour into demitasse cups. Place in refrigerator to gell. Just before serving, put dab of whipped cream on each cup.

Mrs. John L. Haverkampf

SHERRY GELATIN DESSERT   (Serves 6)

4 envelopes plain gelatin
½ cup water (cold)
1 cup boiling water
2½ cups cream sherry
2 / 3 cups sugar
1 cup fresh orange juice
4 T. lemon juice

Soak gelatin in cold water; heat orange juice, lemon juice, sherry, sugar. Add to boiling water; dissolve gelatin in mixture. Pour into mold.

Soak honeydews and cantaloupe in cointreau mixed with powdered sugar, and serve around gelatin mold.

Mrs. Herbert Watt

PRUNE DESSERT

1 lb. Prunes (pitted)
1½ cups sugar
1 lemon
¾ cup sherry wine
3 envelopes of gelatin
4 egg whites

Cook prunes with a little sugar until soft. Put
through a colander, add rest of sugar and cook for
a few minutes. Then add wine, rind and juice of a
lemon. Add gelatin which has been dissolved in ½
cup cold water. Cool. Stir in 4 egg whites beaten
stiff.

Mrs. Eben Erikson

COEUR A LA CREME

¼ lb. cream cheese
¼ pint heavy cream
1 T. confectioners sugar
dash of paprika
pinch of salt
rich fruit preserves or
fresh strawberries, sugar, and cream

Blend cheese, cream, sugar, paprika and salt
together thoroughly but lightly. Dampen a piece
of cheesecloth and spread as smoothly as possible
in heart-shaped mold. Pack cheese mixture into
this and chill in refrigerator for several hours.
Unmold the coeur on a wreath of shiny green
leaves, and remove cloth. Serve with rich
preserves or fresh strawberries, sugar, and
cream.

Mrs. Arthur W. McGrath

MOCHA PARFAIT   (Serves 6)

½ cup sugar
1 cup (6-oz. package) semi-sweet chocolate chips
½ cup water
2 eggs
2 tsp. instant coffee powder
1½ cups whipping cream—well whipped
cognac to taste

Boil sugar, water and coffee powder for 3 minutes. Place chocolate chips in blender. Add the syrup made from the sugar, water and coffee. Blend for 6 seconds. Add eggs and blend for 1 minute more. Add cognac...about 2 T....depending upon the one you have on hand.

Fold this mixture into the whipped cream and freeze.

Let stand at room temperature for 10 minutes before serving.

Mrs. H. Alexander Vance, Jr.

COFFEE CHARLOTTE SQUARES   (Serves 8-10)

2 T. instant coffee (or Sanka)
1 cup hot water
½ lb. (32) marshmallows
1 cup heavy cream, whipped
18 lady fingers, split

Dissolve coffee in hot water; add marshmallows.
Place over low heat and stir until marshmallows
are completely melted; chill until slightly
thickened. Fold in whipped cream. Line bottom of
shallow oblong serving dish about 7x11x1½ inches
with half of split lady fingers. Cover with half of
coffee mixture; add another layer of lady fingers
and top with remaining coffee mixture. Chill 8
hours or overnight. Cut in squares (8-10) to serve.
A dab of whipped cream and shaved chocolate on
top is decorative.

Mrs. Gordon D. Sharvy

COFFEE TORTONI   (Serves 12)

2 egg whites
2 T. instant coffee
¼ tsp. salt
4 T. sugar
2 cups heavy cream
½ cup sugar
2 tsp. vanilla
¼ tsp. almond extract
¾ cup toasted almonds, finely chopped

Add coffee and salt to egg whites, and beat until stiff but not dry.

Gradually beat in 4 T. sugar. Continue beating until stiff and shiny. Whip cream, adding ½ cup sugar, vanilla and almond extract, continuing to beat until stiff.

Fold cream and ½ cup almonds into egg mixture.

Spoon into 12 paper cups inserted in muffin tin. Sprinkle remaining almonds on top.

Freeze quickly.

Mrs. Herbert Watt

DOUBLE BOILER CHOCOLATE SOUFFLE
(Serves 4-6)

2 squares baking chocolate
1 cup milk
1)3 cup sugar
dash of salt
3 unbeaten eggs

Melt chocolate in milk in top of double boiler; beat until smooth. Add sugar, salt, and eggs; beat 1 minute. Cover and cook over boiling water for 20 minutes without lifting cover. Serve warm with ice cream or whipped cream.

Mrs. Richard P. Connette

CHERRY CHOCOLATE SOUFFLE

Per Portion:

2 eggs
1 T. confectioners sugar
1-2 / 3 T. unsweetened cocoa

Separate the eggs. Beat the whites until stiff. Beat the yolks thoroughly and add, little by little, the sugar and cocoa. Fold in the whites. Place the mixture in a buttered baking dish on the bottom of which has been spread a thin layer of preserved black cherries. Bake near top of a 425 degree oven where the heat rises and cooks the top surface until souffle rises (about 10 minutes). Remove from oven and serve at once. If doubling recipe, bake not more than 12 minutes.

Dorothy M. Nixon
(Mrs. Carles A.)

APRICOT SOUFFLE   (Serves 6)

1 pkg. dried apricots
½ cup sugar
whites of 5 eggs
½ tsp. lemon juice

Pick over and mash fruit. Cook in water (enough
to almost cover fruit). When soft rub through a
Foley Food Mill or put through a meat grinder.
Add sugar.Cook 5 minutes or until the consistency
of marmalade. Cool. Beat whites of eggs until
stiff. Fold into fruit and add lemon juice. Heap
lightly into buttered souffle dish or tiny individual
baking dishes. Bake in slow oven—275 degrees, 30
to 45 minutes. Serve cold with whipped cream.

Marian Braddock

ORANGE MARMALADE SOUFFLE   (Serves 4)

4 egg whites, well beaten
4 T. sugar
3 T. orange marmalade
1 tsp. orange extract

Fold sugar, marmalade, and extract into beaten whites. Pour into well buttered top of double boiler covered with well buttered lid. Cook over hot water for one hour. Serve with sauce.

Sauce:

2 egg yolks beaten
½ cup confectioners sugar
pinch salt
1 cup whipped cream
generous dash sherry

Sprinkle with toasted almonds.

Mrs. John Brewer

LEMON SOUFFLES (Serves 8)

1 cup sugar
¼ cup flour
⅛ tsp. salt
2 T. melted butter
5 T. fresh lemon juice
1 T. grated lemon rind
3 eggs separated
1½ cups milk

Blend sugar, flour, and salt; add melted butter, lemon juice and rind and mix well. Stir in well beaten egg yolks and milk. Fold in stiffly beaten egg whites and pour into greased custard cups; place in pan of water and bake at 350 degrees for 45 minutes.

Ruth F. Crawford
(Mrs. W. F.)

MACAROON SOUFFLE (Serves 6)

6 egg whites
pinch of cream of tartar
1½ cups granulated sugar
1 scant cup finely ground macaroons

Beat the egg whites until they foam. Add the pinch of cream of tartar and continue beating until very stiff. Beat at low speed with an electric beater gradually adding sugar. Last, fold in the macaroons. Bake 45 minutes in 300 degree oven. Serve hot with whipped cream.

Mrs. Frank R. Milnor

BABA AU RUM WITH APRICOT SAUCE
(Serves 8

½ cup scalded milk, cooled to warm
½ cup of confectioners sugar, sifted twice
¼ cup of sweet butter, melted
Butter to butter mold
1 yeast cake
1 whole egg
vanilla to taste
1-1 / 3 cups flour sifted or a little more
2 egg yolks beaten well

Dissolve yeast in milk. Beat yolks very well and
gradually add the sugar. Beat whole egg very well
and add to yolks beating hard. Add melted butter
and vanilla to eggs and mix with milk. Now add
flour. The dough should be medium thick so add a
little more flour if needed. Let this stand in a
warm place for at least 4 hours. It may stand
overnight, if made for lunch, always covered.
Butter the mold (bundt) generously and fill it half
full with the dough and let the dough rise again
until double in proportions in a warm place,
covered. Bake in a 350 degree oven until a needle
comes out clean (20 minutes). Unmold and cool.
Wash the mold and dry it. Place baba back in
mold.

Syrup:

About 1 cup sugar
2 tsp. of lemon juice to taste
3½-4 juggers rum
2 cups apricot juice
2 T. orange juice

Boil all ingredients excepting rum in a double
boiler for about 10 minutes. Add rum and check
seasonings. When cool pour ½ of the liquid over
baba. When absorbed pour the rest of the liquid

over baba adding more rum if needed. Serve with whipped cream in the center mixed with sugar and rum to taste. You make small babas in little molds the same way. They will bake quicker of course. Just check them with a needle, and proceed the same way as above. Serve with whipped cream or ice cream. A different way of serving small babas is placing them, after marinating in a chafing dish, pour over rum (hot) mixed with hot brandy and igniting them.

Mrs. H. Alexander Vance, Jr.

RHUBARB CRUNCH   (Serves 6)

2 cups rhubarb, cut in chunks
Mix with: ¾ cup white sugar and 2 T. flour

Put in baking dish.

Mix:

¼ cup brown sugar
¼ cup flour
¼ cup dry oatmeal
¼ cup butter

Spread oatmeal mixture over the rhubarb.

Bake 40 minutes in 350 degree oven. Very good served with vanilla ice cream.

Mrs. William J. Hagenah, Jr.

POACHED PEARS IN VELVET SAUCE (Serves 6)

1 cup sugar
1½ cups sauterne (or other white dinner wine)
1½ cups water
6 fresh pears

Combine sugar, wine, water in large sauce pan. Heat until sugar dissolves. Pare skin from pears, remove core from bottom leaving stem and pear whole. Add pears to hot syrup, cover and simmer until barely tender (ten minutes). Remove and chill in syrup. When ready to serve drain and serve with velvet sauce and grated chocolate.

Velvet Sauce: (Makes 2 cups)

4 egg yolks
1 cup sifted confectioners sugar
½ cup cream sherry
⅛ tsp. salt
1 cup whipping cream
grated semi-sweet chocolate

Beat egg yolks till golden. Gradually beat in sugar until creamy and light in color. Blend in sherry and salt and cook until thickened (do not boil). Stir now and then and refrigerate several hours. Fold in whipping cream before serving.

Mrs. Robert Bon Durant

PEARS BAR-LE-DUC   (Serves 6)

6 fresh pears
2 pkg. soft white cream cheese—large
2 jars bar-le-duc—(may use 3 jars if stronger
flavor preferred
cream

Moisten cheese with cream and work together
until the consistency of heavy cream. Mix in bar-
le-duc and add pears peeled and quartered. Heap
in bowl **and** serve cold.

Mrs. Philip S. Clarke

CHERRY DESSERT   (Serves 16)

3 cups all purpose flour
1½ cups granulated sugar
1 can or small pkg. shredded coconut
½ lb. margarine or butter
1 tsp. salt
3 cans cherry pie filling

Mix flour, sugar and salt. Cut in margarine or
butter. Add coconut. Save ¾ cup mixture for
topping. Press the mixture lightly into ungreased
large oblong pan. Top with cherry filling. Sprinkle
rest of mixture on top. Nuts may be added 15
minutes before dessert is done. Bake at 350
degrees for 30 to 35 minutes.

Mrs. H. H. Kittleman

BAKED PEARS "MARGERY"

Peel fresh Bartlett pears, halve and core. Put slice of lemon in each cavity. Make a syrup of 1 cup sugar to ½ cup water and boil to a thread (dropped in test glass of water) consistency. Pour syrup over pears and bake at 350 degrees until pears are tender. Simple and delicious light dessert.

Lessie B. Davison
(Mrs. Charles Hamilton Davison)

FORT RILEY DESSERT   (Serves 4)

Remove excess moisture from 12 Kadota figs and chill them thoroughly. When time to serve, place the cold figs on dish and cover with a sauce made of 6 T. of sour cream and 6 T. of creme de cacao. Top with grated Baker's bitter chocolate.

Elizabeth W. Arnold

BRAZILIAN BANANAS   (Serves 8)

8 bananas
2 T. rum
2 dessert tsp. instant coffee
2 dessert tsp. super-fine sugar
8-oz. whipping cream
few almonds, browned and flaked

Peel bananas, slice thickly into serving dish, and
sprinkle with the rum. Dissolve coffee in 3-4 T. of
boiling water, add sugar, and leave until cold.
Whip cream very stiff, and fold in the coffee
mixture. Cover the bananas with the coffee cream
mixture, scatter a few almonds on the top, and
serve very well chilled.

Mrs. Ralph Daniel

MINCEMEAT PEACHES   (Serves 4)

8 canned peach halves, drained
mincemeat, brandy added
preserved ginger, finely minced or
ground ginger
ice cream, whipping cream, or
cream, optional

Place 1 heaping T. of mincemeat in the hollow of
each peach. Sprinkle with ginger. Preheat oven to
350 degrees and bake 10-15 minutes.

Mrs. William F. Regnery

PEACH BELLEVUE   (Serves 6)

6 ripe peaches
juice of 1 lemon
1/3 cup of sugar
1/3 cup brandy
1/3 cup water

Select ripe and unblemished peaches, drop into boiling water for a couple of minutes. Remove and peel by sliding the skin off with fingers. Place in an oven proof dish with a cover. Mix the juice of one lemon, sugar, water and brandy together and pour over peaches. Bake in a 400 degree oven for up to an hour. Size of fruit determines length of time and should be checked after 40 minutes in order to avoid overcooking. Excellent served chilled in own juice or with sabayon or custard sauces.

Anne P. Nicholson

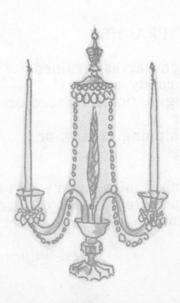

CLAIRE'S FUDGE SAUCE

6 squares unsweetened chocolate
½ stick butter
3 cups sugar
1 T. cornstarch
pinch salt
½ cup white corn syrup
1 13oz. can evaporated milk
1 tsp. vanilla

Melt chocolate and butter in double boiler.

Mix sugar, cornstarch, salt and add to melted chocolate.

Add corn syrup, evaporated milk, and vanilla.

Cook all 20 minutes. Store in refrigerator. Serve hot over ice cream.

Always reheat in double boiler—never spoils.

Mrs. Thomas D. Hodgkins

EASIEST CHOCOLATE SAUCE

Melt one large Hershey Almond Bar (or, a plain one, if you wish) over hot water. When melted stir in one tablespoon White Karo and ¼ cup milk which has been brought to the boiling point. If well-hidden in the refrigerator it will keep for a couple of weeks. The almonds, incidentally, will remain crisp.

Mrs. Hays MacFarland

CHOCOLATE ALMOND SAUCE

3-1oz. squares unsweetened chocolate
1¾ cups light cream or milk
1 cup sugar
¼ cup flour
¼ tsp. salt
1 T. butter
1 tsp. vanilla
½ cup toasted almonds

Melt chocolate in cream over hot water, cook until smooth. Stir occasionally. Combine sugar, flour and salt; add enough chocolate mixture to make a smooth paste. Add to remaining chocolate mixture. Cook until smooth and slightly thickened...about 10 minutes. Remove from heat and add vanilla, butter, and almonds. Serve hot or cold on ice cream.

Dorothy Jane Cook

BANANA FRITTERS

½ tsp. salt
1 tsp. baking powder
1 cup all purpose flour
½ cup water
½ cup milk
½ tsp. black pepper
1 tsp. accent
1 T. paprika
1 egg, well beaten

Mix all ingredients together and stir until smooth.
Set aside for an hour or more and stir again before
cooking. Dip bananas one by one into the batter.

Cut each banana in three sections. Cut each setion
in lengthwise pieces. Dip in batter. Put some oil in
a frying pan and heat. Place bananas in pan and
brown on both sides. Place on paper towel to dry.
Place in warm oven until time to serve. Sprinkle
lightly with sugar before serving.

Mrs. Ferdinand A. Bunte

SWISS APPLE TORTE

¼ cup soft butter
1 cup sugar
1 egg
1 cup all purpose flour
1 tsp. cinnamon
½ tsp. baking powder
½ tsp. nutmeg
½ tsp. ginger
¼ tsp. soda
⅛ tsp. salt
⅛ tsp. cloves
3 apples—peeled, cored, but into ⅛ inch thick
  slices (3 cups)

Mix butter, sugar and egg; then add other ingredients which have been sifted together; then apples. Bake in 9 inch greased pie pan and spread smooth. Bake at 350 degrees for 1 hour. Serve with vanilla ice cream or whipped cream.

Mrs. Barry J. Carroll

Miscellaneous and Quick Cuisine

ENGLISH TOFFEE

1 cup butter (2 sticks)
1 cup sugar (granulated)
1/3 to ½ cup pecans
3 small plain Hershey chocolate bars

Melt butter and sugar in sauce pan (preferably copper bottom). Stir constantly and cook briskly for approximately 9 minutes. The mixture is done when it has turned from a butter color to a light brown taffy color. Do not scorch. May take a little longer depending upon size of flame and pan. Pour into a square or oblong cake tin which has the bottom covered with pecans (pan is un-buttered). Break three Hersheys into small pieces over the top. Let stand for 5 minutes and when melted, spread over the entire surface. When thoroughly cool and hard, break into desired pieces.

Mrs. Irvin E. Houck

TOFFEE

1½ cups of cane sugar
1½ cups broken pecans
1 cup butter (room temp.)
salt
scant ⅛ cup of water

Combine all ingredients in a heavy sauce pan. Stir *constantly* over medium heat until dark toffee color. Do not undercook as candy will sugar. Do not burn. Candy should have reached the finished stage when it moves freely in a mass as you stir it. The stirring goes on for fifteen minutes to half an hour. Color and texture is your clue to pouring it on a marble or enamel table after you have buttered the top. Spread quickly to thin sheet. Let cool and crack up into pieces. This will freeze well.

Mrs. Wm. Jewett Fulton

PICKLES

1 qt. best quality plain dill pickles
3 cups sugar
2 cups water
1 cup vinegar
1 T. mixed pickling spices

Slice pickles lengthwise (about 4-5 slices per pickle) and place in bowl.

Boil then simmer sugar, water, vinegar & pickling spices. Pour hot solution over pickles. Cool to room temperature.

Place in refrigerator for three days before serving.

Mrs. Peter Economou

INSTANT RUSSIAN TEA

1 cup instant tea (unsweetened plain)
1 cup sugar
2 cups Tang
1 pkg. sweetened lemonade mix
1 tsp. cinnamon
½ tsp. ground cloves

Mix together.

Use 2 rounded tsps. per cup of boiling water.

Maria Braddock

CAPPUCINO

1/3 Expresso Coffee
1/3 reg. hot chocolate mixture made with coffee
cream
1/3 each Tia Maria Rum and Brandy—total of 1
jigger

Top with whipped cream and served hot.

Mrs. William Wrigley

HOT MUSTARD FOR SANDWICHES

Coleman's mustard (½ of a ¼ lb. tin)
1 tsp. cider vinegar
1 tsp. worcestershire sauce
½ tsp. sugar
½ tsp. salt
warm water to mix

Mix all ingredients. Store in covered container.

Mrs. Albert D. Williams, Jr.

MICKEY'S CUCUMBERS

2 cucumbers, pared
1 cup granulated sugar
½ cup water
2 tsp. salt
1 cup white vinegar
2 tsp. snipped fresh dill

Slice cucumber very thinly. In a saucepan combine everything but cucumbers. Bring mixture to a boil. Pour this hot vinegar mixture over cucumber slices in a 1 quart jar; cover tightly & refrigerate. These must marinate one week before they are served.

Mrs. Allan E. Bulley, Jr.

RUM PUNCH

18 lemons
1 gallon boiling water
¾ gallon rum
1 pint green tea
1 pint brandy

To the juice of 18 lemons and the grated rinds of 9, add 1 gallon of boiling water. When nearly cold pour in ¾ gallon of rum, 1 pint of green tea, 1 pint of brandy. Strain through muslin and sweeten to taste. (I must admit that I did not go to the trouble of straining and found that the lemon rinds mattered not at all.)

Mrs. William H. Arnold

OLIVE OIL PICKLES

Soak whole pickles in ice water for 60 minutes. Combine 2 quarts sliced pickles with 1 cup thinly sliced onion rings and ½ cup salt. Let stand 2 hours. Drain off liquid. Add 2 tsp. each of celery and mustard seed, 1 cup cider vinegar, ½ cup olive oil, ½ tsp. sugar. Let stand one hour, stirring often. Taste—and add more vinegar (or sugar) if desired. Put in jars and refrigerate—delicious!

MERCERSBERG QUAKER PEANUT BRITTLE

Boil together until a little dropped in cold water is brittle:

1½ cups New Orleans molasses
1½ tsp. of vinegar
1½ cup brown sugar
3 T. butter

Remove from fire and quickly add 1½ tsp. of soda and 1 tsp. of vanilla. Beat this well for a few minutes and then pour into pans which have been well buttered and lined with peanuts.

A LADY'S COCKTAIL

Pink Lady

4 egg whites
4 T. grenadine
4 small ice cubes
¾ cup gin (8-oz. cup)
4 small scoops of vanilla ice cream

All in a blender and mix well and serve.

Winifred Marx

QUICKIE CHICKEN SALAD

2 cups of diced chicken
½ cup diced celery
½ cup sour cream
¼ cup mayonnaise

Mix well and garnish with chives.

Mrs. Edward A. Hurley

Cut celery root in THIN 2 inch long, small strips. Marinate raw in thinned mayonnaise; serve on a bed of crisp lettuce leaves for salad.

QUICKIE FRENCH DRESSING

Whip slightly ½ cup cream; add 2 or 3 T. of French dressing, mix well and pour over your salad.

FRESH GINGER ROOT

Fresh ginger root—grated for chicken, etc. keeps very well if put in a jar of sherry wine and kept in the refrigerator.

QUICK DELICIOUS SUNDAES

Soak a can of bing cherries in brandy overnight. Serve on Lemon Sherbert.

Flavor whipping cream with cognac and instant coffee. Serve over coffee ice cream with grated chocolate on top.

Mrs. H. Earl Hoover

QUICKIE FIRST COURSE FOR SPECIAL OCCASIONS (Serves 4)

2 cans of beef consomme
½ cup sour cream

Garnish with sour cream and chives or caviar and sour cream.

Mrs. Edward A. Hurley

QUICK CHEESE STRAW

1 package pie crust mix prepared according to directions on the package EXCEPT mix a few drops of Tabasco Sauce in the water; 1 package shredded Cheddar cheese. Roll out pie crust, sprinkle with grated cheese. Fold over and roll a second time. Fold a third time and roll until about ¼ inch thick. Cut in strips and bake until light brown. Serve hot.

In the bottom 2/3's of a bouillon cup, put cold jellied Madrilene; fill cup with Vichyssoise and finish with a garni of your preference...minced parsley, watercress, chives, etc.

FOR A FIRST COURSE IN THE SPRING

Tie about six fresh green onions in a bunch...one bunch for each serving...leaving three or four inches of the green tops on the onions. Boil gently in salted water until tender...do not overcook. Place each bunch on a piece of toast, cut the string holding them together. Serve with melted butter or hollandaise on top...if hollandaise is used the assembled serving—with the hollandaise on top—may be "run" under the broiler for a minute...to lightly brown the hollandaise.

TO MAKE BAY'S ENGLISH MUFFINS CRISP

Plunge quickly in & out of cold water. Blot well.

Split apart and cut into four pieces.

Spread each piece on innerside thickly with butter.

Place on a tin—butter side up.

Bake at 375 degrees for half an hour or until an even brown.

Wait 5 minutes and serve hot.

Winifred Marx

Use a thin slice of celery or cucumber...about the size of a pencil as a stirrer for **Bloody Mary**s or for a **Virgin Mary** (no gin!)

ZUCCHINI OR YELLOW SQUASH

Split. Boil in salted water until tender. Drain thoroughly. Put in shallow baking dish. Brush with butter. Sprinkle top with onion flakes, cracker crumbs and grated Parmesan cheese. Bake until hot.

QUICKIE

Next time you serve spinach make it "extra special" by serving it with sour cream to which grated horseradish has been added.

Cook thin slices of celery in lightly salted water until partially done...NOT soft. Cool. Mix with seeded tomatoes, slightly undercooked green beans and marinate in French dressing until well-seasoned. Serve on chilled lettuce leaf.

Scoop out medium-sized tomatoes...fill center with cooked pureed frozen peas...add a dash of nutmeg and a dollop of sour cream. Bake in hot oven for 15 minutes.

To keep in your freezer and serve on a moment's notice:

Make ice cream balls. Roll in toasted coconut or finely shaved chocolate or crushed and rolled vanilla wafers or chocolate wafer or slivered toasted almonds. Serve with a variety of sauces: butterscotch, chocolate, creme de menthe, maple syrup or marshmallow. (Thin marshmallow sauce with a little hot water and flavor the sauce with mint. Try adding a bit of green food coloring to the mint flavored marshmallow sauce and serve it with chocolate ice cream.) As you shape the balls and roll them in whichever coating you prefer, place on wax paper about an inch apart and put in freezing compartment as you make each ball.

A QUICK AFTER-SCHOOL TREAT

Split left-over muffins, baking powder biscuits, rolls or doughnuts. Spread with currant jelly and toast for a few minutes...watch carefully as the jelly burns quickly.

INSTEAD OF A TEA OR A COFFEE

Just soup and sandwiches, you can get it up in a twinkling

—A lot of fun is to use your silver tea set—the kettle and sugar bowl and tray only. In the sugar bowl have an assortment of Lipton's "Cup-a-soup." There are quite a few varieties. Each soup is in a little bright colored envelope. Let guests choose variety of bouillon or soup that appeals to them.

—All you need are a cup, a person, a plate, a napkin and a spoon, a few crackers or sandwiches.

—Have the hot water in your silver kettle boiling hot. Content of envelope guest shakes into cup and the hot water required is poured from kettle.

—A brass kettle can be used—anything that looks "elegant."

—The audience participation is part of the fun. It loosens tongues and people talk and laugh and have a good time—it's all so nice and informal.

Frances Hooper

ORANGE ENERGY BUILDER

Put in blender 2 whole eggs, 2 cups orange juice and 1 T. sugar. Whip until well mixed; then add ½ cup crushed ice (the addition of the crushed ice is optional).

One can of Apricot Nectar may be substituted for the orange juice.

Soak pitted prunes in half sherry and half cognac. Serve with cocktails or as garnish on meat or fowl platters; or, stuff with a nut and serve with wine. (The largest prunes may usually be purchased at Health Food Stores.)

Roast lamb is delicious basted with left-over coffee...try it. The flavor is pleasant and the gravy improved in color and flavor by the addition of the small amount of coffee.

MY GRANDMOTHER'S FUDGE RECIPE

2 cups of sugar
¾ cup of milk
2 squares of chocolate
butter, size of walnut

Combine these ingredients and boil until a soft ball is formed when dropped into a glass of cold water. Remove from stove, add 1 tsp. vanilla and beat until just ready to harden, then pour into buttered pyrex dish quickly. It will have a smooth glossy top. Add chopped nuts before beating, if desired.

Mrs. H. H. Kittleman

PEACHES FLAMBES FOR ICE CREAM

2 packages frozen peaches...let thaw just enough to drain off the juice. Put juice in sauce pan, stir in full tablespoon cornstarch...cook until thick and clear...stirring constantly. Put peaches in chafing dish, add thickened juice. Ignite 2 jiggers of bourbon or brandy and stir into peaches. Serve over vanilla ice cream. (Enough for 4 or 5 servings)

The use of frozen patty shells is an excellent source for puff paste...especially good for a fruit tart: stretch the shells over the back of a muffin tin.

APRICOT WHIP

Pit whole canned apricots and press through strainer or food mill. Mix with equal amounts of heavy cream whipped stiff. Add dash of brandy...put in serving dish and refrigerate at least six hours.

CHOCOLATE BAKED ALASKA

At serving time, brush top of chocolate ice cream roll (from your market's frozen food section) with brandy. Place roll on baking sheet and cover frozen roll with meringue made with 2 egg whites beaten with 2 T. sugar until stiff. Brown in hot oven—450 degrees—for 3 minutes. Serve at once.

Advice, Tips, Short Cuts

- To make a smooth cut when slicing hard boiled eggs in half, use a wet sharp knife.
- If you want to cool gelatin quickly, take a pan of ice cubes and cover ice with salt.
- To prevent crusts from browning too quickly cover them with brown paper.
- Butter the lip of a cream pitcher to prevent it from dripping.
- If serving a chocolate or butterscotch sauce in a pitcher, coat the pitcher with melted butter.
- When cooking bacon, remove from refrigerator and let stand until it reaches room temperature. Separate slices and bake in oven slowly until brown and crisp. Drain on paper towel. Cook a pound or more at a time as you can always reheat it.
- To make CROUTONS: Cut bread in ¼ inch cubes, dry and brown in a slow oven. Pour melted butter over browned croutons and sprinkle with Beau Monde salt.
- Instead of basting eggs when frying, after egg whites are firm add about 1 tsp. water to frying pan and cover. Continue cooking until eggs are to your liking.
- When cooking rice or potatoes, butter sides of the pan to avoid water boiling over.
- Save all your fruit juice and freeze to make jello (use instead of water).
- Boil vegetables in salted water uncovered if they are grown OVERGROUND. If grown UNDERGROUND, boil covered.

- Do not add salt when boiling corn, but a little sugar.
- Boil eggs in salted water, putting them in wet. They will not crack.
- To freeze eggs, always separate and break yolks. 2 tablespoons of white makes one egg and 1 tablespoon of yolk makes one egg.
- Perfect vanilla extract: 1 pint of brandy plus 5 to 6 vanilla beans cut in 3 inch pieces. Keep in a well closed jar for 5 weeks before using.
- Add honey to whipping cream for stiff peaks. Add ice milk by teaspoons if cream is over whipped.
- Onion cut and peeled keeps a long time in refrigerator in a well closed jar.
- Celery sticks keep a long time, wrapped with a few slices of peeled potato.
- Cut difficult cheeses with a wet warm knife.
- Skins come off more easily from oranges and lemons if you pour boiling water over them and let stand 5 minutes. White skin of the same fruits comes off more easily if peeled under running cold water.
- To degrease a sauce in a hurry, throw some ice cubes in the hot sauce and then remove them.
- Classical BOUQUET GARNI: 1 or ½ bay leaf and a dash of thyme tied in a piece of cloth or linen with a few sprigs of parsley tied on the outside.
- Always boil potatoes with the skins on otherwise too much water is absorbed.
- Defrost all frozen vegetables before cooking them (except those in plastic cooking bags). Then pour salted boiling water over them. They will cook more quickly and look and taste much better.

Index

Hor d'Oeuvres and Appetizers

Soups

Breads, Coffee Cakes, Pancakes

Luncheon Dishes

Sandwiches

Salads

Salad Dressings

Entrees – Meats

Entrees – Poultry

Entrees – Fish

Cakes

Dessert Sauces

Notes

Notes

Notes

Notes

WOMAN'S ATHLETIC CLUB COOKBOOK

PLEASE SEND ME _____ COPIES OF YOUR COOKBOOK AT

$5.50 EACH PLUS $.75 POSTAGE AND HANDLING PER COPY.

ENCLOSED IS MY CHECK FOR _____.

NAME _____

STREET _____

CITY _____ STATE _____ ZIP _____

ILLINOIS RESIDENTS MUST ADD TAX

WOMAN'S ATHLETIC CLUB COOKBOOK

PLEASE SEND ME _____ COPIES OF YOUR COOKBOOK AT

$5.50 EACH PLUS $.75 POSTAGE AND HANDLING PER COPY.

ENCLOSED IS MY CHECK FOR _____.

NAME _____

STREET _____

CITY _____ STATE _____ ZIP _____

ILLINOIS RESIDENTS MUST ADD TAX

WOMAN'S ATHLETIC CLUB COOKBOOK

PLEASE SEND ME _____ COPIES OF YOUR COOKBOOK AT

$5.50 EACH PLUS $.75 POSTAGE AND HANDLING PER COPY.

ENCLOSED IS MY CHECK FOR _____

NAME _____

STREET _____

CITY _____ STATE _____ ZIP _____

ILLINOIS RESIDENTS MUST ADD TAX

WOMAN'S ATHLETIC CLUB COOKBOOK

626 NORTH MICHIGAN AVENUE

CHICAGO, ILLINOIS 60611

WOMAN'S ATHLETIC CLUB COOKBOOK

626 NORTH MICHIGAN AVENUE

CHICAGO, ILLINOIS 60611

WOMAN'S ATHLETIC CLUB COOKBOOK

626 NORTH MICHIGAN AVENUE

CHICAGO, ILLINOIS 60611